# Managing
# Quality

# Managing Quality

## The Strategic and Competitive Edge

## David A. Garvin

**THE FREE PRESS**
*A Division of Macmillan, Inc.*
NEW YORK

Maxwell Macmillan Canada
TORONTO

Maxwell Macmillan International
NEW YORK   OXFORD   SINGAPORE   SYDNEY

The Free Press
A Division of Macmillan, Inc.
866 Third Avenue, New York, N.Y. 10022

Maxwell Macmillan Canada, Inc.
1200 Eglinton Avenue East
Suite 200
Don Mills, Ontario M3C 3N1

Macmillan, Inc. is part of the Maxwell Communication
Group of Companies.

Printed in the United States of America

printing number

8  9  10  11  12  13  14  15  16  17  18  19  20

**Library of Congress Cataloging-in-Publication Data**

Garvin, David A.
  Managing quality.

  Includes index.
  1. Quality of products—United States—Management.
2. Quality assurance—United States—Management.
3. Quality of products—United States—Management—
Case studies. 4. Quality assurance—United States—
Management—Case studies.   I. Title.
HF5415.157.G37      1988      658.5'62      87–15145
ISBN 0–02–911380–6

*To My Family*

# Contents

# Part III
# Japanese Quality Management
# 177

# Acknowledgments

This book is the product of six years of writing and research. During that time, I was assisted by many people, and would like to take this opportunity to express my thanks.

Two of my colleagues at Harvard Business School, Robert Hayes and Robert Stobaugh, were especially supportive and influential. They helped me frame the original research project, met with me repeatedly to review work-in-progress, and commented extensively on drafts of each chapter. I have benefited enormously from their insights, which have vastly improved the final manuscript.

Other Harvard Business School colleagues also provided sage advice. Earl Sasser introduced me to the subject of quality and gave me a number of valuable comments on early drafts. Two directors of the Business School's Division of Research, E. Raymond Corey and Benson Shapiro, provided funding for the project, as well as thoughtful guidance as it evolved. Both commented extensively on the manuscript. Helpful comments were also provided, on selected chapters as well as early papers, by Kenneth Andrews, C. Roland Christensen, Colyer Crum, Kenneth Goodpaster, Barbara Jackson, Alan Kantrow, Janice Klein, Theodore Levitt, John Quelch, Wickham Skinner, and the editors and referees of *Harvard Business Review, Sloan Management Review, Columbia Journal of World Business, Business Horizons,* and *Academy of Management Journal,* where several of the ideas in this book first appeared.

A number of other people supported the project and ensured its completion. John Coleman and Helena Reilly provided extraordinarily skillful research assistance. Kathryn Neeld May made sure that funding was available when it was most needed; David Good did the same for computer time. The staff of the Word Processing Center cheerfully typed each chapter, with a rare combination of speed and accuracy. The Nomura School of Advanced Management in Tokyo arranged and coordinated my trip to Japan; without their help that phase of the project would have been impossible. I am grateful to Colyer Crum for my initial contacts with Nomura. I am also grateful to the hundreds of managers, first-line supervisors, and appliance servicemen and -women who filled out questionnaires, consented to interviews, provided factory tours, and otherwise assisted in the room air conditioning study that lies at the heart of this book.

I wish to thank the following publications for permission to use material that appeared in my articles: "Quality on the Line," *Harvard Business Review,* September–October 1983, pp. 64–75; "Product Quality: An Important Strategic Weapon," *Business Horizons,* March–April, 1984, pp. 40–43; "Japanese Quality Management," *Columbia Journal of World Business,* Fall 1984, pp. 3–12; "What Does 'Product Quality' Really Mean?," *Sloan Management Review,* Fall 1984, pp. 25–43; and "Quality Problems, Policies, and Attitudes in the United States and Japan: An Exploratory Study," *Academy of Management Journal,* December 1986, pp. 653–673.

My deepest thanks, however, go to the members of my family. My wife, Lynn, sustained me in countless ways—with humor, love, and suggestions on almost every chapter. My daughter, Diana, now all of two and one-half years old, provided diversion and delight; her enthusiasm has invariably been contagious. And my parents were enormously supportive cheerleaders; they have been my best teachers, as well as my most discerning readers. To these four very special people, I dedicate this book.

# Introduction

Quality is fast becoming one of the competitive issues of the 1980s and 1990s. A wave of imports, federal and state programs, and increased customer sensitivity have combined to give it new visibility. Pressures for improvement have become intense. The result is a heightened interest in quality management at many U.S. companies and a growing recognition of quality's strategic importance.

The challenge is vast. A 1981 survey reported that nearly 50 percent of U.S. consumers felt that the quality of American products had dropped during the previous five years.[1] Other surveys, repeated between 1973 and 1983, found that one-quarter of respondents were "not at all confident" that they could depend on industry to deliver reliable products.[2] In selected businesses, the picture is even bleaker. In 1973, 12 percent of U.S. consumers felt that Japanese cars were of better quality than American cars; a decade later, the figure had more than tripled, to 40 percent.[3]

The need for quality improvement is thus painfully evident. Yet, despite intense application, progress has been slow. Few U.S. companies have achieved dramatic breakthroughs in quality peformance; still fewer have matched the quality and reliability levels of their overseas competitors. The problem has not been a lack of interest, for managers in countless industries have joined the quality bandwagon. Programs have proliferated, as have tools and techniques. A lack of understanding, however, has impeded progress on several fronts.

Quality is an unusually slippery concept, easy to visualize and yet exasperatingly difficult to define. It remains a source of great confusion to managers, leading to the frequent but empty claim, "I know it when I see it."[4] Quality improvement is unlikely in such settings. Moreover, even when quality has been defined precisely, programs have lacked competitive impact. Many programs have been narrowly focused on the factory floor or have relied primarily on traditional methods of quality control. Little attention has been paid to the underlying sources of superior quality: the relative contributions of product design, vendor selection and management, and production and work force management. Tools and techniques have dominated instead, with short-term improvement projects often pursued at the expense of long-term quality planning. Links to competitive strategy have been few and far between.

Japanese companies provide an instructive contrast. Their quality performance has been enviable, with dramatic improvements since World War II. Today the quality and reliability of Japanese products are sources of great competitive advantage. Moreover, progress has been achieved through a carefully orchestrated campaign of micro and macro policies, top management involvement, and shop-floor activities. Little has been left to chance. An overriding philosophy has encouraged a holistic approach rather than a focus on technique. Short-term projects have therefore meshed neatly with long-term objectives, lending a strategic character to Japanese quality programs.

The aim of this book is to provide a deeper understanding of successful quality management by drawing on evidence from both the United States and Japan. Part I focuses on conceptual issues: the history and meaning of quality in the United States. Chapter 1 begins by tracing the history of the American quality movement from its roots in inspection through statistical quality control and quality assurance. It provides background and context, while also introducing a number of basic techniques: process control charts, sampling plans, cost of quality calculations, and reliability engineering. Chapter 2 focuses on strategic quality management, the last, and least understood, period in America's quality evolution. Elements of the strategic approach are carefully enumerated, and several examples are provided to distinguish the era from preceding ones, since many companies mistakenly assume that they have already adopted its precepts. Chapters 3 and 4 take the strategic approach a step further, reviewing the literature on quality and then breaking the concept into eight separate dimensions: performance, features, reliability, conformance, durability, serviceability, aesthetics, and perceived quality. Each of these dimensions can be a source of competitive advantage. And because tradeoffs among the dimensions are inevitable, positioning on quality becomes vastly more complex. Chapter 5 pursues the empirical implications of this argument. It reviews the evidence connecting quality and price, market share, advertising, cost, productivity, and profitability, and then shows that the direction and strength of these relationships depend largely on how quality has been defined.

The analysis in Part II is more focused, for it involves a case study of quality in a single U.S. industry, room air conditioning. Limiting the analysis in this way avoids mixing apples with oranges and ensures that all comparisons are firmly grounded. It also permits a rigorous application of the concepts of the preceding section. Chapter 6 begins by exploring consumers' perceptions of room air conditioner quality using the eight dimensions introduced in Chapter 4; it then compares consumers' quality rankings with the rankings of three expert panels: *Consumer Reports,* appliance servicemen and -women, and first-line supervisors. Chapter 7 presents objective measures of quality for the same industry. Both in-plant and field measures are reviewed, cross-sectionally and over time. The resulting industry portrait shows wide and persistent gaps between the best and poorest quality performers. Chapters 8 and 9 attempt to explain these gaps, the former by examining such sources of quality as product design, vendor selection and management, and production and work force management; and the latter by examining differences in companies' quality policies and management attitudes. Appendixes A, B, and C supplement the chapters in Part II with a fuller description of the room air conditioning study, an explanation of the methods used to classify plants by quality performance, and several statistical analyses.

In Part III, U.S. and Japanese approaches to quality management are compared. Chapter 10 begins with a historical review of the quality movement in Japan and then contrasts that movement, which was enormously successful, with the less effective American quality movement described in Chapter 1. Japan's success is traced to a combination of forces, including massive training programs, government policies such as the Industrial Standardization Law, and the leadership of such organizations as the Union of Japanese Scientists and Engineers. Chapter 11 takes a more microanalytic approach, exploring Japanese quality management at the factory level. Again, data from the room air conditioning industry are used. Seven Japanese plants are compared with the eleven U.S. plants examined in Chapters 6 through 9, using such categories as attitudes and philosophy; quality programs, policies, and systems; product design; vendor selection and management; and production and work force management. The last chapter of the book provides a brief conclusion, including a summary of key findings and a discussion of their implications for managers and researchers.

Throughout, a single theme dominates the analysis: the importance of understanding quality well enough to manage it. There are already far too many books on quality that emphasize methods and techniques at the expense of implementation. At the same time, most management guides lack rigor, offering simple solutions to quality problems but little supporting evidence. *Managing Quality* takes a different approach. By blending theory and practice, analysis and action, it shows how a more sophisticated understanding of quality can lead to long-term competitive advantage.

Part
I

The
Concept
of
Quality

# Chapter

# 1

# History and Evolution

$\mathbf{A}$s a concept, quality has been with us for millennia. Only recently has it emerged as a formal management function. The discipline is still evolving. In its original form, it was reactive and inspection-oriented; today, quality-related activities have broadened and are seen as essential for strategic success. Once the exclusive province of manufacturing and operations departments, quality now embraces functions as diverse as purchasing, engineering, and marketing research, and commands the attention of chief executive officers.

How have these changes come about? Most modern approaches to quality have emerged gradually, arriving through steady evolution rather than dramatic breakthroughs. They are the product of a series of discoveries stretching back over a century. In the United States, these discoveries can be organized into four distinct "quality eras": inspection, statistical quality control, quality assurance, and strategic quality management.[1] The first three are discussed in this chapter; the fourth, a more recent innovation, is reserved for Chapter 2.

## THE RISE OF INSPECTION

In the eighteenth and nineteenth centuries, quality control as we know it today did not yet exist. Most manufacturing was performed by artisans and skilled craftsmen or by journeymen and apprentices who were supervised by masters at the trade.[2] Goods were produced in small volumes; parts were matched to one another by hand, and after-the-fact inspection to ensure high quality was conducted informally, if at all. A well-performing product was viewed as the natural

3

outgrowth of reliance on skilled tradesmen for all aspects of design, manufacturing, and service.[3]

Formal inspection became necessary only with the rise of mass production and the need for interchangeable parts. As volumes increased, parts could no longer be fitted to one another by hand: The process required a large pool of skilled labor and was both costly and time-consuming. Prices were often beyond the reach of the average consumer, especially for machinery and equipment. Nor was the federal government able to purchase large quantities of high-quality firearms at low cost.

These pressures gave rise to what has been called the American system of manufacturing: the use of special-purpose machinery to produce interchangeable parts by following a preestablished sequence of operations.[4] Most initial efforts were connected with the military's demand for armaments and were closely coordinated by the United States Ordnance Department, the national armory at Springfield, Massachusetts, and the Harpers Ferry Armory. In consumer products, the Singer Company, which manufactured sewing machines, and the McCormick Harvesting Company, which made farm equipment, later adopted the same techniques.

From a quality control standpoint, the key breakthrough was the development of a rational jig, fixture, and gauging system in the early 1800s.[5] Jigs and fixtures are devices that position tools or hold parts while they are being worked on, keeping them fixed to the equipment so that machining operations can be performed accurately and precisely. Since every part that is worked on is held in place in exactly the same way—all jigs and fixtures having been designed from a standard model of the product to be manufactured—a high degree of interchangeability is assured. Nevertheless, parts may still deviate from one another: They may have been mounted improperly during machining, built from imperfect raw materials, or made on worn tooling. To minimize problems at final assembly, when parts are matched together for the first time, accurate inspection is required during the process of manufacture. A system of gauges is often used for that purpose; like jigs and fixtures, gauges are based on a standard model of the product to ensure uniformity.

By 1819, an elaborate gauging system was in place at the Springfield Armory. It gave inspection a new respectability, for activities that were previously conducted by eye were replaced by a more objective, verifiable process.[6] Two inspectors using a gauge were much more likely to reach the same result than two who were relying on personal judgment alone.

As the American system of manufacturing matured, gauging became more refined, and inspection became even more important. In the early 1900s, Frederick W. Taylor, the father of "scientific management," gave the activity added legitimacy by singling it out as an assigned task for one of the eight functional bosses (foremen) required for effective shop management:

> The inspector is responsible for the quality of the work, and both the workmen and the speed bosses [who see that the proper cutting tools are used, that the work is properly driven, and that cuts are started in the right part of the piece] must see that the work is finished to suit him. This man can, of course, do his work best if he is a master of the art of finishing work both well and quickly.[7]

Inspection activities were linked more formally to quality control in 1922, with the publication of G. S. Radford's *The Control of Quality in Manufacturing*.[8] For the first time, quality was viewed as a distinct management responsibility and as an independent function. The book even touched on a number of principles regarded as central to modern-day quality control: the need to get designers involved early in quality activities, the need for close coordination among the various departments affecting quality, and the association of quality improvement with increased output and lower costs. Its primary focus, however, was inspection. Nine of the book's twenty-three chapters were devoted to that subject alone. Topics included the purpose of inspection (to "exercise the duty of viewing the work closely and critically so as to ascertain the quality, detect the errors, and present them to the attention of the proper persons in such a way as to have the work brought up to standard");[9] the evolution of inspection (from visual to dimensional checks); types of inspection (material, office, tool, and process); sampling methods (including 100 percent and random sampling, but without any statistical foundation); gauging techniques; and the organization of the inspection department. Throughout, the emphasis was on conformance and its link with inspection; according to Radford, the purchaser's "principal interest in quality [was] that evenness or uniformity which results when the manufacturer adheres to his established requirements."[10]

Here matters stood for several years. Quality control was limited to inspection and to such narrow activities as counting, grading, and repair. Troubleshooting was considered beyond the reach of the average inspection department.[11] In the next decade, however, the role of the quality professional would be redefined. The stimulus for change was research conducted at Bell Telephone Laboratories; the result was what is today called statistical quality control.

## STATISTICAL QUALITY CONTROL

The year 1931 marked a watershed for the quality movement. W. A. Shewhart's *Economic Control of Quality of Manufactured Product* was published that year, giving the discipline a scientific footing for the first time.[12] Much of modern-day quality control can be traced to that single volume. In it, Shewhart gave a precise and measurable definition of manufacturing control, developed powerful techniques for monitoring and evaluating day-to-day production, and suggested a variety of ways of improving quality.

Shewhart was in fact part of a larger group at Bell Telephone Laboratories that was investigating problems of quality. The group's research was prompted by the concerns of engineers at Western Electric, the manufacturing arm of the Bell System, who were seeking greater standardization and uniformity in the nationwide telephone network. Most attention was focused on the complex equipment being built at the company's Hawthorne Works. How, the engineers wondered, could the maximum amount of information about the quality of these units be extracted from the minimum amount of inspection data? And how should that data be presented? In 1924, an Inspection Engineering Department was established at Western Electric to address such questions; it later became the Quality Assurance Department of Bell Laboratories. The group, which included such luminaries as Shewhart, Harold Dodge, Harry Romig, G. D. Edwards, and later Joseph Juran, was largely responsible for creating the present-day discipline of statistical quality control.[13]

### Process Control

The initial breakthrough was Shewhart's. He was the first to recognize that variability was a fact of industrial life and that it could be understood using the principles of probability and statistics. Shewhart observed that no two parts were likely to be manufactured to precisely the same specifications. Raw materials, operator skills, and equipment would all vary to some degree. Even the same part produced by a single operator on a single machine was likely to show variation over time. From a management standpoint, this required a rethinking of the problem of quality. The issue was no longer the existence of variation—it was certain to continue at some level no matter what actions were taken—but how to distinguish acceptable variation from fluctuations that indicated trouble.

The entire analysis grew out of Shewhart's concept of statistical control:

> A phenomenon will be said to be controlled when, through the use of past experience, we can predict, at least within limits, how the phenomenon may be expected to vary in the future. Here it is understood that prediction means that we can state, at least approximately, the probability that the observed phenomenon will fall within the given limits.[14]

Shewhart then developed simple statistical techniques for determining these limits, as well as graphic methods for plotting production values to assess whether they fell within the acceptable range. The result, the process control chart illustrated in Figure 1.1, is one of the most powerful tools used by today's quality professionals.[15] By segregating abnormal (assignable) causes of variation from those that are inherent in a production process, it ensures that genuine problems are distinguished from those due purely to chance. Moreover, it does so by drawing samples of output during the course of production, rather than waiting until after a unit has been fully assembled.

At the same time that Shewhart was pursuing his work on process control, other researchers at Bell Laboratories were advancing the practice of sampling, the second critical element in the growth of statistical quality control. Harold Dodge and Harry Romig were the prime movers in this effort.

### Sampling

Sampling techniques start from the simple premise that 100 percent inspection is an inefficient way of sorting good products from bad. Checking a limited number of items in a production lot, then deciding on that basis whether the entire lot is acceptable, is clearly an alternative. The process, however, entails certain risks. Because samples are never fully representative, one may occasionally accept

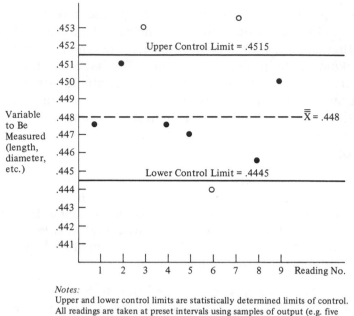

Notes:
Upper and lower control limits are statistically determined limits of control.
All readings are taken at preset intervals using samples of output (e.g. five
    parts in a row).
$\bar{\bar{X}}$ = grand average of all readings.
● = readings falling within limits (variations due to chance).
○ = readings falling outside limits (assignable causes to be corrected).

FIGURE 1.1    A Typical Process Control Chart

a production lot that in reality contains a large number of defective items. A related error is also possible: One may reject a production lot that is actually of perfectly acceptable quality.

Dodge and Romig recognized these problems, called consumer's and producer's risk, and devised plans for dealing with them systematically. They were able to develop sampling plans that ensured that for a given level of defects, the probability of unwittingly accepting an unsatisfactory lot would be limited to a certain percentage.[16] A certain number of items would be checked for a specified lot size. If according to the sampling tables the number of defective items in that group exceeded the number allowable, the entire lot would be rejected.

Useful as it was, the method was limited in application. It applied only to individual production lots, rather than to the overall level of quality produced by a manufacturing process. A new concept, the average outgoing quality limit (AOQL), was developed to meet that deficiency. It indicated the maximum percentage of defective units that a process would produce under two conditions: sampling inspection by lots, and the individual separation of good from bad items in all lots that had already been rejected on the basis of sampling.[17] A typical AOQL sampling table, showing the relationship between process quality, lot size, sampling rules, and outgoing quality, is illustrated in Figure 1.2.

These breakthroughs were instrumental in improving the quality of telephone equipment and service. Inspection costs fell, quality improved, and with fewer defects to correct, employees became more productive. Surprisingly, however, neither sampling techniques nor process control charts had much of an immediate impact outside the Bell System. Most of the original research was published in technical journals with limited circulation. Only with the advent of World War II and the need to produce munitions in large volumes did the concepts of statistical quality control gain a wider audience.

### The Impact of World War II

In December 1940, a committee was formed by the War Department to draft standards in the area of quality. The standards were published in 1941 and 1942. Their primary focus was the development and use of control charts. At roughly the same time, the Ordnance Department of the U.S. Army was facing the problem of how to get large quantities of arms and ammunition from multiple suppliers at acceptable levels of quality. Two alternatives were under consideration: extensive training of contractors in the use of process control charts and the development of a system of acceptance sampling procedures to be applied by government inspectors. The second approach won out, and in 1942 a Quality Control section was established in the War Department, staffed largely by statisticians from Bell Laboratories.[18]

This group soon developed a new set of sampling tables based on the concept of acceptable quality levels (AQL): the poorest quality (maximum percent defective) that a supplier could maintain over time and still be considered satisfactory. Two kinds of inspection were involved. Normal inspection, which required fewer checks, was used when the products under review had recently proved to have a defect rate lower than or equal to the AQL. Tightened inspection was used when the defect rate had recently exceeded the AQL. The tables also contained rules showing when to switch from one method of inspection to the other.[19]

AVERAGE OUTGOING QUALITY LIMIT = 0.75%

| Process Average % | 0-.015 | | | .016-.15 | | | .16-.30 | | | .31-.45 | | | .46-.60 | | | .61-.75 | | |
|---|---|---|---|---|---|---|---|---|---|---|---|---|---|---|---|---|---|---|
| Lot Size | n | c | $P_t\%$ | n | c | $P_t\%$ | n | c | $P_t\%$ | n | c | $P_t\%$ | n | c | $P_t\%$ | n | c | $P_t\%$ |
| 1-25 | All | 0 | — | All | 0 | — | All | 0 | — | All | 0 | — | All | 0 | — | All | 0 | — |
| 26-50 | 25 | 0 | 6.4 | 25 | 0 | 6.4 | 25 | 0 | 6.4 | 25 | 0 | 6.4 | 25 | 0 | 6.4 | 25 | 0 | 6.4 |
| 51-100 | 33 | 0 | 5.6 | 33 | 0 | 5.6 | 33 | 0 | 5.6 | 33 | 0 | 5.6 | 33 | 0 | 5.6 | 33 | 0 | 5.6 |
| 101-200 | 39 | 0 | 5.2 | 39 | 0 | 5.2 | 39 | 0 | 5.2 | 39 | 0 | 5.2 | 39 | 0 | 5.2 | 39 | 0 | 5.2 |
| 201-300 | 42 | 0 | 5.0 | 42 | 0 | 5.0 | 42 | 0 | 5.0 | 42 | 0 | 5.0 | 42 | 0 | 5.0 | 42 | 0 | 5.0 |
| 301-400 | 44 | 0 | 4.9 | 44 | 0 | 4.9 | 44 | 0 | 4.9 | 44 | 0 | 4.9 | 90 | 1 | 4.0 | 90 | 1 | 4.0 |
| 401-500 | 45 | 0 | 4.8 | 45 | 0 | 4.8 | 45 | 0 | 4.8 | 90 | 1 | 4.1 | 90 | 1 | 4.1 | 90 | 1 | 4.1 |
| 501-600 | 45 | 0 | 4.9 | 45 | 0 | 4.9 | 45 | 0 | 4.9 | 95 | 1 | 3.9 | 95 | 1 | 3.9 | 95 | 1 | 3.9 |
| 601-800 | 46 | 0 | 4.9 | 46 | 0 | 4.9 | 100 | 1 | 3.8 | 100 | 1 | 3.8 | 100 | 1 | 3.8 | 100 | 1 | 3.8 |
| 801-1000 | 47 | 0 | 4.8 | 47 | 0 | 4.8 | 100 | 1 | 3.8 | 100 | 1 | 3.8 | 100 | 1 | 3.8 | 155 | 2 | 3.2 |
| 1001-2000 | 48 | 0 | 4.7 | 48 | 0 | 4.7 | 105 | 1 | 3.7 | 105 | 1 | 3.7 | 170 | 2 | 3.1 | 170 | 2 | 3.1 |
| 2001-3000 | 48 | 0 | 4.7 | 110 | 1 | 3.5 | 110 | 1 | 3.5 | 170 | 2 | 3.1 | 170 | 2 | 3.1 | 240 | 3 | 2.8 |
| 3001-4000 | 48 | 0 | 4.7 | 110 | 1 | 3.5 | 110 | 1 | 3.5 | 175 | 2 | 3.1 | 245 | 3 | 2.7 | 315 | 4 | 2.5 |
| 4001-5000 | 49 | 0 | 4.6 | 110 | 1 | 3.6 | 175 | 2 | 3.1 | 175 | 2 | 3.1 | 245 | 3 | 2.7 | 320 | 4 | 2.5 |
| 5001-7000 | 49 | 0 | 4.6 | 110 | 1 | 3.6 | 180 | 2 | 3.0 | 250 | 3 | 2.7 | 325 | 4 | 2.5 | 400 | 5 | 2.3 |
| 7001-10,000 | 49 | 0 | 4.6 | 110 | 1 | 3.7 | 180 | 2 | 3.0 | 255 | 3 | 2.6 | 405 | 5 | 2.3 | 560 | 7 | 2.1 |
| 10,001-20,000 | 49 | 0 | 4.6 | 110 | 1 | 3.7 | 255 | 3 | 2.6 | 335 | 4 | 2.4 | 495 | 6 | 2.1 | 750 | 9 | 1.9 |
| 20,001-50,000 | 110 | 1 | 3.7 | 180 | 2 | 3.0 | 260 | 3 | 2.6 | 420 | 5 | 2.2 | 675 | 8 | 1.9 | 1130 | 13 | 1.6 |
| 50,001-100,000 | 110 | 1 | 3.7 | 185 | 2 | 2.9 | 335 | 4 | 2.4 | 590 | 7 | 2.0 | 955 | 11 | 1.7 | 1720 | 19 | 1.5 |

Notes:

n = size of sample. Entry of "All" indicates that each piece in lot is to be inspected.

c = allowable defect number for sample. If more than this number of defects is found, the lot should be rejected.

$P_t$ = lot tolerance percent defective corresponding to a consumer's risk (Pc) = 0.10. This means that under the given sampling plan, the probability of inadvertently accepting a lot whose quality (measured in percent defective) is $P_t$, is at most 10 percent.

Process average = the average percentage of defective units produced by the manufacturing process.

FIGURE 1.2  A Typical AOQL Single Sampling Table

SOURCE: H. F. Dodge, "Notes on the Evolution of Acceptance Sampling Plans, Part I," *Journal of Quality Technology*, April 1969, p. 85. Copyright © 1969 American Society for Quality Control. Reprinted with permission.

These techniques were immensely successful. The primary bottle-neck slowing the production of war materials had occurred in inspection; it was soon eliminated.[20] In the first eight months after the methods were introduced on a large scale, inspectors were able to process far higher volumes. The number of Ordnance Department inspectors per million dollars of accepted material dropped from 42 to 12.[21] Substantial improvements in quality were realized as well.

Meanwhile, additional training programs were being organized by the Office of Production Research and Development (OPRD) of the War Production Board. Researchers at Bell Laboratories again played a leading role, this time in cooperation with major universities. Walter Shewhart, for example, was instrumental in selling the initial proposal to OPRD. At the time, the techniques of statistical quality control had still seen little application outside the telephone company. As one of the early academic participants in the program remarked: "What we professors had at the time was faith—faith that statistical techniques would prove to be widely useful in the control of quality in many different kinds of manufacturing."[22] The aim of the programs that were finally developed was the rapid dissemination of these techniques to other branches of industry.

Courses were first offered at the Carnegie Institute of Technology in 1941 and Stanford in 1942. By the end of the war, institutions in twenty-five states were involved. A total of 8,000 people were trained in courses ranging from one-day executive programs to intensive eight-day seminars for engineers, inspectors, and other quality control practitioners.[23]

Most early trainees made little effort to apply the techniques they had learned. Statistical concepts were still something of a novelty, with only a brief track record. A few companies, however, achieved spectacular gains; these were reported in follow-up seminars and proved instrumental in inducing other companies to experiment with process control and sampling methods.[24]

Soon the students who had attended the courses began to form local societies for quality control. In October 1945, thirteen of these groups banded together to become the Society of Quality Engineers; a year later they merged with another federation to become the American Society for Quality Control (ASQC). Today, the ASQC remains the field's dominant professional group. Meanwhile, the first U.S. journal on the subject, *Industrial Quality Control,* was published in July 1944 by the Buffalo Society of Quality Control Engineers. It later became *Quality Progress,* the official magazine of the ASQC.[25]

By the late 1940s, then, quality control was established as a recognized discipline. Its methods were primarily statistical, however, and its impact was confined largely to the factory floor. Little would change until several key works were published in the 1950s and early 1960s. These ushered in the next major quality era, that of quality assurance.

## QUALITY ASSURANCE

During the period of quality assurance, quality evolved from a narrow, manufacturing-based discipline to one with broader implications for management. Problem prevention remained the primary goal, but the profession's tools expanded far beyond statistics. Four separate elements were involved: quantifying the costs of quality, total quality control, reliability engineering, and zero defects.

### Costs of Quality

Until the 1950s, most efforts to improve quality were based on the unstated assumption that defects were costly. How costly was a matter of conjecture, for few companies had gone to the trouble of tallying up the expenses they incurred because products were not built right the first time. In the absence of such a yardstick, managers accustomed to making decisions on the basis of hard numbers had little to go on. For them, a critical question remained: How much quality was enough?

In 1951 Joseph Juran tackled the question in the first edition of his *Quality Control Handbook,* a publication that would shortly become the profession's bible.[26] Its initial chapter discussed the economics of quality and proposed the now famous analogy to "gold in the mine." Juran observed that the costs of achieving a given level of quality could be divided into avoidable and unavoidable costs. The latter were the costs associated with prevention—inspection, sampling, sorting, and other quality control initiatives. Avoidable costs were those of defects and product failures—scrapped materials, labor hours required for rework and repair, complaint processing, and financial losses resulting from unhappy customers. Juran regarded failure costs as "gold in the mine" because they could be reduced sharply by investing in quality improvement. The payoff from these efforts could be substantial: At the time, Juran estimated that avoidable quality losses were typically in the range of $500 to $1,000 per productive operator per year.[27]

Managers now had a way of deciding how much to invest in quality improvement. Additional expenditures on prevention were likely to be justified as long as failure costs remained high. The concept also illustrated another important principle: that decisions made early in the production chain—for example, when engineers first sketched out a new product's design—had implications for the level of quality costs incurred later on, in both the factory and the field.

### Total Quality Control

In 1956 Armand Feigenbaum took this principle a step further by proposing "total quality control." High-quality products, he argued, were unlikely to be produced if the manufacturing department was forced to work in isolation:

> The underlying principle of this total quality view . . . is that, to provide genuine effectiveness, control must start with the design of the product and end only when the product has been placed in the hands of a customer who remains satisfied . . . the first principle to recognize is *that quality is everybody's job.*[28]

Feigenbaum noted that all new products, as they moved from design to market, involved roughly the same activities. From a quality standpoint, they could be grouped into three categories: new design control, incoming material control, and product or shop floor control. The first, for example, involved preproduction assessments of a design's "manufacturability" as well as the debugging of new manufacturing techniques through pilot runs. To be successful, these activities required the cooperation of multiple departments. In fact, as products moved through the three principal stages, groups as varied as marketing, engineering, purchasing, manufacturing, shipping, and customer service had to become involved. Otherwise, mistakes might be made early in the process that would cause problems to appear later—during assembly or, worse yet, after the product was in a customer's hands.

To make the system work, many companies developed elaborate matrices, like the one in Figure 1.3, listing departmental responsibilities across the top and required activities down the left-hand side.

| Activity or Function | Group or Department | | | | | | | |
|---|---|---|---|---|---|---|---|---|
|  | General Management | Finance | Marketing | Engineering | Manufacturing | Quality Control | Purchasing | Service |
| Establish product reliability and quality policies | x | o | o | o | o | o | o | o |
| Analyze quality costs | o | x |  |  |  | x |  |  |
| Perform in-process quality audits |  |  |  | o | o | x |  |  |
| Ensure that new product designs meet the test of manufacturability and ease of service |  |  |  | x | x | o |  | x |
| Establish specifications for purchased parts and materials and qualify vendors |  |  |  | x |  | o | x |  |

x  indicates the departments primarily responsible for an activity.
o  indicates other departments that should be involved in an activity.

FIGURE 1.3    A Typical Matrix of Quality Responsibilities

SOURCE: Adapted from A. V. Feigenbaum, *Total Quality Control* (New York: Mc-Graw-Hill, 1961), p. 65. Reprinted with permission.

The matrices typically showed considerable overlap among functions, for few activities were likely to be error-free if they were assigned to a single department or were pursued seriatim. Interfunctional teams therefore became essential: They ensured that diverse viewpoints were represented and that otherwise autonomous departments worked together. Top management was ultimately responsible for the effectiveness of the system; to maintain its interest, Feigenbaum, like Juran, proposed careful measurement and reporting of the costs of quality.

The two experts also agreed on the need for a new type of quality professional. Statistical methods were still important—both authors devoted large sections of their books to explanations of process control and sampling—as were traditional techniques of inspection and gauging. But the quality system now included new product development, vendor selection, and customer service, in addition to manufacturing control. To deal with these responsibilities, both Feigenbaum and Juran argued that a new function, quality control engineering, was necessary.[29] It would be involved in high-level quality planning, coordinating the activities of other departments, setting quality standards, and providing quality measurements. These activities required a mix of management skills. They implied that a statistics background was no longer enough to guarantee competence as a quality professional.

Reliability Engineering

Yet, at about the same time that Feigenbaum and Juran were making these arguments, another branch of the discipline was emerging that relied even more heavily on probability theory and statistics: reliability engineering, which had as its objective the assurance of acceptable product performance over time.[30] The field was closely aligned with the postwar growth of the aerospace and electronics industries in the United States; as a result, the military was a prime supporter. In 1950 the Department of Defense formed an Ad Hoc Group on Reliability of Electronic Equipment, and in 1957 a major report was issued on the subject.[31] The report eventually resulted in a number of military specifications setting out the requirements for a formal reliability program.

These efforts were stimulated by the plummeting reliability of military components and systems. In 1950 only one-third of the Navy's electronic devices were working properly at any given time. A study by the Rand Corporation at the time estimated that every vacuum tube the military had plugged in and working was backed by nine others in warehouses or on order. Equally serious problems were encountered with missiles and other aerospace equipment.[32]

Clearly, greater attention needed to be paid to product performance over time. The first step was to define reliability more precisely—as "the probability of a product's performing a specified function without failure, for a given period of time, under specified conditions."[33] Coupled with the tools of modern probability theory, this definition led to formal methods for predicting equipment performance over time. It also resulted in techniques for reducing failure rates while products were still in the design stage.

Much of the analysis rested on the concept of a probability distribution. This was no more than a mathematical relationship specifying a product's reliability (or inversely, its failure rate) as a function of time. Engineers soon found that different operating conditions and different products were better approximated by different mathematical forms. Among the most popular were the exponential life function, which assumed that a product's failure rate remained relatively unchanged over its entire operating life; the Weibull distribution, which allowed failure rates to increase or decrease over time as products improved or deteriorated with age; and the "bathtub curve"—so called because of its distinctive shape—which dropped the assumption that failure rates were constant or changed steadily over time and argued instead for a break-in period (when failure rates were high), a normal operating period (when failure rates were constant and relatively low), and a wear-out phase (when failures rose steadily as the product deteriorated).[34] These relationships were then coupled with careful testing programs designed to simulate extreme operating conditions, to estimate reliability levels even before products reached full-scale production.

Prediction, however, was only the first step. The discipline's real goal was to improve reliability and reduce failure rates over time. To accomplish these ends, a variety of techniques were employed: failure mode and effect analysis (FMEA), which systematically reviewed the ways a product could fail and on that basis proposed alternative designs; individual component analysis, which computed the probability of failure of key components and then tried to eliminate or strengthen the weakest links; derating, which required that parts be used below their specified stress levels; and redundancy, which involved the use of parallel systems to ensure that backups were available whenever an important component or subsystem failed.[35] An effective reliability program also required close monitoring of field failures. Otherwise, engineers would be denied vital information—a product's actual operating experience—useful for planning new designs. Field failure reporting normally involved comprehensive systems of data collection as well as efforts to ensure that failed parts were returned to the laboratory for further testing and analysis.[36]

Like total quality control, reliability engineering was aimed at preventing defects from happening in the first place. It too emphasized engineering skills and attention to quality throughout the design process. Zero defects, the last significant development in the quality assurance era, took a different tack: It focused on management expectations and the human relations side of the equation.

### Zero Defects

Zero defects had its genesis at the Martin Company in 1961–62.[37] At the time, Martin was building Pershing missiles for the U.S. Army. Their quality, though generally good, was achieved only through massive inspection. Incentives were offered to workers to lower the defect rate still further; together with even more intensive inspection and testing, these efforts led, on December 12, 1961, to the delivery of a Pershing missile to Cape Canaveral with zero discrepancies.

A defect-free missile could therefore be made, although it was likely to require extensive debugging before shipment. A month later, Martin's general manager in Orlando, Florida, accepted a request from the U.S. Army's missile command to deliver the first field Pershing one month ahead of schedule. He went even further—he promised that the missile would be perfect, with no hardware problems, no document errors, and all equipment set up and fully operational ten days after delivery (the norm was ninety days or more). Two months of feverish activity followed. Since little time was available for the usual inspection and after-the-fact correction of errors, all employees were asked to contribute to building the missile exactly right the first time. The result was still a surprise: In February 1962 a perfect missile was delivered. It arrived on time and was fully operational in less than twenty-four hours.

This experience was an eye-opener for Martin. After careful review, management concluded that the project's success was primarily a reflection of its own changed attitude: "The reason behind the lack of perfection was simply that perfection had not been expected. The one time management demanded perfection, it happened!"[38] Similar reasoning suggested a need to focus on workers' motivation and awareness. Of the three most common causes of worker errors— lack of knowledge, lack of proper facilities, and lack of attention— management concluded that the last had been least often addressed. It set out to design a program whose overriding goal was to "promote a constant, conscious desire to do a job (any job) right the first time."[39]

The resulting program was called zero defects. It was very heavy on philosophy, motivation, and awareness, and much leaner when it came to specific proposals and problem-solving techniques. A key step, in fact—the identification of problems at their source and the design of remedial efforts (called error cause removal)—was developed by the Small Engine Department of General Electric, an early adopter of the program, and not by Martin. Martin's contribution lay primarily in articulating a philosophy—that the only acceptable quality standard was zero defects—and in showing how it could be instilled in the work force through training, special events, the posting of quality results, goal-setting, and personal feedback. That was no small achievement. Since the prevailing quality ethic at the time was acceptable quality levels (AQL)—the idea, associated with sampling techniques, that some non-zero level of defects was good enough—Martin was fighting nearly thirty years of quality control history. Even today, the debate continues. One of the most popular—and controversial—recent books on quality is *Quality Is Free,* written by Philip B. Crosby, an advocate of zero defects who worked at Martin in the 1960s.[40] Crosby's claim that perfect quality is both technically possible and economically desirable has rekindled many of the old arguments about how much quality is enough.

## EVOLUTION AND CHANGE

Zero defects was the last major movement in the quality assurance era. Together with reliability engineering, total quality control, and the costs of quality, it helped expand the boundaries of the quality profession. Design, engineering, planning, and service activities were now as relevant as statistics and manufacturing control. New management skills were required, especially in the area of human relations. Interfunctional coordination became a primary concern, and quality professionals shifted their attention to program design, standard setting, and monitoring the activities of other departments.

Table 1.1 charts the evolution from inspection to quality assurance in more detail. It shows how quality management in the United States has expanded in ever widening circles, each era incorporating elements of the one that preceded it. Quality assurance, for example, acknowledged the role of statistical analysis while placing it in the larger context of the production chain, just as quality control saw gauging and measurement as a small part of the problem of efficient inspection. Early breakthroughs were seldom rejected; rather, they were subsumed within larger categories.

The resulting pattern of change reflects, in microcosm, the evolution of U.S. industry and the escalating demand it faced for technically sophisticated products. When American manufacturing involved only simple fabrication and assembly and low production volumes, informal inspection was enough to ensure high quality. Larger volumes, however, required tighter control and led to separate inspection departments and precise systems of gauging. The nationwide telephone network resulted in a further leap forward. It involved still more complex equipment and even higher degrees of standardization; both enhanced the desirability of statistical meth-

TABLE 1.1  *From Inspection to Quality Assurance*

|  | | Stage of the Quality Movement | |
|---|---|---|---|
| Identifying Characteristics | Inspection | Statistical Quality Control | Quality Assurance |
| Primary concern | detection | control | coordination |
| View of quality | a problem to be solved | a problem to be solved | a problem to be solved, but one that is attacked proactively |
| Emphasis | product uniformity | product uniformity with reduced inspection | the entire production chain, from design to market, and the contribution of all functional groups, especially designers, to preventing quality failures |
| Methods | gauging and measurement | statistical tools and techniques | programs and systems |
| Role of quality professionals | inspection, sorting, counting, and grading | troubleshooting and the application of statistical methods | quality measurement, quality planning, and program design |
| Who has responsibility for quality | the inspection department | the manufacturing and engineering departments | all departments, although top management is only peripherally involved in designing, planning, and executing quality policies |
| Orientation and approach | "inspects in" quality | "controls in" quality | "builds in" quality |

19

ods. Scale effects played a role in the discipline's later evolution as well. The war years were a fertile period for quality control for just this reason.

Quality assurance continued these trends. It was born of necessity: the need to meet the tightened specifications and performance criteria demanded by the country's military, electronics, and space programs. Product design became more exacting, giving rise to reliability engineering and the need for better coordination among departments before new products were released. At the same time, a number of new ideas were emerging in American thinking about human resource management. Such concepts as Theory Y and the Scanlon Plan encouraged companies to offer greater autonomy to workers.[41] The zero defects movement, with its emphasis on motivation and employee initiative, was remarkably similar in spirit.

Yet, in spite of these changes, approaches to quality remained largely defensive throughout this period. The main objective of the quality department was still the prevention of defects. Even though a proactive approach was now being pursued, quality was still viewed negatively—as something that could hurt a company if ignored—rather than as a possible basis for competition. That view finally changed in the 1970s and 1980s, when the strategic aspects of quality were recognized and embraced.

# Chapter
# 2

---

# Strategic Quality
# Management

The beginnings of strategic quality management cannot be dated precisely, for no single book or article marks the transition. Many American managers, in fact, appear to believe that quality assurance was the discipline's last important development. The quality programs they are now adopting are strikingly similar to those that emerged twenty years earlier. They rely on such well-established principles as interfunctional coordination, zero defects, the costs of quality, and statistical quality control.[1] Based on this evidence, the quality movement's last two decades would seem to have been little more than business as usual, with few advances over past practice.

In a growing number of companies, however, a new vision has begun to emerge. It embodies a dramatic shift in perspective. For the first time, top managers, at the level of presidents and chief executive officers, have expressed an interest in quality. They have linked it with profitability, defined it from the customer's point of view, and required its inclusion in the strategic planning process. In the most radical departure of all, many have insisted that quality be viewed as an aggressive competitive weapon.

## CHALLENGE AND RESPONSE

These changes did not appear overnight. A variety of external forces, each linking losses of profitability and market share to poor quality, paved the way. Together, they awakened companies to quality's competitive potential. Among the most important influences were increased foreign competition, a sharp jump in the number of product

21

liability suits, and pressures from the government on several fronts. For many American managers, however, the rudest awakening came from the dramatic inroads made by Japanese manufacturers because of their superior quality and reliability.[2]

The semiconductor industry provides an instructive example. Until recently, evidence on companies' comparative quality performance was scarce and closely held. But in March 1980, Richard W. Anderson, General Manager of Hewlett-Packard's Data Systems Division, reported that after testing 300,000 16K RAM chips from three American and three Japanese manufacturers, Hewlett-Packard had discovered wide disparities in quality. At incoming inspection, the Japanese chips had a failure rate of *zero*; the comparable rate for the three U.S. manufacturers was between 0.11 and 0.19 percent. After 1,000 hours of use, the failure rate of the Japanese chips was between 0.010 and 0.019 percent; after the same period, the American chips had a failure rate between 0.059 and 0.267 percent.[3]

The extent of these differences shocked the industry. Several U.S. companies reacted with complaints of selective shipping, claiming that the Japanese were sending only their best components to important U.S. customers such as Hewlett-Packard. Others disputed the basic data. Yet the differences in quality fitted well with the rapid ascendancy of Japanese chip manufacturers, who in a few years had gone from a standing start to large market shares in both the 16K and 64K chip markets.[4] Remedial efforts quickly began at most American semiconductor manufacturers, and in 16K chips the quality gap soon closed. But the lesson was not lost on other U.S. managers, in industries as diverse as machine tools, radial tires, and color televisions, who had seen their positions erode in the face of Japanese competition. For them, quality took on a new importance.

A few years earlier, a number of government agencies had begun to scrutinize quality; their efforts soon had a similar effect. Programs took several forms, although all included a closer policing of defects and unsatisfactory performance. For example, product recalls rose dramatically during the 1970s. In 1973, just over 7 million units of various products were recalled because of campaigns to correct potential safety hazards by the National Highway Traffic Safety Administration, the Environmental Protection Agency, and the Consumer Product Safety Commission. In 1978, the total number of units recalled by these agencies had jumped to more than 29 million.[5] The recalls were often extremely expensive. In October 1978, Firestone Tire and Rubber began a recall of its Firestone 500 steel-belted radial tires; three years later, the recall had cost the company $182 million.[6]

Not all defects, of course, involve potential safety hazards. Some are simply aggravating and expensive. In recent years, federal and state governments have begun to take action on these problems as well. For example, the U.S. Federal Trade Commission now has a product defects program that holds manufacturers responsible for failures incurred shortly after warranties expire.[7] Complaints are filed by the agency if three conditions are met: The product contains systematic, known defects; the company could have disclosed information to buyers about likely problems but failed to do so; and the agency sees action to be "in the public interest" and likely to increase consumer welfare. Among the companies cited for violations under the program have been Mobil, General Motors, and Champion Home Builders. Corrective action has ranged from repairs and reimbursement to the disclosure of additional product information.

In a similar vein, several states have recently enacted "lemon laws."[8] These statutes apply to automobiles with recurrent defects. If dealers are unable to repair major problems in a reasonable period of time—even though the repairs occur early in the car's life and are covered by warranty—consumers may be entitled to a comparable new car or a refund. "Lemons" have generally been defined as vehicles that have not been fixed after four separate attempts to repair the same defect or as vehicles that have spent at least thirty days in the repair shop during the warranty period. Should disputes arise over consumers' claims, they are normally referred to special arbitration panels.

In combination, such programs have sharply increased the cost of producing defective products. A rising tide of product liability suits has further raised the stakes. Between 1974 and 1981, the number of product liability suits filed in federal district courts grew at an annual average rate of 28 percent.[9] Damages rose as well, and today multimillion-dollar awards are not uncommon.

Because of the large sums involved, these external forces had the predictable effect of sensitizing top managers to product quality. With their companies' reputations, market shares, and profitability at risk, the topic could no longer be ignored. Nor could it be relegated to lower levels of the organization, where functional loyalties might interfere with a broader strategic vision. What emerged from this environment was a new approach to quality, one strongly shaped by the concerns of upper management.[10]

## ELEMENTS OF THE STRATEGIC APPROACH

To accommodate these concerns, quality first had to be redefined. Defect-free production, the object of both quality assurance and statistical quality control, was too limited in scope. A more outward-looking perspective was needed to gain the commitment of top managers, whose interests were strategic and competitive. The solution was to define quality from the customer's point of view.

The essence of the approach has been well summarized by a recent report to the American Society for Quality Control:

- It is not those who offer the product but those whom it serves— the customers, users, and those who influence or represent them—who have the final word on how well a product fulfills needs and expectations.
- Satisfaction is related to competitive offerings.
- Satisfaction, as related to competitive offerings, is formed over the product lifetime, not just at the time of purchase.
- A *composite* of attributes is needed to provide the most satisfaction to those whom the product serves.[11]

Here, quality has been defined comparatively—relative to competitors—rather than against fixed, internal standards. Customers, and not internal departments, have been given the final say in determining whether or not a product is acceptable. By implication, meeting specifications has become a secondary concern to be pursued only after users' needs have been carefully defined. Otherwise, excellence in process control provides little advantage, for it is easily misdirected.

This perspective suggests several new requirements. Market research on quality becomes more important; otherwise, companies would have no way of knowing how to position their products on the basis of quality.[12] Methods might include careful reviews of competitors' products, as well as surveys to establish exactly what customers mean when they say one product is of higher quality than another.[13] In addition, attention shifts from initial prices, at the time of purchase, to life-cycle costs, which include expenditures on service and maintenance over time and so reflect users' total costs more accurately.[14] Even consumer complaints may have a new role to play. As valuable sources of market information, they acquire high visibility through such devices as toll-free telephone hot lines and are no longer squirreled away as potentially damaging bad news.[15]

Managers at leading companies have embraced such programs, which can be quite expensive, because they see a clearer link between quality and profitability. Today's consumers are thought to be more sensitive to quality differences and more likely to direct their purchases accordingly. For example, high quality is expected to produce greater customer loyalty; over time, that should translate into an increased repurchase rate for products.[16] The payoff from such allegiance can be substantial. One automobile manufacturer has estimated that a loyal customer is worth at least $100,000 in revenues over his or her lifetime. Several banks have concluded that holding onto a customer for five years is worth $400 in profits.[17] Other research, first published in the 1970s, has confirmed quality's impact on the bottom line. The Profit Impact of Marketing Strategies (PIMS) studies, discussed at length in Chapter 5, have been especially influential.[18] They showed not only that companies whose products were of higher quality had a higher return on investment (ROI) for any given market share but that gains in quality were also associated with market share gains.

New evidence from the market place, then, convinced many managers that improving quality could be a profitable pursuit. A review of the production side usually pointed in the same direction. Managers have long known of the costs of quality, but only recently have they discovered the connection between quality and productivity.[19] Chapter 5 summarizes the available evidence, which suggests that a manufacturing process without defects runs far more efficiently than one that is constantly interrupted for rework and repair. Machine utilization is likely to be higher, buffer inventories smaller, and labor more productive.

Faced with such evidence, a growing number of companies came to the same conclusion: Quality was a powerful competitive weapon. On both the market and cost sides, it offered great leverage. Aggressive managers soon went a step further. If quality and profitability were so closely linked, they could see no reason to match competitors' quality levels. Why not exceed them instead?

That called for a rethinking of traditional approaches to quality, since dramatic—and continuing—improvement was desired. Competitors were unlikely to stand pat once they discovered that their quality had been surpassed; they too would try to improve. Quality goals would then become moving targets, reset continually at higher and higher levels. Continuous improvement would become the objective, rather than the achievement of stable AQLs.[20] That required a dedication to the improvement *process* as well as the commitment of the entire company. An important prerequisite quickly became clear: Top management had to be actively involved in the process.[21] Such high-level commitment was considered essential to establishing seriousness of purpose and long-run devotion to quality. In fact, many companies found that it was only after their highest executives devoted time to quality that employees took notice. For example, at the Materials and Controls Group of Texas Instruments, top managers were the first to take courses in quality control; they then spread the word by personally instructing employees at lower levels. The results were a program widely accepted by employees and steady improvement in quality.

In most cases, these programs have shared the same goal: the creation of an organizationwide commitment to quality. Top management participation has been one approach used; another has been extensive training and team-building.[22] To internalize a quality ethic often requires attitude change at various levels of the company. Otherwise, employees continue to view quality as the job of the quality department rather than a responsibility of their own. Broader understanding and personal involvement are usually necessary for improvement. Many companies have unknowingly fallen short here: They provide training in the tools of quality control but have failed to emphasize quality's connection with basic business objectives. The resulting programs have been long on technique but lacking in motivation and purpose.

The strategic approach to quality also places new demands on quality professionals.[23] Technical expertise remains desirable, but an understanding of the company's strategic goals becomes more important. Education and training become key responsibilities, as do program assessment, goal-setting, and consultative work with other departments. Overall, there is a clear shift away from a narrow policing role toward one that emphasizes more of a general management perspective.

To support that perspective, quality is often included explicitly in the strategic planning process. Annual goals are set for quality improvement and made specific and actionable.[24] Goals normally take into account the customer's perspective and are also matched against the expected performance of competitors. GTE, for example, as part of its strategic planning process, requires that each business unit identify the place of quality in its business strategy, define the important quality elements in its strategic programs, establish long-range quality-related goals, and explain how it will develop the commitment and coordination of line and staff functions to meet those goals. Both internal cost of quality measures and external customer-related measures are involved. For a division like Sylvania, which manufactures light bulbs, the customer-related side would include such goals as product life and field failure rates, both carefully matched against competitors.

Efforts of this sort are clearly innovations in quality management. But the strategic approach to quality also incorporates elements of the movements that preceded it. For example, statistical quality control continues to be an important tool. Interfunctional teams are still employed to ensure that engineering and manufacturing needs are coordinated. Considerable effort is devoted to shaking down designs before they are produced. Even though the precise techniques have evolved—reliability methods, for example, now rest on principles of experimental design and go by the name of "off-line quality control"[25]—the earlier movements have contributed much to the success of the strategic approach.

Strategic quality management, then, is more an extension of its predecessors than a denial of them. Aspects of both quality assurance and statistical quality control can be seen at companies adopting the new approach. But the three movements should not be confused. The strategic approach to quality is more comprehensive than its predecessors, more closely linked to profitability and basic business objectives, more sensitive to competitive needs and the consumer's point of view, and more firmly tied to continuous improvement. Many companies mistakenly think that they have adopted the new approach when their programs merely include elements of quality assurance and quality control. For the most part, these companies are still thinking defensively about quality. They have yet to see its competitive potential.

## THREE EXAMPLES

There is no single successful model of strategic quality management. Companies have differing business needs, which require attention to different issues and a focus on different operating departments.

Organizational cultures are equally diverse. A successful implementation program at one company might well fall flat at another. Even so, there are a number of common themes. Three examples of the strategic approach in action—at Hewlett-Packard, Xerox, and Corning Glass—are presented here. They have been selected because of their diversity and because they are representative of efforts at other leading U.S. companies. Together, they provide a hint of the wide variety of programs that fall under the heading of strategic quality management.

### Hewlett-Packard

Hewlett-Packard has long been known for the quality of its computers, test instruments, and other electronic devices.[26] But in the early 1980s it began to face increased pressure from customers for higher quality products. Japanese competitors also provided a strong challenge. A detailed study of quality was soon initiated; the company found, to its surprise, that as much as 25 percent of manufacturing assets were tied up in reacting to quality problems. Management recognized that continuing quality improvement was necessary if Hewlett-Packard was to retain a position of market leadership.

Its first step was to awaken the organization to the task ahead. Management selected a dramatic goal—a tenfold reduction in the field failure rates of the company's products in a single decade—and communicated it to all employees According to John A. Young, Hewlett-Packard's President and Chief Executive Officer:

> We knew this represented a difficult challenge. But we also suspected
> that anything less dramatic wouldn't convey the importance we
> attached to this issue. By establishing a far-reaching goal and getting
> people to feel in their guts that the goal was reasonable, we felt some
> serious movement would begin to occur.[27]

Management's next step was to develop champions for the cause and to convince them that such dramatic improvement was possible. A study team of a dozen first-line and second-line managers was assembled and sent to Japan. Its mission was to find the explanation for the Japanese success in producing high-quality products. Several themes that would dominate the company's later quality efforts emerged from this trip: the importance of top management commitment, the need for specific goals, the importance of manufacturing and design simplification, and the need to emphasize continuous improvement and doing things exactly right the first time. Perhaps most important, members of the team became convinced that quality improvement led ultimately to lower costs, increased productivity, and a sustainable long-term advantage. Members of the study team had become believers in quality; the task management then faced was how to harness their enthusiasm and spread the message throughout the company. Several methods were employed, including training sessions, newsletters, and informal discussions. By far the most important, however, was an approach carefully tailored to Hewlett-Packard's culture: peer competition through quality teams.[28]

Specific, detailed goals were first set in major quality areas and were eventually incorporated into the management-by-objectives (MBO) process. Interfunctional teams were then organized to pursue these objectives. Teams were established at both divisional and operating levels, the former to provide guidance and the latter to work on problem-solving. Studies soon found that the most successful teams were fully integrated into their group's business strategy; operated in environments where continuous improvement was the goal; had close involvement with managers, who had developed a sense of ownership in their projects; were provided with training in problem-solving, team-building, and other necessary skills; and were found in settings that encouraged teamwork and cooperation. These ideas were then spread throughout the organization. Frequently a small number of pilot programs served as the forerunners of more extensive efforts, because management felt that visible early successes were the best way of encouraging active involvement. The impact of these initial steps was dramatic: In a short time, more than a thousand quality teams were active in the company. Successful programs were rewarded with special plaques, free trips, recognition from top management, and other honors.

These efforts eventually filtered down to the lowest levels of the company. Each division added wrinkles of its own, depending on local needs. For example, the Computer Systems Division focused much of its early efforts on improving customer-oriented measures such as reliability. Extensive field data were collected, both formally and informally, and design changes were made where necessary. By the end of the program's first year, the reliability of the division's HP 3000 computer, as measured by its mean time between failures, had improved 100 percent. Later efforts then shifted to process improvement, eliminating waste, and integrating total quality control

(TQC) with just-in-time (JIT) production methods. The results were again impressive, especially for printed circuit boards. In two years, wave soldering defects fell from 5,500 parts per million to fewer than 100 parts per million, while in one year final assembly defects dropped by more than 90 percent.

The company's Greeley, Colorado, division, which manufactures flexible-disc drives, started with a different approach, although it too eventually embraced TQC and JIT methods. Greeley focused initially on internal measures, such as the costs of quality, and on developing corrective action programs to ensure that systemic problems were identified and fully resolved. Organizational changes—including a redefined role for the quality department and the use of problem-solving teams in research, new product development, and manufacturing—were emphasized, as were new systems and procedures. Considerable time was devoted to upgrading manufacturing standards and to working with vendors. Progress was swift. In less than two years, Greeley's total costs of quality as a percentage of value added fell 50 percent; its acceptance rate for incoming parts and subassemblies rose 15 to 20 percent; and line shutdowns for bad material became much less of a problem.

That these two divisions followed different routes to quality improvement was no accident. Hewlett-Packard's top management was unwilling to demand uniformity from divisions with dissimilar environments and competitive needs. Local initiative was valued, and each division was evaluated on the basis of its own special circumstances. On the other hand, the two programs were strikingly similar in key areas: unswerving support from upper (division) management; organizationwide commitment based on extensive communication, training, and shared goals; heavy use of problem-solving teams; and the perception that quality improvement was a competitive necessity because of pressure from Japanese manufacturers. All are hallmarks of strategic quality management. Together, they produced enormous gains. Six years into the program, Hewlett-Packard's field failure rates were decreasing at more than 20 percent annually, and several parts of the business were fast approaching the initial target of a tenfold reduction in failures.

### Xerox Corporation

External threats played an equally important role in sparking Xerox's interest in quality.[29] In the mid-1970s a number of Japanese manufacturers took aim at the low-priced copier market. Several of them introduced models that were inexpensive, reliable, and easy to use. Xerox had historically ignored this segment of the market and at first paid little attention to the new entrants. The Japanese machines, however, soon forced the company to take notice. Between 1970 and 1980, Xerox's share of U.S. copier revenues fell from 96 percent to 46 percent, largely because of Japanese competition.

These inroads led to a restructuring of the company. Corporate staff was cut, and decision-making was decentralized. A new structure emerged, based on relatively autonomous strategic business units (SBUs). About the same time, management began to study Japanese approaches to quality and productivity, including careful assessments of the methods used by Fuji-Xerox, its joint venture in Japan. Top managers were determined to beat the Japanese at their own game.[30] Several ambitious quality programs were initiated as a result.

The first was competitive benchmarking. Comprehensive surveys were developed to monitor customer satisfaction and to compare customers' reactions to Xerox's products and to competitors'. Quality of products, services, and practices was then checked against the performance of world leaders. Considerable attention was devoted to teaching managers the mechanics of collecting competitive information, using public sources, consultants, personal contacts with leading firms, the insights of other divisions, and even surveys by students at graduate business schools. Analysis of the data was then organized around four basic questions:

1. Is the competition better? If so, by how much?
2. Why are they better?
3. What can we learn from them?
4. And how can we apply what we have learned to our business?

Targets for improvement were developed on this basis, with all benchmarks incorporated into annual operating plans and five-year business plans.

These steps marked a sharp change in company philosophy. Xerox historically had been self-contained and introspective. As a virtual monopolist, it measured progress by tracking its own performance over time, rather than by watching competitors. Benchmarking was more outward-looking and comparative. It focused on relative improvement and on identifying and closing performance gaps. It also produced two important discoveries: Many of the measurements that the company had been using to assess customer satisfaction did not reflect market realities, and the gap between Xerox's quality performance and that of competitors was so large that it was unlikely to be overcome by traditional methods. The first of these problems was addressed by changing the measurement system; the second took a bit longer, because it required fundamental changes in the way products were made.

Design problems were attacked first. The new product development process was completely overhauled; large investments were made in professional workstations and computer-aided design (CAD) capabilities; engineering and design teams were located closer together and given shared responsibility for design, ease of manufacture, and ease of service; designers were provided with additional training, including exposure to such advanced techniques as "off-line quality control"; and design teams began to work with suppliers much earlier in the development cycle. These efforts produced real progress. Even so, management decided that wider participation was necessary if Xerox was ever to close in on its competitors. According to Frank J. Pipp, President of the Reprographic Business Group: "Management was just not smart enough to do th[e] job by itself."[31] The result was a new emphasis on employee involvement, including the use of quality circles and problem-solving teams. Extensive training was provided and coupled with systems of feedback, recognition, and reward. Managers were also urged to develop more facilitative styles.

Xerox's top management, however, was still somewhat removed from the quality improvement process. Without its involvement, the program stood little chance of succeeding over the long term. Senior management recognized this need and convened a series of meetings for twenty-five of the company's top managers. Leading quality experts were also invited to present their views. Eventually a consensus emerged: Xerox needed to introduce a companywide quality control process, anchoring it in a clear statement of philosophy and goals. The group then developed the Xerox Quality Policy:

> Quality is *the* basic business principle for Xerox. Quality means providing our external and internal customers with innovative products and services that fully satisfy their requirements. Quality improvement is the job of every Xerox employee.[32]

This policy, which strongly emphasized the customer's perspective, was soon followed by a set of quality principles (e.g. "Error-free work is the most cost-effective way to improve quality.''), a description of required actions and behaviors (e.g., ''We will set quality objectives and measurement standards.''), and a listing of tools to support the process (e.g. ''a method for measuring the cost of nonconformance''). A Corporate Quality Office, headed by a vice president, was established, as were implementation teams at both corporate and operating levels. These efforts underscored the commitment of Xerox's top management to continuing quality improvement. But many employees remained skeptical. One manager observed that in the program's earliest days it was viewed as no more than a passing fad—what he termed ''the flavor of the month.'' Only after a new product launch was held up for three months because of a comparatively small engineering flaw—despite intense pressure from Xerox's operating companies and sales force—did the approach gain credibility. It soon produced impressive results. Assembly quality in the Reprographic Business Group improved 63 percent in two years. During the same period, the reliability of the group's products, as measured by customer reporting, increased 40 percent, and an index of customer satisfaction, compiled from monthly surveys of 50,000 customers, increased 30 percent.

### Corning Glass Works

Unlike Xerox and Hewlett-Packard, Corning's approach to quality has emerged gradually over time, rather than as a sudden response to foreign competition.[33] The company has long been a leader in specialty glass and is known for its ability to research a customer's needs, develop a design, and meet the resulting manufacturing requirements. Success has required a range of abilities: R&D expertise, tight process control, and above all, close contact with customers, who have usually been large original equipment manufacturers. Customer acceptance has always been one of Corning's guiding principles; today the corporate quality policy explicitly acknowledges its importance:

> It is the policy of Corning Glass Works to achieve total quality performance in meeting the requirements of external and internal customers. Total quality performance means understanding who the customer is, what the requirements are, and meeting those requirements without error, on time, every time.

This philosophy has long shaped behavior at the company, although it was formalized only recently. During the 1960s, for example, Corning entered a number of new consumer markets, offering such well-known brands as Pyrex and Ovenware cooking products and Pyroceram dinnerware. To ensure sensitivity to customers' needs, three separate quality groups, each responsible for a different stage of the development process, were formed within Corning's Consumer Affairs Department. Quality Assurance was concerned with product characteristics and reviewed criteria such as the number of detergent washings a plate decoration had to withstand; Product Appraisal ran test kitchens and assessed new product performance and the need to upgrade old lines; and the Service Panel surveyed test homes that had been equipped with products yet to be released, reviewing use patterns and expected performance. Despite their different roles, all three groups were focused on the same end: ensuring customer satisfaction.

At Corning, such market sensitivity has historically been coupled with close attention to internal quality. Process control has been an area of special expertise, and in the early 1970s Corning established a separate Manufacturing and Engineering Division (M&E) to consolidate these technical skills. (The group was disbanded a decade later, and its activities were dispersed to operating divisions.) M&E served largely as an intermediary, helping to transfer products from R&D to full-scale production, and also as a troubleshooter. Its quality responsibilities fell into several areas. The division was home to the company's quality engineering group and to much of its statistical expertise. It was also involved in quality education. For example, one of its projects was the replacement of 100 percent inspection with statistical quality control techniques at the operator level. Corning had long used these techniques—they were first applied in 1946 to control the manufacture of light bulb blanks—but usually through the involvement of managers and engineers. M&E helped to shift attention to the shop floor. Later efforts, coordinated by a newly established Quality Institute, helped broaden the base of expertise. Extensive training was offered to the company's 28,000 employees worldwide, and especially to skilled operators, who feared that statistical techniques would remove the craft element from their work. A large number of quality circles were also introduced to encourage employee involvement.

What distinguished Corning's approaches in these areas from those of other companies was the close tie between its internal quality programs and customers' needs. Process improvement, for example, was not pursued in a vacuum. Engineers and plant managers met regularly with customers to determine whether the specifications they had been using were realistic. Their aim was to avoid setting excessively tight tolerances on dimensions that were not critical to product performance, while maintaining or improving standards on those that were essential. Similarly, many of the company's plants had established programs to educate employees about customers' needs. Operators, quality circles, and problem-solving teams used this information to propose new ideas and to sustain their interest in continuous improvement. In several cases, Corning's production workers actually corresponded directly with production workers at customers' facilities to ensure that their needs were met.

Top management has consistently supported these efforts. In fact, an impressive new quality initiative was started in 1983 at the direction of J. R. Houghton, Corning's newly elected chairman. He, along with the company's two vice chairmen and three group presidents, then attended the very first program at the company's Quality Institute. Productivity improvement, which in a yield-sensitive business like glassmaking is often identical to quality improvement, has received equally strong support from top management. In the early 1980s these programs, together with reductions in personnel, lowered Corning's break-even point from an estimated 63 percent of capacity to 55 percent. But even when attention to quality threatened to lower profits temporarily, management maintained its interest. After receiving reports of coffee percolator failures several years ago, Corning issued a voluntary recall—even though the number of failures was extremely low when measured against the 19 million percolators that had been sold. Management felt that the company's reputation for quality was too important to jeopardize.

Corning's approach to quality, then, like those of Hewlett-Packard and Xerox, has been strategic in character. The programs share a number of common elements. All three have been aimed squarely at the consumer and have been deeply concerned with increasing customer satisfaction. Internal quality improvements have often been little more than means toward this end. At each company, top managers have played a pivotal role, first as catalysts and then as promoters, cheerleaders, and participants in programs and projects. At some point, most have also found it necessary to send unequivocal signals, through such measures as product recalls and delayed product launches, to sensitize employees to quality and awaken them to the tasks ahead. Moreover, even in the face of active resistance, managers at all three companies have insisted on building their quality programs on the widest possible base. Each has used a slightly different approach—at Hewlett-Packard, it was project teams; at Xerox, it was competitive benchmarking; and at Corning, it was process control and statistical training—but each has worked to unite workers and managers behind quality by linking it directly with basic business objectives. It is this theme, more than any other, that unifies the programs, despite their superficial differences. In combination, they illustrate the richness and variety of strategic quality management: the range of approaches, each tailored to a particular market and corporate culture, that can be traced to the same small set of guiding principles.

## MANAGING QUALITY

Today's quality professionals bear little resemblance to their turn-of-the-century predecessors. They are managers, not inspectors; planners, not controllers; sensitive to markets as well as to manufacturing. Competitive pressures have broadened their perspective and forced them to link quality with other business needs. The result is a discipline that now attracts the interest of managers at all levels.

The discipline's center of gravity, in fact, has been shifting steadily toward greater and greater emphasis on management. Quality is no longer an isolated, independent function, dominated by technical experts. At a growing number of companies, it has entered the corporate mainstream, becoming an activity as worthy of attention as marketing or finance.

Table 2.1 charts these changes in more detail. It shows, with the help of information already summarized at the end of the previous chapter, how strategic quality management contrasts with its predecessors. The new approach incorporates important elements of the first three quality eras but goes a crucial step further, linking quality with competitive success. Market research on quality, pressures for continuous improvement, and high levels of communication and participation are now required. These responsibilities broaden the job of general managers, who must attend to quality if they hope to succeed in the face of intense global competition.

Strategic quality management is thus the capstone of a trend that began more than a century ago. In its original incarnation, quality was the responsibility of the manufacturing department; today it has emerged from the factory and has entered the boardroom. The ac-

TABLE 2.1  *The Four Major Quality Eras*

Stage of the Quality Movement

| Identifying Characteristics | Inspection | Statistical Quality Control | Quality Assurance | Strategic Quality Management |
|---|---|---|---|---|
| Primary concern | detection | control | coordination | strategic impact |
| View of quality | a problem to be solved | a problem to be solved | a problem to be solved, but one that is attacked proactively | a competitive opportunity |
| Emphasis | product uniformity | product uniformity with reduced inspection | the entire production chain, from design to market, and the contribution of all functional groups, especially designers, to preventing quality failures | the market and consumer needs |
| Methods | gauging and measurement | statistical tools and techniques | programs and systems | strategic planning, goal-setting, and mobilizing the organization |
| Role of quality professionals | inspection, sorting, counting, and grading | troubleshooting and the application of statistical methods | quality measurement, quality planning, and program design | goal-setting, education and training, consultative work with other departments, and program design |
| Who has responsibility for quality | the inspection department | the manufacturing and engineering departments | all departments, although top management is only peripherally involved in designing, planning, and executing quality policies | everyone in the organization, with top management exercising strong leadership |
| Orientation and approach | "inspects in" quality | "controls in" quality | "builds in" quality | "manages in" quality |

companying shift in perspective is crucial to understanding modern thinking about quality. A succinct summary of the new view appears in a report prepared for the 1983 White House Conference on Productivity:

> Managing the quality dimension of an organization is not generically different from any other aspect of management. It involves the formulation of strategies, setting goals and objectives, developing action plans, implementing plans, and using control systems for monitoring feedback and taking corrective action. If quality is viewed only as a control system, it will never be substantially improved. Quality is not just a control system; quality is a management function.[34]

# Chapter

# 3

# Concepts and Definitions

Despite the interest of managers, quality remains a term that is easily misunderstood. In everyday speech, its synonyms range from luxury and merit to excellence and value. Different companies also appear to mean different things when they use the word, as do different groups within the same firm. Without further refinement, continued ambiguity and confusion are inevitable.

A better understanding of the term is therefore essential if quality is to assume a strategic role. The academic literature on the subject provides a convenient starting point; moreover, it has seldom been reviewed extensively. The problem is one of coverage. Scholars in four disciplines—philosophy, economics, marketing, and operations management—have explored quality, but each group has viewed it from a different vantage point. Philosophy has focused on definitional issues; economics, on profit maximization and market equilibrium; marketing, on the determinants of buying behavior and customer satisfaction; and operations management, on engineering practices and manufacturing control. The result has been a host of competing perspectives, each based on a different analytical framework and employing its own terminology.

At the same time, a number of common themes are apparent. On the conceptual front—the focus of Chapters 3 and 4—each discipline has wrestled with the following questions: Is quality objective or subjective? Is it relative or absolute? Is it timeless or socially determined? Can it be divided into narrower and more meaningful categories? Empirically, interest has focused on the correlates of quality—its relationship to variables such as price, advertising, market share, cost, productivity, and profitability. Those relationships are discussed in Chapter 5.

## DEFINING QUALITY

Five principal approaches to defining quality can be identified: the transcendent, product-based, user-based, manufacturing-based, and value-based. Table 3.1 presents representative examples of each approach.

TABLE 3.1    *Five Definitions of Quality*

I. *Transcendent:*

- "Quality is neither mind nor matter, but a third entity independent of the two . . . even though Quality cannot be defined, you know what it is." (Robert M. Pirsig, *Zen and the Art of Motorcycle Maintenance* [New York: Bantam Books, 1974], pp. 185, 213)
- " . . . a condition of excellence implying fine quality as distinct from poor quality. . . . Quality is achieving or reaching for the highest standard as against being satisfied with the sloppy or fraudulent." (Barbara W. Tuchman, "The Decline of Quality," *New York Times Magazine,* November 2, 1980, p. 38)

II. *Product-based:*

- "Differences in quality amount to differences in the quantity of some desired ingredient or attribute." (Lawrence Abbott, *Quality and Competition* [New York: Columbia University Press, 1955], pp. 126–27)
- "Quality refers to the amounts of the unpriced attributes contained in each unit of the priced attribute." (Keith B. Leffler, "Ambiguous Changes in Product Quality," *American Economic Review,* December 1982, p. 956)

III. *User-based:*

- "Quality consists of the capacity to satisfy wants . . ." (Corwin D. Edwards, "The Meaning of Quality," *Quality Progress,* October 1968, p. 37)
- "In the final analysis of the marketplace, the quality of a product depends on how well it fits patterns of consumer preferences." (Alfred A. Kuehn and Ralph L. Day, "Strategy of Product Quality," *Harvard Business Review,* November–December 1962, p. 101)
- "Quality is fitness for use. (J. M. Juran, ed., *Quality Control Handbook,* Third Edition [New York: McGraw-Hill, 1974], p. 2-2)

IV. *Manufacturing-based:*

- "Quality [means] conformance to requirements." (Philip B. Crosby, *Quality Is Free* [New York: New Americn Library, 1979], p. 15)
- "Quality is the degree to which a specific product conforms to a design or specification." (Harold L. Gilmore, "Product Conformance Cost," *Quality Progress,* June 1974, p. 16)

V. *Value-based:*

- "Quality is the degree of excellence at an acceptable price and the control of variability at an acceptable cost." (Robert A. Broh, *Managing Quality for Higher Profits* [New York: McGraw-Hill, 1982], p. 3)
- "Quality means best for certain customer conditions. These conditions are (a) the actual use and (b) the selling price of the product." (Armand V. Feigenbaum, *Total Quality Control* [New York: McGraw-Hill, 1961], p. 1)

## Transcendent

According to the transcendent view, quality is synonymous with "innate excellence."[1] It is both absolute and universally recognizable, a mark of uncompromising standards and high achievement. An implicit assumption of the transcendent view is that there is something timeless and enduring about works of high quality, an essence that rises above changes in tastes or styles. Occasionally the transcendent approach equates quality with fine craftsmanship and a rejection of mass production.[2] But more often it claims that quality cannot be defined precisely, that it is a simple, unanalyzable property we learn to recognize only through experience.

The approach borrows heavily from Plato's discussion of beauty.[3] In the *Symposium,* Plato argues that beauty is one of the "platonic forms," and thus a term that can be understood only after exposure to a succession of objects that display its characteristics. In the transcendent approach, the same is said of quality. Michelangelo, for example, may not enjoy universal appeal, but after seeing a number of his statues, it is difficult to deny the quality of his work. An advertising brochure for Cadillac uses similar reasoning. After asking, "How is it that one American car became a world symbol for meticulous quality and outstanding craftsmanship?'' the brochure responds by citing ''vision . . . goals . . . achievement . . . and . . . pride. . . . Today, the Cadillac commitment to quality is best expressed by the car itself.''[4]

The difficulty with this view it that is offers little practical guidance. To argue that the hallmarks of quality are ''intensive effort'' and ''honesty of purpose'' tells us little about how quality products differ from those that are run-of-the-mill.[5] Quality remains maddeningly elusive. In fact, at its most primitive this definition amounts to no more than the claim that whatever quality consists of, managers will know it when they see it.[6]

### Product-Based

Product-based definitions are quite different: They view quality as a precise and measurable variable. Differences in quality thus reflect differences in the quantity of some ingredient or attribute possessed by a product.[7] High-quality ice cream has a high butterfat content, just as fine rugs have a large number of knots per square inch. This approach lends a vertical or hierarchical dimension to quality, for goods can be ranked according to the amount of the desired attribute they possess. An unambiguous ranking, however, is possible only if the attributes in question are ranked in the same order by virtually all buyers.[8]

Product-based definitions of quality first appeared in the economics literature, where they were quickly incorporated into theoretical models. In fact, the early economic research on quality focused almost exclusively on durability, simply because it was so easily translated into the above framework.[9] Since durable goods provide a stream of services over time, increased durability implies a longer stream of services—in effect, more of the good. Quality differences could therefore be treated as differences in quantity, considerably simplifying the mathematics.

There are two obvious corollaries to this approach. First, higher quality can be obtained only at higher cost. Because quality reflects the quantity of attributes that a product contains, and because attributes are considered to be costly to produce, higher-quality goods will be more expensive. Second, quality is viewed as an inherent characteristic of goods rather than as something ascribed to them. Because quality reflects the presence or absence of measurable product attributes, it can be assessed objectively and is based on more than preferences alone.

While the objective nature of the approach is an important strength, it has limitations as well. A one-to-one correspondence between product attributes and quality does not always exist. Sometimes high-quality products are simply different; instead of possessing more of a particular attribute, they are based on entirely different concepts. When quality is a matter of aesthetics, the product-based approach is also lacking, for it fails to accommodate differences in tastes.

### User-Based

User-based definitions start from the premise that quality "lies in the eyes of the beholder." Individual consumers are assumed to have different wants or needs, and the goods that best satisfy their preferences are the ones they regard as having the highest quality.[10] This is an idiosyncratic and personal view of quality, and one that is highly subjective. In the marketing literature, it has led to the notion of "ideal points": precise combinations of product attributes that provide the greatest satisfaction to a specified consumer.[11] In the economics literature, it has led to the view that quality differences are captured by shifts in a product's demand curve.[12] And in the operations management literature, it has given rise to the concept of "fitness for use."[13] Each of these concepts, however, faces two problems. The first is practical: how to aggregate widely varying individual preferences so that they lead to meaningful definitions of quality at the market level. The second is more fundamental: how to distinguish those product attributes that connote quality from those that simply maximize consumer satisfaction.

The aggregation problem is usually resolved by assuming that high-quality products are those that best meet the needs of most consumers. A consensus of views is implied, with virtually all users agreeing on the desirability of certain product attributes. Unfortunately, this approach ignores the different weights that individuals normally attach to quality characteristics and the difficulty of devising an unbiased statistical procedure for aggregating such widely varying preferences.[14] For the most part, these problems have been ignored by theorists. Economists, for example, have typically specified models in which the market demand curve responds to quality changes without explaining how that curve, which represents the summation of individual preferences, was derived in the first place.[15]

A more basic problem with the user-based approach is its equation of quality with maximum satisfaction. While the two are related, they are by no means identical. A product that maximizes satisfaction is certainly *preferable* to one that meets fewer needs, but is it necessarily *better* as well? The implied equivalence often breaks down in practice. For example, books on best seller lists are clearly preferred by a majority of readers, even though few would argue that they represent the finest available literature. Similarly, consumers may enjoy a particular brand because of its unusual taste or features but may still regard some other brand as being of higher quality. In the latter assessment, the product's objective characteristics are also being considered.

Even perfectly objective characteristics, however, are open to varying interpretation. Today durability is regarded as an important element of quality. Long-lived products are generally preferred to products that wear out more quickly. But that was not always true. Until the late nineteenth century, durable goods were primarily possessions of the poor, for only wealthy individuals could afford delicate products that required frequent replacement or repair.[16] The result was a long-standing association between durability and inferior quality, a view that changed only with the mass production of luxury items made possible by the Industrial Revolution.

### Manufacturing-Based

While user-based definitions of quality are rooted in consumer preferences—the determinants of demand—manufacturing-based definitions focus on the supply side of the equation and are primarily concerned with engineering and manufacturing practices.

Virtually all manufacturing-based definitions identify quality as "conformance to requirements."[17] Once a design or a specification has been established, any deviation implies a reduction in quality. Excellence is equated with meeting specifications and with "making it right the first time." In these terms, a well-made Mercedes is a high-quality automobile, as is a well-made Chevette. The same approach is relevant to service businesses, even though it has traditionally been associated with manufacturing. In service settings, conformance normally means accuracy or timeliness. Examples include correctly tallied bank balances and airlines that arrive and depart on schedule.[18]

While the manufacturing-based approach recognizes the consumer's interest in quality—a product or service that deviates from specifications is likely to be poorly made or unreliable, providing less satisfaction than one that is properly constructed or performed—its primary focus is internal. That is a serious weakness, for little attention is paid to the link, in customers' minds, between quality and product characteristics other than conformance. Rather, quality is defined in a manner that simplifies engineering and production control. On the design side, that has led to an emphasis on reliability engineering. On the manufacturing side, it has meant an emphasis on statistical quality control. As Chapter 1 has indicated, both techniques are designed to weed out deviations early—the former, by analyzing a product's basic components, identifying possible failure modes, and then proposing alternative designs that enhance reliability; the latter, by employing statistical techniques to discover when a production process is performing outside acceptable limits.

Each of these techniques is focused on the same end: cost reduction. According to the manufacturing-based approach, improvements in quality (which are equivalent to reductions in the number of deviations) lead to lower costs, for preventing defects is viewed as less expensive than repairing or reworking them.[19] Firms are therefore assumed to be performing suboptimally. Were they only to increase their expenditures on prevention and inspection—testing prototypes more carefully or weeding out a larger number of defective components before they become part of fully assembled units—they would find their rework, scrap, and warranty expenses falling by an even greater amount.[20] Such reasoning is simply an updated version of Juran's analogy to "gold in the mine." The supporting evidence is examined in Chapter 5.

### Value-Based

Value-based definitions take such ideas a step further: They actually define quality in terms of costs and prices. Thus, a quality product is one that provides performance or conformance at an acceptable price or cost.[21] By this reasoning, a $500 running shoe, no matter how well constructed, could not be a quality product, for it would find few buyers.

A recent survey of consumer perceptions of quality in twenty-eight product categories suggests that the value-based view is becoming more prevalent.[22] While ingredients and materials were seen as the key quality indicators in such categories as food, clothing, personal care, and beauty products—reflecting a product-based approach to the subject—the study's overall conclusion was that "quality is increasingly apt to be discussed and perceived in relationship to price." A recent study of major home appliances provides further evidence. After creating quality ratings for different brands based on their performance in tests by *Consumer Reports,* the study developed rough measures of value by comparing quality rankings with prices. High market shares were consistently associated with brands like General Electric and Whirlpool, which scored high on value, rather than with brands that ranked high on quality or price alone.[23]

Despite its obvious importance, this approach is difficult to apply in practice. It blends two related but distinct concepts: excellence and worth. The result is a hybrid—"affordable excellence"—that lacks well-defined limits and is often highly subjective.


## COMPETING VIEWS AND SHIFTING PERSPECTIVES

Most existing definitions of quality fall into one of the categories listed above. The coexistence of these differing approaches has several important implications. First, it helps to explain the often competing views of quality held by members of the marketing, engineering, and manufacturing departments. Marketing people typically take a user-based or product-based approach to the subject; for them, higher quality often means better performance, enhanced features, and other improvements that increase cost. Their sensitivity to customers also means that they are primarily concerned with what happens to products once they are in the field.

Engineers characteristically take a different approach, as do manufacturing people. Engineers frequently think in terms of specifications; their role is to translate product performance into precise tolerances and dimensions. That suggests a product-based approach to quality. Most manufacturing people, on the other hand, are more comfortable with the idea that quality means conformance to specifications and "doing things right the first time." They often associate poor quality with high levels of rework and scrap. For this reason, they expect quality improvements to result in cost reductions.

These three views are obviously in conflict and can cause serious breakdowns in communication. Remedial efforts may become paralyzed if the coexistence of the competing perspectives is not openly acknowledged. For example, a large division of a major consumer goods company recently reviewed its quality management practices. The firm was especially interested in assessing its new product introduction process, for new products were regarded as the key to competitive success. Two divergent views emerged. One group, primarily marketing and R&D experts, felt that the process had been quite successful: New products appeared regularly and performed as expected, customer complaints were few, and defective items had not been shipped to the trade in any large number. Another group, primarily manufacturing people, felt that the process had to be revamped because quality was so poor: New product releases were frequently delayed while designs were reconfigured to adapt to manufacturing requirements, and material and labor variances of several hundred thousand dollars had been incurred because of unanticipated expenditures on rework and scrap. Because of these disagreements, the project quickly stalled. Further progress required the recognition that one group was employing user-based and product-based definitions of quality while the other was employing a manufacturing-based approach. Only then were the two groups able to agree on the nature of the problems they faced.

Despite the potential for conflict, companies can benefit from such multiple perspectives.[24] Reliance on a single definition of quality is a frequent source of problems. For example, a Japanese paper manufacturer recently discovered that its newsprint rolls failed to satisfy customers even though they met the Japanese Industrial Standard. Conformance was excellent, reflecting a manufacturing-based approach to quality, but acceptance was poor. Other rolls of newsprint, however, generated no customer complaints even though they failed to meet the standard.[25] A leading U.S. manufacturer of room air conditioners faced the opposite problem. Its products were well received by customers and highly rated by *Consumer Reports*. Reject, scrap, and warranty costs were so high, however, that large losses were incurred. While the product's design matched customers' needs, the failure to follow through with tight conformance in manufacturing cost the company dearly.

In both examples, managers felt that they were producing high-quality products. And they were, but according to only one of the approaches to quality described above. Because each approach has predictable blind spots, companies are likely to suffer fewer problems if they employ multiple perspectives on quality, actively shifting the approach they take as products move from design to market. Initially, they may wish to employ a user-based approach, identifying the characteristics that connote quality through careful market research. A product-based approach can then be used to translate the desired characteristics into parts, subassemblies, and specifications. Finally, a manufacturing-based approach can help to ensure that equipment and production methods are providing products that match specifications.

In such a process, members of the marketing, engineering, and manufacturing departments have distinctive roles to play. Each is primarily responsible for a single approach to quality and a single phase of the development process. Success normally requires close coordination of the activities of each function; if departments work in isolation, they are unlikely to be sensitive to the pressures that other groups feel to comply with their own definitions of quality.[26] Poor communication, long new product development cycles, and frequent slip-ups are often the result.[27] Avoiding these problems is likely to require broader perspectives on quality within each function. Engineers, for example, may benefit from exposure to customers and their needs, just as marketing people may be assigned to work closely with manufacturing in order to understand the limitations of existing machinery and equipment. In this way, user-based, product-based, and manufacturing-based approaches to quality can be blended and coordinated.

But even with improved coordination, all the principal approaches to quality share a common problem: Each is vague and imprecise when it comes to describing the basic elements of product quality. Relatively few analysts have shown an interest in these details.[28] The oversight is unfortunate, for as the next chapter will show, much can be learned by treating quality in a less homogeneous fashion.

# Chapter

# 4

# The Multiple Dimensions
# of Quality

According to a 1981 survey, 68 percent of CEOs felt that U.S. product quality had improved in the previous five years. Consumers were less sanguine: Only 25 percent of them thought that U.S. quality had improved during the same period.[1] Even after discounting the natural optimism of executives, that is a large and disturbing gap and demands further explanation.

In part, the problem is one of terminology. Complex concepts like quality are difficult to penetrate. As the previous chapter has shown, marketing, engineering, and manufacturing experts often interpret the term differently. There is no reason to assume that business leaders and consumers will be any more in agreement. Until a more precise vocabulary is developed, such problems are likely to continue. For this reason, Chapter 4 is devoted to disaggregating the concept of quality and exploring its basic elements.

## DIMENSIONS OF QUALITY

Eight dimensions or categories of quality can be identified as a framework for analysis:

- Performance
- Features
- Reliability
- Conformance
- Durability

- Serviceability
- Aesthetics
- Perceived quality

Each category is self-contained and distinct, for a product or service can be ranked high on one dimension while being low on another. However, in many cases the dimensions are interrelated. Sometimes an improvement in one may be achieved only at the expense of another; at other times two dimensions, like reliability and conformance, may move together. The interrelationships suggest the framework's relevance to strategic quality management. According to Chapter 2, a basic tenet of the strategic approach is that quality should be defined from the customer's point of view. To do so requires an in-depth understanding of the term. Moreover, the more disaggregated the concept of quality becomes, the wider the options open to firms wishing to compete on this basis. Narrow, targeted strategies become possible, with several companies in the same industry capable of pursuing quality in different ways. Tradeoffs among the various dimensions must also be faced. Because multiple dimensions allow for multiple strategies, quality competition becomes vastly more complex.

### Performance

First on the list of dimensions is performance, which refers to the primary operating characteristics of a product. For an automobile, they would be traits like acceleration, handling, cruising speed, and comfort; for a television set, they would include sound and picture clarity, color, and the ability to receive distant stations. In service businesses such as fast foods and airlines, an important aspect of performance is often service speed or the absence of waiting time.[2]

This dimension of quality combines elements of both the product-based and user-based approaches of the previous chapter. Measurable product and service attributes are involved, and brands can usually be ranked objectively on at least one dimension of performance. Overall performance rankings, however, are more difficult to develop, especially when they involve benefits that lack universal appeal. Then specific applications must be examined, for products cannot be compared in the abstract. For example, in comparing two power shovels, one with a capacity of 100 cubic yards per hour and the other with a capacity of 10 cubic yards per hour, an obvious ordering exists. The first shovel has a larger capacity and thus offers superior performance. Suppose, however, that the two shovels possessed the identical capacity—60 cubic yards per hour—but achieved it differently: one with a 1-cubic-yard bucket operating at sixty cycles per hour, and the other with a 2-cubic-yard bucket operating at thirty cycles per hour. The capacities of the shovels would then be the same, but their capabilities would be completely different. The shovel with the larger bucket could handle massive boulders, while the shovel with the smaller bucket could perform precision work. Which of the two offers superior performance? That depends entirely on the task to be performed.[3]

The connection between performance and quality is equally dependent on circumstances. Whether performance differences are perceived as quality differences normally depends on individual preferences. Users typically have a wide range of interests and needs; each is likely to equate quality with high performance in his or her area of immediate interest. Some cosmetics wearers, for example, judge quality by a product's resistance to smudging; others, with more sensitive skin, assess it by ease and comfort in application and wear. Each group is likely to rank a different brand highest in quality.

The connection between performance and quality is also affected by semantics. The words that describe product performance include terms frequently associated with quality, along with terms that fail to carry the association. For example, a 100-watt light bulb provides greater candlepower (performance) than a 60-watt bulb, yet few consumers would regard the difference as a measure of quality. The products simply belong to different performance classes. The quietness of an automobile's ride, however, is typically viewed as a direct reflection of its quality. Quietness is therefore a performance dimension that readily translates into quality, while candlepower is not. These differences appear to reflect the conventions of the English language as much as they do personal preferences.[4]

Features

Similar thinking can be applied to product features, a second dimension of quality. Features are the "bells and whistles" of products, those secondary characteristics that supplement the product's basic functioning. Examples include free drinks on a plane flight, permanent press as well as cotton cycles on a washing machine, and automatic tuners on a color television set. In many cases, the line separating primary product characteristics (performance) from secondary characteristics (features) is difficult to draw. Features, like product performance, involve objective and measurable attributes; their translation into quality differences is equally affected by individual preferences. The distinction between the two is largely a matter of centrality or degree of importance to the user.

### Reliability

Reliability reflects the probability of a product's malfunctioning or failing within a specified period of time. Among the most common measures of reliability are the mean time to first failure (MTFF), the mean time between failures (MTBF), and the failure rate per unit time.[5] Because these measures require a product to be in use for some period, they are more relevant to durable goods than to products and services that are consumed instantly.

Reliability normally becomes more important to consumers as downtime and maintenance become more expensive. Farmers, for example, are especially sensitive to downtime during harvest season, when the time available for work is short. Reliable equipment may mean the difference between a good financial year and spoiled crops. For similar reasons, consumers in other markets have become increasingly attuned to reliability. Both computers and copying machines are now advertised on this basis. Recent market research shows that reliability has become an automobile's most desired attribute, especially among young women.[6] The Defense Department, after seeing its expenditures for major weapons repairs jump from $7.4 billion in fiscal 1980 to $14.9 billion in fiscal 1985, has begun cracking down on contractors whose weapons fail frequently in the field.[7] The most important reason for the surge in interest in reliability, however, has been the success of Japanese manufacturers, whose superiority on this dimension of quality has given them a competitive edge in industries as diverse as cameras, consumer electronics, machine tools, and industrial robots.

### Conformance

A related dimension of quality is conformance, or the degree to which a product's design and operating characteristics meet preestablished standards. There are two distinct approaches to conformance. The first, which dominates most American thinking on the subject, equates conformance with meeting specifications.[8] All products and services involve specifications of some sort. When new designs or models are developed, dimensional standards must first be set for parts, and purity requirements for materials. These specifications are seldom defined as a single value. Normally, they include a target or centering dimension, as well as a permissible range of variation or tolerance. Some parts specify drilled holes that are 1.4 inches in diameter ± .05 inches; others require machined surfaces that are within ± .004 inches of being perfectly level. As long as the stipulated tolerances are not exceeded—the first set of parts, for example, might legitimately include diameters between 1.35 and 1.45 inches—quality is deemed acceptable, and parts are not rejected for dimensional reasons.

This view of conformance is closely associated with process control and sampling techniques. Specification limits are matched against the inherent capabilities of a manufacturing process—the greatest precision and least variability that it is capable of producing under controlled operating conditions—and the process is centered as well as possible, ensuring that the majority of parts produced will comply with the specified limits. Because this definition of conformance equates good quality with operating inside a tolerance band, there is little interest in whether the centering dimension has been met exactly. For the most part, dispersion *within* specification limits is ignored.

One drawback of this approach is the problem of "tolerance stack-up."[9] When two or more parts are to be matched together, the size of their tolerances often determines how well they will fit. Should one part fall at the lower limit of its specification and a matching part at its upper limit, a tight fit is unlikely. Even if the parts are mated initially, the link between them is likely to wear more quickly over time than one made from parts whose centering dimensions have been met exactly. Eventually, reliability will suffer.

The same problem can be stated more formally.[10] If four parts, each with a specification requiring dimensions of 1" ± .001", are to be lined up one on top of the other, the resulting unit will *not* have measurements of 4" ± .001". The tolerance of the sum will be larger than that of an individual part, but not four times as large. Oversizes and undersizes may combine to produce a total variation that is more extreme than the variation of the individual parts.

To address this problem, a second approach to conformance has emerged. It is closely associated with Japanese manufacturers and the work of Genichi Taguchi, a prize-winning Japanese statistician.[11] Taguchi begins with the idea of a "loss function" that measures the losses a product imparts to society from the time it is shipped. Such losses include warranty costs, dissatisfied customers, and other problems due to performance failures. Taguchi then compares the losses resulting from two alternative approaches to quality. The first is conventional: Conformance means meeting specifications. The second equates conformance with the degree of variability (inversely, the degree of uniformity) around the target dimension or center line. Variation within specification limits is thus explicitly acknowledged by this approach. Figure 4.1 illustrates the differences between the two definitions. Advocates of the traditional approach to conformance normally prefer process 2. Even though it is poorly centered, all items fall within specification limits and none are rejected for failure to conform. Followers of Taguchi, however, favor process 1, for according to Taguchi's loss function, it will result in lower long-term costs. Even though some items fail to meet specifications and will eventually be rejected by consumers, the vast majority are clustered tightly around the target, suggesting fewer problems due to tolerance stack-up. Because of the link between conformance and reliability, overall losses will be smaller. While hard evidence supporting this claim is still scarce, the approach is regarded as espe-

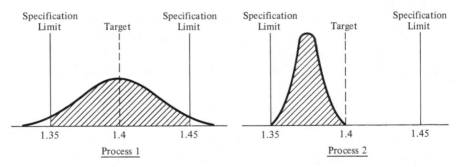

*Notes:*
Curves are frequency distributions showing the number (percentage) of items having the indicated dimensions.

Shaded areas under the curves indicate items meeting specifications; unshaded areas indicate items falling outside specification limits.

FIGURE 4.1    Process Distributions Illustrating Different Approaches to Conformance

SOURCE: L. P. Sullivan, "Reducing Variability: A New Approach to Quality," *Quality Progress*, July 1984, p. 16. Copyright © 1984 American Society for Quality Control. Reprinted by permission.

cially desirable for products, like automobiles, that require the mating of large numbers of parts, and whose reliability is an important selling point.[12]

Despite their differences, both approaches to conformance rely on similar data for monitoring production. Within the factory, measures of the incidence of defects—the proportion of all units that fail to meet specifications and so require rework and repair—form the basic building blocks. If the traditional approach to conformance is being used, simple counts or defect percentages are usually enough. If Taguchi's approach is being followed, more elaborate measures of the distribution of output are required. These include the process capability ratio, which measures the width of specification limits relative to the spread of the process, and the process location ratio, which locates the center of the process relative to the target dimension or center line. Without such measures, improvements in conformance within specification limits are impossible to track.[13]

In the field, data on conformance are more difficult to obtain and proxies are frequently used. Two common measures are the incidence of service calls for a product and the frequency of repairs under warranty. These measures, while suggestive, neglect other deviations from standard, such as misspelled labels or shoddy construction, that do not lead to service or repair. In service businesses, measures of conformance are normally focused on accuracy and timeliness, and include counts of processing errors, unanticipated delays, and other frequent mistakes.

Both reliability and conformance are closely tied to the manufacturing-based approach to quality. Improvements in both measures normally translate directly into quality gains, because defects, field failures, and processing errors are regarded as undesirable by virtually all consumers. They are therefore relatively objective measures of quality and are less likely to reflect individual preferences than are rankings based on performance or features.

### Durability

Durability, a measure of product life, has both economic and technical dimensions. Technically, durability can be defined as the amount of use one gets from a product before it physically deteriorates. A light bulb provides the perfect example. After so many hours of use, the filament burns up and the bulb must be replaced. Repair is impossible. Economists call such products "one-hoss shays,'' after the implement in the Oliver Wendell Holmes poem that was designed by the deacon to last a hundred years, and whose parts broke down simultaneously at the end of the century. Economists have used this formulation extensively in modeling the production and consumption of capital goods.[14]

Durability becomes more difficult to interpret when repair is possible. Then the concept takes on an added dimension, for product life will vary with changing tastes and economic conditions. Durability becomes the amount of use one gets from a product before it breaks down and replacement is regarded as preferable to continued repair. Consumers are faced with a series of choices. Each time a product fails, they must weigh the expected cost, in both dollars and personal inconvenience, of future repairs against the investment and operating expenses of a newer, more reliable model. In such circumstances, a product's life is determined by repair costs, personal valuations of time and inconvenience, changing fashions, losses due to downtime, and relative prices as much as it is by the quality of components or materials.

This approach to durability has two important implications. First, it suggests that durability and reliability are closely linked. A product that fails frequently is likely to be scrapped earlier than one that is more reliable; repair costs will be correspondingly higher and the purchase of a competitive brand will look that much more desirable. Because of the linkage, companies sometimes try to reassure customers by offering lifetime guarantees on their products, as 3M has done with its videocassettes.[15] Second, this approach suggests that durability figures should be interpreted with care. An increase in product life may not be due to technical improvements or to the use of longer-lived materials; the underlying economic environment may simply have changed. For example, the expected life of an automobile has risen steadily over the last decade and now averages fourteen years.[16] Older automobiles are held for longer periods and have become a greater percentage of all cars in use.[17] Among the factors thought to be responsible for these changes are rising gasoline prices and a weak economy, which have reduced the average number of miles driven per year, and federal regulations governing gas mileage, which have resulted in a reduction in the size of new models and an increase in the attractiveness to many consumers of retaining older cars. In this case, environmental changes have been responsible for much of the reported increase in durability.

Yet when assessments are made at a single point in time and comparable levels of maintenance are assumed, durability still varies widely among brands. In 1981, for example, estimated product lives for major home appliances ranged from 9.9 years (Westinghouse) to 13.2 years (Frigidaire) for refrigerators, 5.8 years (Gibson) to 18.0 years (Maytag) for washers, 6.6 years (Wards) to 13.5 years (Maytag) for dryers, and 6.0 years (Sears) to 17.9 years (Kirby) for vacuum cleaners.[18] Such wide dispersion suggests that durability is a potentially fertile area for further quality differentiation.

### Serviceability

A sixth dimension of quality is serviceability, or the speed, courtesy, competence, and ease of repair. Consumers are concerned not only about a product's breaking down but also about the elapsed time before service is restored, the timeliness with which service appointments are kept, the nature of their dealings with service personnel, and the frequency with which service calls or repairs fail to correct outstanding problems. In those cases where problems are not immediately resolved and complaints are filed, a company's complaint-handling procedures are also likely to affect customers' ultimate evaluation of product and service quality.

Some of these variables can be measured quite objectively; others reflect differing personal standards of what constitutes acceptable service. For example, a recent study of consumer satisfaction with such professional services as medical care found the chief complaints to be that "the service was provided in a careless, unprofessional manner" and that "I feel I was treated as an object rather than as an individual."[19] These comments clearly reflect subjective views of what constitutes acceptable professional behavior. Other aspects of service can be assessed more objectively. Responsiveness is typically measured by the mean time to repair (MTTR), while technical competence is reflected in the incidence of multiple service calls required to correct a single problem. Because most consumers equate more rapid repair and reduced downtime with higher quality, these elements of serviceability are less subject to personal interpretation than are those involving evaluations of courtesy or standards of professional behavior.

Even reactions to downtime, however, can be quite complex. In certain environments, rapid response becomes critical only after thresholds have been reached. Farming again presents a vivid example. During harvest season, farmers generally accept downtime of one to six hours on harvesting equipment such as combines with little resistance. As downtime increases, they become more and more concerned; beyond eight hours of downtime they become frantic and frequently go to great lengths to continue harvesting even if it means purchasing or leasing additional equipment.[20] In markets like this, superior service can be a powerful selling tool. Among the strategies open to firms are improved parts availability, such as Caterpillar Tractor's guarantee that it will deliver repair parts anywhere in the world within forty-eight hours; the provision of substitute equipment, such as the decision by a major farm equipment manufacturer to offer free loans of tractors to those customers whose tractors break down during critical periods;[21] and the provision of more rapid service, such as the policy of GCA, a maker of semiconductor manufacturing equipment, that one of its service representatives will arrive at the customer's facility to fix malfunctioning equipment within two hours of any breakdown.[22] Each of these strategies requires a clear understanding of customers' reactions to differing amounts of downtime. Otherwise, service levels are likely to be set either too high or too low.

Occasionally, customers will remain dissatisfied even after repairs have been completed. Sometimes they will object to the prices they have been charged; more frequently, problems have not been fully resolved or service has been otherwise unsatisfactory.[23] Some customers will be unhappy even if products have not had to be repaired. Such dissatisfaction often leads to complaints; how these complaints are handled has an important bearing on a company's reputation for quality and service.[24] Eventually, profitability is likely to be affected as well. A 1976 consumer survey found that among households that initiated complaints to resolve problems, more than 40 percent were not at all satisfied with the results. More significantly, the degree of satisfaction with complaint resolution was closely correlated with consumers' willingness to repurchase the offending brands.[25]

Companies differ widely in their approaches to complaint handling and in the importance they attach to this element of serviceability. Some do their best to resolve complaints; others use legal gimmicks, the silent treatment, and similar ploys to rebuff dissatisfied customers.[26] Recently, General Electric, Pillsbury, Procter & Gamble, Polaroid, Whirlpool, Johnson & Johnson, and other companies have taken a proactive approach, installing toll-free telephone hotlines to improve access to customer complaints.[27] Their efforts have been prompted by a recognition of serviceability's competitive potential and a desire to differentiate themselves through increased responsiveness. As the director of a major mutual fund has observed: "People will bear you for underperformance, but if you screw up their accounts or can't answer their questions, you're done for."[28]

### Aesthetics

The final two dimensions of quality are the most subjective. Both aesthetics and perceived quality are closely related to the user-based approach to quality described in Chapter 3. Aesthetics—how a product looks, feels, sounds, tastes, or smells—is clearly a matter of personal judgment and a reflection of individual preferences. In fact, the marketing concept of "ideal points"—those combinations of product attributes that best match the preferences of a specified consumer—has often been applied to just this dimension of quality.[29] Nevertheless, there appears to be some uniformity in consumers' rankings of products on the basis of aesthetics. Judgments are not wholly idiosyncratic. A recent study of quality in thirty-three food categories, for example, found that high quality was most often associated with "rich/full flavor, tastes natural, tastes fresh, good aroma, and looks appetizing." The brands most successful in establishing strong market positions were the ones most clearly differentiated on these characteristics.[30]

### Perceived Quality

Consumers do not always possess complete information about a product or a service's attributes. Frequently, indirect measures are the only basis for comparing brands. A product's durability, for example, can seldom be observed directly; it must usually be inferred from various tangible and intangible aspects of the product. In such circumstances, cues and other signaling devices become important for drawing inferences about quality.[31] Images, advertising, and brand names—perceptions of quality rather than the reality itself—can be critical. Recently, market research has found that a product's country of manufacture is viewed by many consumers as an indication of its quality.[32] For this reason, both Honda, which manufactures automobiles in Marysville, Ohio, and Sony, which manufactures color televisions in San Diego, have been cautious about publicizing their "made in America" connections, even though by objective measures their locally made products are of excellent quality.[33]

These forces even affect scholarly judgments. When professors around the country were asked to rank the departments in their fields by quality, their rankings were only partially explained by such objective measures as the number of books or articles in leading journals published by members of the department. Both reputation (the historical strength of the department) and affiliation (the quality of the university to which a department was attached) were equally important in explaining the rankings.[34]

Reputation is in fact one of the primary contributors to perceived quality. Its power comes from an unstated analogy: that the quality of products manufactured by a company today is similar to the quality of products it manufactured in earlier periods, or the quality of goods in a newly developed product line is similar to the quality of a company's more established products.[35] Reputation is valued for precisely this reason. In the early years of a new product—especially a capital good, whose reliability and durability may take years to demonstrate—consumers often have little other information on which to base their purchases. For example, in the early 1980s Maytag introduced a new line of dishwashers. Salespeople immediately emphasized the product's reliability and durability—drawing on the reputation of the company's washers and dryers—even though the superiority of that particular product line had yet to be proved.

That completes the list of the eight dimensions of quality. Together, they cover a broad range of concepts. Several of the dimensions involve measurable product attributes; others reflect individual preferences. Some are objective and timeless; others shift with changing fashions. Some are inherent characteristics of goods, while others are ascribed characteristics.

The diversity of these concepts helps to explain the differences among the approaches to quality discussed in Chapter 3. Each of the principal approaches focused implicitly on a different dimension of quality: the product-based approach on performance, features, and durability; the user-based approach, on aesthetics and perceived quality; and the manufacturing-based approach, on conformance and reliability. Conflicts among these approaches were inevitable, because each defined quality from a different point of view. Once the concept is unbundled, however, and each dimension is considered separately, the sources of disagreement become clear.

## COMPETING ON QUALITY

A recognition of the eight dimensions is also important for strategic purposes. Competing on quality becomes far more complex; multiple dimensions imply that products can be differentiated in a multitude of ways. Performance alone is a multifaceted variable, as are several other dimensions. For example, the quality of an automobile tire may reflect its rate of treadwear, its handling, its traction in dangerous driving conditions, its rolling resistance (expected gas mileage), its noise levels, its resistance to punctures, or its appearance.[36] High-quality furniture may be distinguished by its uniform finish, an absence of surface flaws, reinforced frames, comfort, or superior design.[37] Even the quality of a less tangible product like computer software can be evaluated on multiple dimensions. They include reliability, ease of maintenance, match with users' needs, integrity (the extent to which unauthorized access can be controlled), portability (the ease with which a program can be transferred from one hardware or software environment to another), efficiency (the amount of resources required to perform a function), and testability (the effort required to test a program to ensure that it performs as designed).[38]

With variety comes choices. A company that elects to compete on quality can do so in various ways; it need not pursue all eight dimensions at once. In fact, that is seldom possible, unless exorbitant prices are charged. Technological limitations impose a further constraint. In some cases, a product or service can be improved on one dimension of quality only if it becomes worse on another. Manufacturers of motors, for example, are forced to trade off speed against fuel economy; manufacturers of paper towels find it difficult to offer both toughness and softness.[39] Proliferating features may interfere with streamlined service, just as an eye-catching design may impede a product's basic performance. Cray Research, a manufacturer of supercomputers, has faced particularly difficult choices of this sort. According to the company's chairman: "If a machine doesn't fail every month or so, it probably isn't properly optimized."[40] In pursuit of higher operating speeds, Cray has consciously sacrificed reliability, leaving it vulnerable to competitors.

### Quality Niches

Tradeoffs like the ones indicated above suggest that companies wishing to compete on quality will be more successful if they pursue segmentation strategies, singling out a few dimensions of quality as their focus instead of striving to be number one in all categories. Across-the-board excellence is seldom a competitive necessity. Provided the dimensions selected are well matched to market needs, the targeted approach can yield great gains. Consider the following examples:

• Japanese manufacturers have traditionally entered U.S. markets by emphasizing the reliability and conformance of their products while downplaying the other dimensions of quality. The superior "fits and finishes" and low repair rates of Japanese automobiles are well known; less frequently recognized are their poor safety records (performance) and low corrosion resistance (durability).[41] Despite these drawbacks, Japanese automobiles have come to symbolize the very best in quality for many American consumers.

• Tandem Computers has based its business on superior reliability. For computer users like telephone companies and utilities, which find downtime intolerable, Tandem has devised a fail-safe system: two processors working in parallel, linked by software that shifts responsibility between the two if an important component or subsystem should fail. The result, in an industry already well known for quality products, has been spectacular growth. In 1984, after less than ten years in business, Tandem's annual sales topped $500 million.

• New York's Chemical Bank upgraded its lock box services not long ago. A user survey was first conducted; it indicated that quality in this business (collecting payments for corporations) was synonymous with rapid response to customers' queries for account information. After a computerized system was installed to answer calls, the ranking of the bank's lock box services jumped from fourth to first in the industry. When a competitor withdrew from the market, the bank attracted virtually all of its customers.

These examples suggest that firms can successfully pursue a selective quality niche. In fact, they may have no other choice, if competitors have already established broad reputations for excellence. Then new entrants may be able to secure a defensible position only if they focus on an as yet untapped dimension of quality.

This pattern clearly fits the piano industry. For many years, Steinway & Sons has been the quality leader. Its instruments are known for their even voicing (the evenness of character and timbre of each of the eighty-eight notes on the keyboard), the sweetness of their registers (the roundness and softness of tone throughout the piano's entire range), the duration of their tone, their long lives, and their fine cabinet work.[42] Each piano is handcrafted, and each is unique in sound and style. Despite these advantages, Steinway has recently been challenged by Yamaha, a Japanese manufacturer that has developed a strong reputation for quality in a relatively short time. Yamaha has done so by emphasizing reliability and conformance, two dimensions of quality that are low on Steinway's list, rather than artistry and uniqueness. Its pianos are put together on a moving assembly line rather than in a traditional job shop. Yet despite their widely varying approaches to quality, both companies have enjoyed great success.

Strategies aimed at identifying and securing a quality niche, then, can be quite effective. Few products rank high on all eight dimensions of quality; those that do, like Cross pens, Rolex watches, and Rolls-Royce automobiles, are frequently handcrafted and expensive.[43] For companies targeting the mass market, this option is seldom available. Nor is pursuing all eight dimensions at once even necessary for establishing a reputation for quality. As the experiences of Yamaha and other Japanese manufacturers demonstrate, superiority on one or two dimensions of quality—especially reliability and conformance, which have become increasingly important to consumers—is often enough to establish a dominant position.

### Quality Errors

Yamaha's behavior is noteworthy in another respect. By defining quality in its own terms rather than accepting Steinway's definition, Yamaha has avoided a classic strategic error. A direct—and unnecessary—confrontation with the industry's quality leader has been avoided. As a leading strategist has pointed out:

> Never attack head-on with a strategy merely imitative of the leader's, even if you have the resources and staying power . . . the trick is to nullify the leader's advantage while avoiding full-scale retaliation.[44]

Because a recognition of the multiple dimensions of quality expands the choices open to firms, it makes such errors much easier to avoid.

Directly attacking the quality leader is but one of several mistakes companies make in their quality strategies. Most are related in some way to a lack of market research on the eight dimensions of quality. A common error is the pursuit of dimensions of quality that are unimportant to consumers. For example, when deregulation opened up the market for residential telephones, a number of manufacturers, including AT&T, assumed that customers equated quality in this business with a wide range of expensive features. They were soon proved wrong. Fancy telephones sold poorly, while durable, reliable, and easy-to-operate sets gained large market shares.[45] In a similar fashion, a health insurance company set as its quality objective rapid turnaround time on claims. Quick response, however, proved to be much less important to customers than the accuracy of billing and account information. Because most physicians reviewed their accounts receivable only every thirty days, the company's efforts to improve its quality image by expediting payments were of little value.[46]

One version of this quality error deserves special attention because it has arisen in so many different markets. American companies have frequently misread consumers by assuming that reliability and conformance were less important than they ultimately proved to be. As an earlier discussion has indicated, much of the success of Japanese products in this country can be traced to their superiority on these two dimensions of quality. Typically, American manufacturers have been more interested in performance and features—often tied to new technological advances—while Japanese manufacturers have pursued refinements and applications.[47] In an industry such as semiconductor manufacturing equipment, the result has been Japanese machines that generally require less time to set up, break down less frequently, and have few problems meeting their specified performance levels. According to one American plant manager familiar with machines from the two countries: "U.S. equipment is more advanced, but Japanese equipment is more developed."[48]

The fact that U.S. manufacturers have repeatedly misread consumers on this score reflects their lack of attention to the varied meanings of quality. It also suggests another common quality error: relying on the wrong quality metric.[49] The success of programs to evaluate consumers' reactions to quality depends on the accuracy of the measuring sticks employed. If the metrics used by producers fail to match the interests of consumers—because they are poorly designed, rely on technical data that are poor proxies for customer satisfaction, or draw from unrepresentative samples—they will provide little guidance. An especially serious error of this sort is using long-standing quality metrics to set internal quality goals even though the external environment has changed. A major telecommunications firm, for example, had historically evaluated its quality by measuring timeliness—the amount of time it took to provide a dial tone, to connect a call, or to be connected to an operator. On these measures it had performed well. More sophisticated market surveys, however, conducted in anticipation of the industry's deregulation, found that consumers were now much less concerned with the time it took to connect calls (since that time was invariably within acceptable limits) than they were with the clarity of transmission (the degree of crackling and static on the line) once calls had been put through. The company subsequently shifted its internal standards to match better its new understanding of consumer needs.

Quality measures may also be inappropriate in less obvious ways. Some measures are too limited and fail to capture aspects of quality that are important for competitive success; others are too highly aggregated. In either case, the measures will be extremely misleading. For example, Singapore International Airlines (SIA), an air carrier with a reputation for excellent service, saw its market share decline in the early 1980s. The company dismissed quality problems as the cause of its difficulties, because data on service complaints, reported in a number of different ways, showed steady improvement during the period. Only later, after new quality reports had been developed, did SIA see the weakness of relying on complaints as its primary measure of quality. Relative declines in service had indeed been responsible for the loss of market share. Complaint counts, however, had failed to register the change for two reasons: Passengers who wrote complaint letters were a relatively small proportion of all users (in this case, they were primarily Europeans and Americans rather than Asians, the largest percentage of SIA passengers, who filed complaints less frequently), and improvements in service by SIA's competitors were in no way captured by the measures in place.[50]

The pervasiveness of these errors is difficult to determine. Anecdotal evidence suggests that many U.S. companies lack comprehensive comparative quality data and are vulnerable to such mistakes. Several surveys provide indirect support for this conclusion, for they point to the existence of a "quality perception gap." Producers appear frequently to rate the quality of their products and services higher than consumers and to overestimate their quality edge.[51] The surveys cited at the beginning of this chapter are but one prominent example. Another survey found that 65 percent of executives felt that consumers could readily name—without assistance—a good-quality brand in a category such as major home appliances. But when the question was actually posed to consumers, only 16 percent were able to name such a brand for small appliances, and only 23 percent for large appliances.[52] Such figures suggest that many U.S. executives, ill-informed about consumers' true perceptions of quality and lacking the precise vocabulary needed to learn more about them, are inclined to overly optimistic estimates of their standing in the market place.

## IMPROVED INFORMATION, ORGANIZATION, AND IMPLEMENTATION

Both quality errors and quality perception gaps point to the need for better market research on quality. Competitively useful quality information is surprisingly scarce. Many companies *think* they know what quality means in their industry; few appear to have taken the time to back their hunches with careful research. The analysis in this chapter suggests several possible improvements. First, many companies would benefit from explicitly linking measures of customer satisfaction with one or more dimensions of quality. Because satisfaction is such a complex phenomenon, measuring it alone provides little basis for action. More refined measures are frequently required; otherwise, companies are likely to suffer from the same problems that plagued Singapore Airlines. For similar reasons, companies need to understand the precise weight that each dimension of quality plays in shaping consumers' preferences.[53] Does performance matter more than reliability in a particular market, or is aesthetics the primary consideration? What tradeoffs are customers willing to make among the various dimensions of quality? Do thresholds set floors or ceilings on the range of permissible variation, as they do for products like farm equipment?

Having identified the critical dimensions of quality in a market, companies can then relate these dimensions to specific product attributes. That gives designers a set of precise and measurable goals— for example, the need for components that last five years to ensure long product lives desired by consumers, or the need for especially tight tolerances to provide desired levels of fits and finishes. Again, careful market research is required. As an earlier discussion has indicated, traits like durability and reliability can seldom be observed before purchase; more often, customers draw on the experience of friends or infer these characteristics from other aspects of a product. The inference process can be quite complex. Some quality indicators, like taste or materials, are intrinsic to a product and part of its physical makeup; others, like packaging or store image, are extrinsic and more easily observed. Even a product as simple as tomato ketchup can be judged on such varied criteria as taste, color, thickness, labeling, and positioning on store shelves. Because of these complexities, the relationship between product attributes and desired dimensions of quality is seldom immediately apparent. For example, in an effort to understand the relationship between refrigerator quality and product features, General Electric ultimately examined more than a hundred cues, including the presence or absence of glass shelves and portable containers; the nature of shelf trim, door hinges, and drawer material; and the construction of the unit's lining and panels.[54]

Market research of this sort is necessary if products are to offer the dimensions of quality that are of greatest interest to consumers, and if companies are to target a defensible quality niche. The selection of a defensible niche, however, brings additional requirements, for each dimension of quality is likely to impose its own demands on the firm. High performance normally requires careful attention to design and a strong design staff; superior durability normally requires the use of long-lived components and close cooperation between the engineering and purchasing departments; superior conformance normally requires attention to written specifications and precision in assembly; and exceptional serviceability normally requires a strong customer service department and active field representatives. In each case a different function enjoys the leading role, and different tasks are required for success. The managerial implications of this analysis should be obvious: After selecting the dimensions of quality on which it hopes to compete, a firm can benefit by tailoring its organization and operations to meet these specific needs. Otherwise, the wrong departments may be elevated in status or the wrong tasks pursued. A retail store, for example, may choose to cultivate a reputation for high-quality service or a reputation for high-quality merchandise. The two require vastly different personnel and operating policies—varying numbers of salespeople and cashiers per department, more or less lenient merchandise return policies, and contrasting approaches to stocking name brands—and therefore will impose differing management requirements.[55] Disaggregating the concept of quality allows companies to pinpoint these requirements as carefully as they target untapped markets.

Eventually, successful companies try to link their quality improvement programs to the activities of individual work groups. In such efforts, a more precise vocabulary has great advantages. Vague calls for quality improvement typically go unheeded; they lack clear direction and suffer problems of accountability. In contrast, programs aimed at improving reliability, durability, serviceability, or other dimensions of quality are more readily focused and manageable. They can be farmed out to particular departments or interfunctional teams. They can be tied to specific improvement projects. And they permit ready monitoring of progress. Once these steps have been taken—as they have at Hewlett-Packard, Xerox, and Corning Glass, the leading-edge companies described in Chapter 2—the dimensions of quality become more than just theoretical niceties; they become the basis for using quality as a competitive weapon.

# Chapter
# 5

# Correlates of Quality

To be of more than passing interest to managers, quality must have a demonstrable impact on the bottom line. It must be closely associated with such key measures of business performance as cost, market share, and profitability. Otherwise, quality improvement would quickly lose its appeal, for it would lack a strategic rationale.

The success of Japanese products in this country and the increased sensitivity of consumers to quality suggest that such relationships exist. But the American financial community remains unconvinced. According to a 1985 survey of several hundred large institutional investors, the quality of a company's products ranked dead last as a factor influencing stock selection. In contrast, expected earnings ranked near the top of the list.[1]

To these investors—and, no doubt, countless others—the evidence linking quality and corporate performance has been unimpressive. The same success stories have been recounted time and time again. Claims of quality's impact have often been based on dramatic turnarounds, but few generalizations can be drawn from such selective evidence. Sophisticated explanations for the association between quality and key business variables have been rare.

For these reasons, Chapter 5 will summarize the theory and evidence linking quality to price, advertising, market share, cost, productivity, and profitability. In several areas, conflicting findings coexist. Sometimes quality and price are positively related; at other times they are negatively related. In some industries quality and cost move together; in other industries they move inversely. In some studies high quality implies high market shares; in other studies it implies low market shares.

Scholars have found these results difficult to explain, but they are easily interpreted using the framework of Chapter 4. Because few

69

studies have recognized the multiple dimensions of quality, definitional problems have often been severe. Such varied dimensions of quality as performance and conformance have been lumped together. Each dimension, however, is likely to be related to price, cost, or market share in a different way. As the ensuing discussion will show, this insight is enormously helpful in interpreting the evidence on the correlates of quality.

## PRICE

The theoretical argument for a relationship between quality and price takes two forms. One, an outgrowth of the economics literature, focuses on objective measures of quality; the other, driven by marketing scholars, is more concerned with perceived quality. Despite these differences, the two approaches generally agree that quality and price should be positively correlated.

Economists begin with the assumption that higher quality can be produced only at higher cost, because additional labor, materials, or capital are required. Radial tires, for example, cost more to produce than conventional tires because of a more complex production process, but they last 50–100 percent longer, offer improved gas mileage, and ensure better handling. In this formulation, as long as costs and prices are positively related, quality and price will move together as well.[2]

An implicit assumption of this approach is that consumers possess sufficient information to evaluate product quality. If they do not, markets are characterized by "asymmetric information": Sellers know more about the quality of the goods they are selling than do buyers.[3] Used cars are the classic example. Asymmetric information creates a difficult marketing problem for companies whose products are truly of superior quality: How can they convince consumers of their product's quality, and so charge the higher prices that their costs require? The answer, according to theorists, is to invest in brand names, reputation, attractive places of business, and other assets that serve as signals of product quality to consumers.[4] If such investments are made, quality and price should be positively related even in the presence of asymmetric information.

Marketing scholars have also dealt with the problem of imperfect information, but they have approached it from a different angle. They too have recognized that consumers do not always possess full information about a product or service's quality. As Chapter 4 has indicated, in such circumstances other cues will become important for evaluating quality. Comparative prices are one example; others include advertising, recommendations from friends, brand reputation, and packaging. Prices—especially price *differences*—thus serve two functions, allocating resources as well as conveying information:

> [A] price difference may have more than one meaning. Most often, perhaps, we think of high prices negatively, in terms of the sacrifice we must make to get what we want. In other cases, however . . . we think of a higher price positively, as a symbol of extra quality or extra value or prestige.[5]

Subsequent theorizing has tried to differentiate price from other cues that are perceived to be symbols of quality. Most cues can be evaluated on two dimensions: their predictive value ("a measure of the probability with which a cue seems associated with a specific product attribute") and their confidence value ("a measure of how *certain* the consumer is that the *cue* is what she thinks it is").[6] Some theorists have argued that since price is such an obvious, measurable entity, it is likely to have a high confidence value and for this reason will be viewed as an especially low-risk indicator of quality.[7]

The impact of price on perceived quality thus depends on the relative strength of price and nonprice cues. Whether these perceptions accord with *actual* quality differences is another matter. Once managers recognize that consumers are judging quality by price, they may respond by readjusting prices:

> If managers believe that perceptions and perhaps consumer purchase decisions are positively correlated with price, they may set higher prices in order to imply higher product quality. Price, therefore, may become a means of differentiating a product . . . such pricing strategies . . . would likely result in a deterioration of the price–quality relationship within a product category.[8]

The theory, then, is equivocal.[9] Quality and price may or may not be positively correlated, depending on whether perceived or actual quality is being measured and whether or not managers are using price as a means of product differentiation.

Extensive empirical research has been conducted to test these propositions. Studies fall into two general categories: experimental studies, which have focused on the price–perceived quality relationship, and market studies, which have examined the relationship between price and more objective measures of quality. Experimental studies have typically presented a panel of subjects with a product or series of products and then have varied prices—in some cases, other cues as well—to see how assessments of quality were affected. Those studies in which prices and quality perceptions were the only variables measured have found a positive correlation between the two.[10] The relationship breaks down, however, in the more sophisticated experimental studies. Where multiple cues are present for inferring quality—brand name, store image, product features, or country of manufacture in addition to price—the strong price-perceived quality association of the earlier bivariate research weakens or disappears.[11] Moreover, the strength of the relationship has been found to vary with circumstances and with the characteristics of individual consumers.[12] Thus, no single conclusion emerges from the experimental studies.

When market data have been used instead, the results have differed by product category and methodology.[13] All market studies have employed list prices as their measures of price and *Consumer Reports* or *Consumer Research* rankings as their measures of quality. Typically, quality rankings have been based on performance, durability, or aesthetics (especially in foods, where taste is a key factor). In all cases, individual brands were ranked by technical experts employed by a not-for-profit testing organization, who first subjected each brand within a product category to evaluative tests and then assigned points based on the results. A room air conditioner, for example, might be set up in a high-humidity environment and its cooling ability measured, or a frying pan might be assessed for ease of handling and use. Some of these measures are quite objective, while others rely more on the judgment of testers.

Correlation studies based on these measures have shown a relatively weak relationship between quality and price. While correlations have generally been positive, few have been large or significant. Durable goods have normally displayed a stronger relationship between quality and price than nondurables, probably because consumers are better able to make informed decisions about quality in such markets.[14] Yet despite these differences, the overall conclusion one draws from the studies is that "price and quality . . . correlate, but at a level so low as to lack practical significance."[15]

Correlation studies may be flawed, however, by a failure to include variables other than price and quality. Prices are influenced by more than performance alone. They also reflect the cost of materials, levels of advertising, and relative scarcity. *Consumer Reports'* rankings may also be too highly aggregated to provide meaningful results. They not only lump together multiple dimensions of quality but often fail to include dimensions that are of critical importance to users, such as reliability.

One way of overcoming these problems is to use multivariate statistical techniques rather than correlations. An especially useful method is that of hedonic price indexes, which are based on the idea that variations in the prices of different brands or models of a product reflect differences in the amount of certain basic attributes that they possess.[16] For example, the prices of different types of automobiles are likely to reflect differences in their size, horsepower, or trim, while the prices of houses are likely to correspond to variations in square footage, number of rooms, location, or other amenities. Statistical methods are then used to link price directly to these elements, which represent performance and features. Because each dimension of quality can be broken out separately as an independent variable, hedonic techniques have the advantage of measuring the association between each dimension of quality and price after other important influences have already been accounted for.

Surprisingly, few hedonic studies have included measures of quality other than performance or features. Most have sought to explain price variation by differences in size, weight, or other obvious product characteristics. Two important exceptions involved automobiles and new homes.[17] The former study included measures of reliability (repair frequency) while the latter study included measures of reliability and conformance (leaky roofs, interior cracks, toilet breakdowns, and blown fuses). Neither study, however, found a particularly strong relationship between price and conformance or reliability. In only a few equations were the coefficients of the quality variables statistically significant.[18]

A further attempt to explore the relationship between multiple dimensions of quality and price using the hedonic approach appears in Appendix C. It consists of equations estimated from 1979, 1980, and 1982 *Consumer Reports* data on room air conditioners. Three measures of quality have been used: *Consumer Reports* aggregate quality rankings, which group products into broad quality categories based on their performance in tests but do not rank products within categories; *Consumer Reports* specific quality rankings, available for 1980 models only, which rank all products separately rather than using broad groupings; and 1981–82 service call rates under first-year warranty coverage, which measure the percentage of all models sold by the company (and not just the models rated by *Consumer Reports*) requiring service of some sort during their first year of ownership.[19]

Two results stand out. First, neither aggregate nor specific quality rankings contribute much to the equations; they appear with the expected signs but are never statistically significant. Second, service call rates have an impact quite different from quality measures based on performance. Surprisingly, reliability, as measured by first-year service call rates, is negatively related to price in this sample. More expensive models typically have higher service call rates. That finding is difficult to explain, although it does suggest that the sources of superior product performance are different from the sources of superior reliability.

In summary, the hedonic approach yields results that are as equivocal as those of the leading correlation studies.[20] While aspects of performance and features such as horsepower and size are related to price, other dimensions of quality are not. Overall, the price–quality relationship is weak. Confirming evidence comes from a 1983 survey of the characteristics consumers used to judge product quality. It found that price ranked a distant fifth. Only 24 percent of respondents said a high price was always important in their judgments of quality, and only 1 percent cited it as their most important quality indicator.[21] These findings, plus the evidence reviewed here, suggest that there is little empirical support for the predicted positive association between quality and price, except when there are obvious differences in performance or features.

## ADVERTISING

The theoretical argument for a positive association between quality and advertising is based on the distinction between "search" and "experience" goods.[22] The attributes of search goods can be determined prior to purchase, while those of experience goods can be learned only after the product has been purchased and used. The cut and fit of an article of clothing are examples of product characteristics that can be learned through search; the reliability and durability of major home appliances are examples of traits that are learned primarily through experience. Theorists claim that for experience goods, higher levels of advertising will be associated with higher-quality products:

High-quality brands will obtain more repeat purchases . . . than low-quality brands. Thus . . . sellers of high-quality brands will spend more to persuade consumers to try their wares since . . . the present value of a trial purchase is larger . . . this force causes better brands to advertise more in equilibrium as long as consumers respond to advertising at all; the level of advertising for experience goods is thus positively correlated with quality, regardless of what individual ads actually claim. Quality information is provided by the level of advertising, not the claims it makes.[23]

The argument has recently been extended to incorporate consumers' aversion to risk. In the new formulation, firms are assumed to be investing in advertising to signal consumers that their products are less risky (that is, of more uniform quality) than products that are unadvertised.[24]

The evidence on these points is inconclusive. Analysts using both American and British data have found some evidence of a positive relationship between advertising and product quality (with quality again measured by *Consumer Reports* or *Consumers' Bulletin* rankings), but the results have varied widely and unsystematically by product category. For example, an early study reported correlations for 1972 and 1973 between quality rankings and advertising levels in fourteen product categories. It found a strong association only when unadvertised brands were included in the sample and assigned to the lowest rank of advertising expenditures.[25] These results suggest that a consumer seeking a high-quality brand was likely to be more successful if he or she selected a brand that was nationally advertised.[26] But the authors still concluded that their evidence was equivocal: "Advertised products are apparently of better quality than nonadvertised goods for some products, when rated by certain criteria, in some years. . . . But no broad generalizations can be made."[27] Other researchers have expanded on this study by employing multiple measures of advertising levels and brand quality. They have reached similar conclusions; for example: "A heavily advertised product is just as likely to be poor quality as any other."[28] All studies have intermingled search and experience goods, but the same results are found if the analysis is confined to goods in the latter category.

A different conclusion emerges from research based on the Profit Impact of Marketing Strategies (PIMS) data base. All PIMS studies have employed the same highly aggregated measure of quality. Each company in the PIMS survey was first asked the following questions: What was the percentage of sales of products or services from each business in each year which were superior to those of competitors? What was the percentage of equivalent products? What was the percentage of inferior products? Quality indexes were then compiled for each business by subtracting its percentage "inferior" from its percentage "superior."

Unfortunately, the primary PIMS study of pricing and advertising strategies did not test directly for the relationship between advertising and quality.[29] It looked instead at how relative prices and return on investment were affected by variables such as market stability, stage in the life cycle, and quality. The findings, however, are suggestive. Those brands in the study with the highest relative prices were the ones with both the highest quality and the highest advertising. The authors concluded:

> Marketers who *tell* consumers about quality differences in their
> product command higher prices than marketers who depend on high
> quality to communicate *itself* to consumers. For mass produced items,
> advertising is the most efficient way of communicating superior
> quality—especially when consumers may not be able to judge quality
> differences from inspection or use.[30]

A later study using the same data base, however, found a much weaker connection between the two variables.[31]

Such findings are quite similar to those relating quality and price. Overall, the empirical results lack clear direction. Advertising and quality are related in certain circumstances, but the relationship is more complex than predicted by theory. Consumers apparently feel the same way. In a recent survey of consumer attitudes, the majority of respondents felt that advertised products were no more likely to be dependable than were products without advertising.[32] Another survey found that a widely advertised brand name was viewed by consumers as the least important of ten indicators for judging product quality.[33]

## MARKET SHARE

The relationship between quality and market share is likely to depend on how quality is defined.[34] If a high-quality product is one with superior performance or a large number of features, it will generally be more expensive and will sell in smaller volumes. But if quality is defined as fitness for use, superior aesthetics, or improved conformance, it need not be accompanied by premium prices. In that case, quality and market share are likely to be positively correlated.

Virtually all empirical work on this topic has employed the PIMS data base.[35] Each study has therefore used the same measure of quality described above. Each has also found a strong positive association between quality improvements and market share gains. The figures in Table 5.1 are representative. More sophisticated studies using both bivariate and multivariate methods have produced similar results.

Two studies using more consumer-oriented measures of quality have pointed in the opposite direction.[36] In both foods and major home appliances, quality rankings and market shares were not well correlated. Other research suggests that the two variables move together, but only with a lag. Because consumers often lack up-to-date quality information, they sometimes base their purchase decisions on reputation instead of more objective measures of quality. For example, after a product recall for possible safety problems, Firestone Tire & Rubber suffered an erosion of market share. A new quality program was enacted, and quality soon improved. The company's market share, however, rebounded more quickly in the original equipment market, where all new tires were rigorously tested by customers (the major auto companies) for performance, durability, and other aspects of quality, than it did in the replacement market, where customers had much less firsthand information about quality.[37]

Overall, the evidence on the connection between quality and market share is mixed. The PIMS data show that the two are positively

TABLE 5.1   *Changes in Market Share and Quality Improvement*

| Change in Relative Quality | Rate of Change in Share | | |
|---|---|---|---|
| | *Consumer Products Businesses* | *Raw Materials Businesses* | *Industrial Products Businesses* |
| Reduced | +2.1% | −0.9% | +0.7% |
| No change | +0.1 | +0.8 | +2.5 |
| Increased | +4.0 | +2.1 | +4.3 |

correlated, especially where customers are well-informed. But contrary findings in foods and major home appliances suggest a more complex relationship. Additional research, using more objective measures of quality to buttress the PIMS results, is required.


## COST

Theoretical discussions of the relationship between quality and cost fall into three distinct categories. One group, following the product-based approach of Chapter 3, argues that quality and direct cost are positively related. The implicit assumption here is that quality differences reflect variations in performance, features, durability, or other product attributes that require more expensive components or materials, additional labor hours in construction, or other commitments of tangible resources. This view of quality dominates much American thinking on the subject.

A second view draws on the operations management literature. It sees quality and cost as inversely related, because the costs of improving quality are thought to be less than the resulting savings in rework, scrap, and warranty expenses. According to this view, which is widely held among Japanese manufacturers and explains much of their dedication to "continuous improvement," quality is synonymous with the absence of defects, and the costs in question are quality costs.

Quality costs are defined as any expenditures on manufacturing or service in excess of those that would have been incurred if the product had been built or the service had been performed exactly right the first time.[38] In their most comprehensive form, these measures would include the cost of forgone opportunities (lost sales) and the cost of responding to customer complaints, as well as various hidden costs not normally associated with poor quality. For example, the cost of carrying excess raw materials and work-in-process inventory to ensure that defective items do not shut down the production line is a cost that can be ascribed to poor quality, as is the expense of owning and operating excess capacity in order to compensate for machine clogging and downtime. Neither appears in most conventional measures. IBM has identified an even subtler example.[39] Every quarter, the company compiled a phone directory listing its 14,000 employees in the lower Westchester region of New York State. The directory contained errors the day it was printed. Over time the number of incorrect listings increased, since Westchester employees averaged three hundred job and office changes per week. On a percentage basis, this meant that the directory became 2 percent less accurate each week. Combining these inaccuracies with the directory's initial errors and recognizing that directories were reprinted every quarter, the company concluded that each directory was on average 80 percent correct. From a quality standpoint, that meant if an employee used the directory just once a day, a wrong number was likely to be dialed every week. The lost time spent on these calls was the cost of (poor) quality.

In practice, few measures of quality costs are an inclusive as the IBM example. Typically, companies confine quality costs to four broad categories: prevention costs, appraisal costs, internal failure costs, and external failure costs.[40] Prevention costs include expenditures on supplier education, on-the-job training, product redesign, and other efforts to keep mistakes from happening in the first place; appraisal costs include expenditures on inspection, testing, and other activities designed to ferret out mistakes once they have occurred; internal failure costs include expenditures on rework, scrap, and other errors found within the factory; and external failure costs include expenditures on warranty claims, product liability suits, and other problems that arise after a product has reached the customer.

Using these categories, it is easy to see why analysts argue that quality and cost are inversely related. Poor conformance and reliability lead eventually to large failure costs. Defective units must be reworked, scrapped, or repaired in the field. These costs can be quite substantial; as long as they are higher on a per-unit basis than the costs of preventing problems or catching them before a unit has been fully assembled, efforts to improve quality through increased prevention should result in lower total quality costs. In general, the closer one gets to a final product, the higher the failure costs and the greater the possible savings. Richard W. Anderson, general manager of Hewlett-Packard's computer systems division, observes:

> The earlier you detect and prevent a defect the more you can save. If you catch a two cent resistor before you use it and throw it away, you lose two cents. If you don't find it until it has been soldered into a computer component, it may cost $10 to repair the part. If you don't catch the component until it is in the computer user's hands, the repair will cost hundreds of dollars. Indeed, if a $5,000 computer has to be repaired in the field, the expense may exceed the manufacturing cost.[41]

The same phenomenon is illustrated in Figure 5.1. According to estimates by General Electric, error costs rise by an order of magnitude each time a product or component moves a step further along the production chain. An error that costs $.003 if found at the supplier level costs $300—100,000 times more—if left undiscovered until the product is in the field. A study of weapons systems by the Institute for Defense Analysis reached similar conclusions. It estimated repair costs per failure at the part, subassembly, assembly, and field level and found that costs rose from $1 at the outset to $2,000 in the field.[42] In such settings, improvements in quality—even if they require increased expenditures on training, supplier education, or design—should lead eventually to lower quality costs.

A number of analysts have extended this argument to include the claim that improved conformance should also result in reductions in long-run manufacturing costs.[43] Often the justification for the claim

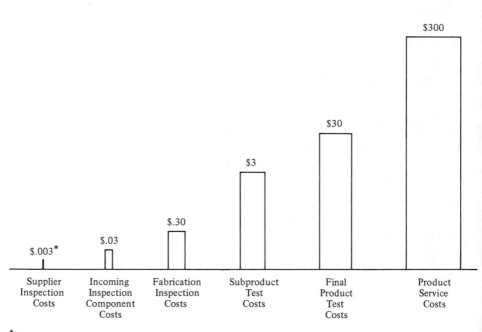

*Estimated cost per defect per product.

FIGURE 5.1    Escalation in Cost of Errors Down the Production Line

SOURCE: Weston Ison, manager of quality control and reliability systems, General Electric Company. Reprinted, by permission of the publisher, from "How to Gain the Competitive Edge: Improving Product Quality Through Continuous Feedback," by Robert E. Cole, *Management Review,* October 1983, p. 10, © 1983 American Management Association, New York. All rights reserved.

has been the expected link between quality improvement and productivity gains, which is discussed in more detail below. A dynamic process may also be at work. Efforts to improve quality normally lead to a better understanding of the manufacturing process; over time, that learning may translate into lower production costs.[44] Finally, quality improvements may lead, through their impact on sales and cumulative production levels, to savings in the form of experience-based scale economies.[45] In each of these cases, long-run manufacturing costs would be reduced.

The evidence in these areas is fragmentary. Occasionally, conflicting findings coexist. For example, the PIMS data base has generally been used to examine the relationship between quality and direct cost. The results have varied considerably by industry. In one study, quality and direct cost were positively related for differentiated-product businesses but negatively related for homogeneous products.[46] In another study, the two were positively related in capital goods businesses but negatively related in components and supplies businesses.[47] However, the experience curve effect, with high quality leading to high market share, increases in cumulative production, and, eventually, experienced-based reductions in costs, was found in all types of businesses.[48]

The varying results of these studies may reflect differences in the definitions of quality used by firms in different industries. The PIMS quality index does not distinguish among performance, features, reliability, or other dimensions of quality discussed earlier. Different industries could therefore be employing different definitions when assessing the quality of their products. That, in turn, would determine whether the relationship between quality and direct cost was positive or negative. For example, in homogeneous product businesses (e.g. chemicals), quality is often defined as meeting specifications.[49] Such a conformance-based view of quality is likely to result in an inverse relationship between quality and direct cost. In differentiated and capital goods businesses, however, quality is likely to be equated with performance or features, suggesting a positive association between quality and direct cost. While these inferences are consistent with the PIMS findings, they require further research in order to be verified.

The data on quality costs are even more limited, for few analysts have collected information on both quality costs and quality performance. The evidence that exists is largely anecdotal, often accounts by companies wishing to publicize successful quality programs. For example, Signetics Corporation, a manufacturer of semiconductors, has reported that between 1980 and 1983 its average outgoing quality levels improved from 7,000 defective parts per million (ppm) to 150 ppm. At the same time, the company reduced its quality costs by $20 million.[50] This example—with innumerable others like it—is suggestive about the relationship between conformance and quality costs but hardly definitive.

A more complete accounting, based on a single industry, appears in Table 5.2. It draws on the study of quality at U.S. and Japanese manufacturers of room air conditioners that serves as the basis for several of the chapters to follow (see Appendix A for a description of the study). Plants were first assigned to quality groupings based

TABLE 5.2    *Quality and Quality Costs in the Room Air Conditioning Industry, 1981–82*

| Grouping of Companies by Quality Performance | Warranty Costs as a Percentage of Sales[a] | | Total Costs of Quality (Japanese companies) and Total Failure Costs (U.S. companies) as a Percentage of Sales[b] | |
|---|---|---|---|---|
| | *Average* | *Range* | *Average* | *Range* |
| Japanese manufacturers | .6% | .2–1.0% | 1.3% | .7–2.0% |
| Best U.S. plants | 1.8 | 1.1–2.4 | 2.8 | 2.7–2.8 |
| Better U.S. plants | 2.4 | 1.7–3.1 | 3.4 | 3.3–3.5 |
| Fair U.S. plants | 2.7 | 1.7–4.3 | 3.9 | 2.3–5.6 |
| Poor U.S. plants | 5.2 | 3.3–7.0 | >5.8 | 4.4–>7.2 |

[a]Because most Japanese air conditioners are covered by a three-year warranty while most U.S. units are covered by a warranty of five years, these figures somewhat overstate the Japanese advantage. The bias is unlikely to be serious, however, because second- to fifth-year coverage in the United States and second- to third-year coverage in Japan are much less inclusive—and therefore less expensive—than first-year coverage. For example, at U.S. companies second- to fifth-year warranty costs averaged less than one-fifth of first-year expenses.
[b]Total costs of quality are the sum of all quality-related expenditures, including the costs of prevention, inspection, rework, scrap, and warranties. The Japanese figures include expenditures in all of these categories, while the U.S. figures, because of limited data, include only the costs of rework, scrap, and warranties (failure costs). As a result, these figures understate total U.S. quality costs relative to those of the Japanese.

SOURCE: Company records and questionnaires distributed by the author.

on their defect and field failure performance—the precise classification system is described in Appendix B—and quality costs were then computed for each plant and averaged by category. According to the table, improved conformance and reliability were strongly associated with lower quality costs. As expected, warranty costs rose as quality declined—an increase in field failures meant an increase in the volume of repair. More significantly, when quality declined, total quality costs rose as well. Japanese manufacturers, with defect and field failure rates between seventeen and sixty-seven times lower than their U.S. competitors, averaged total costs of quality that were 1.3 percent of sales.[51] The best American plants averaged rework, scrap, and warranty costs that alone were 2.8 percent of sales. At the U.S. plants with the poorest quality, these costs exceeded 5.8 percent of sales.

Table 5.2 clearly shows that conformance and reliability are inversely related to quality costs. That analysis, however, is based on a single industry. Other studies have collected more comprehensive data on the costs of quality. They provide indirect support for the above relationships. For example, a 1977 survey found that companies with formal systems for assessing quality costs—which most analysts associate with superior quality management and low failure rates—had lower total costs of quality than companies without such systems. Companies in the former group averaged quality costs that were 5.8 percent of sales; those in the latter, rework, scrap, and warranty costs that alone were 7.8 percent of sales.[52]

Moreover, the amount that companies are spending to prevent quality problems—and, therefore, to ensure lower failure rates—may very well be suboptimal. A recent study found that at least one-quarter of the companies surveyed were spending less than 5 percent of their quality costs on prevention; approximately one-half were spending less than 10 percent.[53] The author concluded that greater expenditures on prevention would result in improved conformance and fewer defects; that, in turn, was likely to produce an overall reduction in the total costs of quality because of significant savings in rework, scrap, and warranty.

In summary, the evidence generally supports the conclusion that improved conformance and reliability lead to lower costs of quality. The relationships between quality and direct cost and between quality and long-run manufacturing cost are more problematic. Not only have the findings varied by industry, but they have also relied on the same PIMS measure of quality. A better understanding of these relationships is likely to require further research at the factory or operating unit level.


## PRODUCTIVITY

For obvious reasons, studies linking cost and quality have usually discussed productivity as well. In this analysis, the two are discussed separately only because productivity is viewed as such a basic index of organizational health.

The argument for a positive correlation between quality and productivity is usually stated in the simplest of terms. Less rework means more time devoted to manufacturing acceptable products, and less scrap means fewer wasted materials.[54] Occasionally, the argument is broadened to include the "hidden plant"—that proportion of (unnecessary) plant capacity, estimated at between 15 and 40 percent of the total, that exists solely to rework unsatisfactory parts or to repair defective units that have been returned from the field.[55] But in either case, the linkage between quality and productivity comes down to changes in the defect rate.

This is a narrow view of the relationship between the two variables, and it provides only limited insight. If productivity reflects the ratio of (defect-free) output to inputs and quality is defined as conformance (that is, the percentage of units produced that are defective), then any improvement in quality must translate directly into increased output. Nor should inputs increase if scrap and rework are reduced, for error-free operation is normally thought to require fewer resources. Yield-sensitive businesses provide an obvious example. If the process yield in semiconductor manufacturing rises from 50 to 60 percent, productivity and quality (conformance) improve simultaneously—almost by definition.

A better understanding of the connection between quality and productivity requires an examination of their common sources of improvement.[56] First, however, productivity must be more carefully defined. Most analysts implicitly associate it with partial measures. Either labor productivity (output per employee or output per labor hour) or materials productivity (output per pound of input or output per dollar of material employed) is normally reported. But more comprehensive measures, reflecting total factor productivity, are also available. They track changes in output according to changes in a combination of inputs—usually labor, materials, capital, and energy—rather than matching output to changes in a single input alone.[57]

Using these definitions, quality and productivity improvement can be traced to similar roots. For example, standardized parts and modular designs simplify the assembly process, reduce opportunities for errors, involve easier-to-stock parts and materials, imply less time devoted to disruptive engineering change orders, and often require less labor for manufacturing and rework. Improved equipment and better maintenance mean less downtime, fewer machine-related errors, and less excess capacity held in anticipation of breakdowns. A more stable and trained work force means that jobs will be performed more efficiently and inadvertent mistakes will be less frequent. Even attitude and tone play an important role:

> How workers feel about their job, about their fellow workers, about management, and about the organization, may be more important in influencing productivity than is the particular way they are instructed to do their work, the formal organization structure, or even financial incentives.[58]

As a later discussion will show, such observations are as relevant to quality improvement as they are to productivity.

In a number of areas, then, common sources of improvement can be identified. Quality and productivity would appear to share many of the same roots. But if the rationale for a positive association between the two is so clear, why do managers often assume otherwise? Is there any basis for the widely held view that gains in quality come only at the expense of reduced productivity?

In the short run, the two variables may indeed move in opposite directions. As quality programs get under way, there are inevitable disruptions: line stoppages, efforts to involve engineers in corrective action programs, meetings to establish new modes of operation, and time off for training and skill development. The immediate impact of these efforts is likely to be a reduction in productivity. New ways of operating are seldom absorbed immediately; they normally require large up-front investments of time and energy. Learning is often slow and painful. But once the programs have been institutionalized, productivity should increase. Thus, managers who equate quality improvements with productivity reductions may simply be limiting their analysis to short-run impacts.

There is another, more insidious reason why quality and productivity may appear to move in opposite directions. Flawed measurements may be to blame. Accounting systems sometimes include both defective and nondefective items when computing figures for total production. Instead of measuring *good* output—which would require that defective units be netted from the totals—they count any and all units produced. The result is a clear bias in favor of "getting it out the door" as well as a measurement system that ensures that quality and productivity improvement will be at odds.[59] Under such a system, any attempt to reduce defects automatically lowers the day's production totals as well.

The theory, then, is relatively straightforward. Quality and productivity should be positively correlated, except in the very short run or where inaccurate measurements are involved. The evidence on the subject is meager, although anecdotal examples abound. Virtually all show a positive association between quality and productivity. For example, General Electric recently modernized its dishwasher plant in Louisville, Kentucky. New designs were developed using modular components, conveyors and assembly systems were automated, and process flows were reconfigured to reduce product handling. Both productivity and quality improved as a result. Between 1980 and 1983 reject rates at mechanical and electrical testing dropped from 10 percent to 3 percent while output per employee rose 33 percent.[60] A similar example comes from banking. Loan-processing productivity at the Continental Bank was measured before and after a quality improvement project was initiated. At the start of the program, approximately 2,080 loan tickets were processed each month at a cost of $7,753. Labor accounted for $7,123 of the total, computer runtime for $500, and ticket forms for $130. After the project was completed and rejects were virtually eliminated through improved communication, tightened procedures, and better training, the number of tickets processed per month rose slightly while total processing costs fell to $6,682. Labor costs dropped by $1,046 (a reduction in hours required of 15 percent), ticket costs dropped $25 (a reduction in forms required of 19 percent), and computer costs remained unchanged.[61] Here too, quality improvement and productivity improvement moved hand in hand.

More systematic studies of the relationship between quality and productivity are relatively scarce. The few that exist have found a positive relationship between the two variables. For example, a study of the sources of productivity at the factory level found that low levels of waste (scrap) were associated with higher total factor productivity.[62] In some cases, the possible operating improvement from further reductions in waste was dramatic. At one plant employing a continuous or flow process of production, a 10 percent reduction in waste for one product group was expected to yield a 3 percent improvement in total factor productivity. Another study of variations in a single plant's total factor productivity over a seven-year period reached similar conclusions.[63] A third study, which focused on productivity differences at ninety-five large North Carolina factories, found that the most productive plants were also those that paid the most attention to quality.[64]

Additional evidence on the association between quality and productivity appears in Table 5.3. It presents findings from the room air conditioning study described earlier. Productivity has been measured in several ways: by output per labor hour on the assembly line, by output per plant employee, and by output per square foot of plant space. The latter two measures include separate entries for dollar and unit output.

Results vary according to the productivity measure employed. For example, the highest-quality producers had the highest assembly-line output per labor hour. On the basis of the number of direct labor hours actually worked on the assembly line, productivity at the best U.S. plants was five times higher than at the worst.

Measuring productivity by standard labor hours blurs the picture somewhat. Although the Japanese plants maintain a slight edge over the best U.S. plants, categories of performance tend to overlap. The figures based on standard hours, however, are rather imperfect indicators of productivity—for example, they fail to include overtime or rework hours, and so overstate productivity levels, particularly at the poorer plants, which devote more of their time to correcting defects. Thus, these figures have less significance than do those based on the number of hours actually worked.

Productivity measures based on annual output per employee yield results similar to those based on actual hours worked in assembly. The primary difference is the greater relative advantage of the Japanese firms, particularly when output is measured in dollar terms. These differences are easily explained. Not only are Japanese room air conditioners more expensive than American units—an average factory price of $390 versus $279 at the time the study was conducted[65]—the Japanese have focused their limited automation efforts outside final assembly. At the assembly stage, manual operations were the norm in both countries. Since plantwide measures of

TABLE 5.3  *Quality and Productivity in the Room Air Conditioning Industry, 1981–82*

| Grouping of Companies by Quality Performance | Units per Assembly-Line Direct Labor Hour | | Annual Output per Plant Employee | | Annual Output per Square Foot of Plant Space | |
|---|---|---|---|---|---|---|
| | Actual Hours | Standard Hours | Units | Dollars | Units | Dollars |
| Japanese manufacturers | N/A | 2.0 | 1,000 | 388,000 | .9 | 331 |
| Best U.S. plants | 1.7[a] | 1.7 | 645 | 149,000 | .6 | 130 |
| Better U.S. plants | .9 | 1.0 | 562 | 134,000 | .9 | 350[a] |
| Fair U.S. plants | .9 | 1.3 | 519 | 135,000 | 1.1 | 290 |
| Poor U.S. plants | .35[a] | 1.2 | 226 | 109,000 | .3 | 150 |

[a]In this quality grouping, data were available only from a single company.

*Notes:* All figures are averages (means) for the category.

Direct labor hours have been adjusted to include only those workers involved in assembly (i.e., where inspectors and repairmen were classified as direct labor, they have been excluded from the totals).

Units per standard labor hour were computed by using the average cycle time to derive a figure for hourly output and then dividing by the number of assembly-line direct laborers (excluding inspectors and repairmen) to determine output per labor-hour.

Plant employment includes all direct and indirect laborers but excludes clerical workers and first-line supervisors. If quality control personnel are added to the Japanese totals for plant employment, their output per employee becomes 846 and their dollar output per employee $291,000.

Annual dollar output for the Japanese manufacturers was computed using a conversion rate of 265 yen to the dollar, the approximate rate at the time the data were collected. Because some of the U.S. figures are based on 1980 dollar sales and some on 1981 dollar sales, the figures were made comparable by including an adjustment for inflation based on changes in the Consumer Price Index.

SOURCE: Company records and questionnaires distributed by the author.

labor productivity capture the impact of automation while measures focused on the assembly line do not, the relative superiority of the Japanese manufacturers naturally increases when plantwide measures are used. In fact, even when quality control personnel, who are normally classified separately, are included in the Japanese totals for plant employment, the Japanese plants still outperform their American counterparts.

When productivity is measured on the basis of output per square foot of plant space, the Japanese advantage disappears. U.S. manufacturers in two other quality groupings had equal or better productivity on a unit basis. One had better productivity on a dollar basis. Nor are the results at all systematic when the U.S. plants are examined alone. In this category, quality and productivity do not vary together.

Clearly, much additional research on the relationship between quality and productivity is needed. The mechanisms connecting the two variables are only dimly understood.[66] But on the basis of the limited evidence that now exists, quality and productivity would appear to be positively correlated, especially when quality is measured as conformance or reliability and productivity is measured as labor productivity or total factor productivity.


## PROFITABILITY

Figure 5.2 shows two ways in which improved quality might lead to higher profitability. The first route is through the market: improvements in performance, features, or other dimensions of quality lead to increased sales and larger market shares or, alternatively, to less elastic demand and higher prices. If the cost of achieving these gains is outweighed by the increases in contribution received by the firm, higher profits will result.[67]

Quality improvements may also affect profitability through the cost side. Fewer defects or field failures result in lower manufacturing and service costs; as long as these gains exceed any increase in expenditures by the firm on defect prevention, profitability will improve.

Empirical studies using the PIMS data base show a strong positive association between quality and profitability.[68] Representative findings appear in Table 5.4. With one exception, higher quality is associated with higher profitability (that is, return on investment), what-

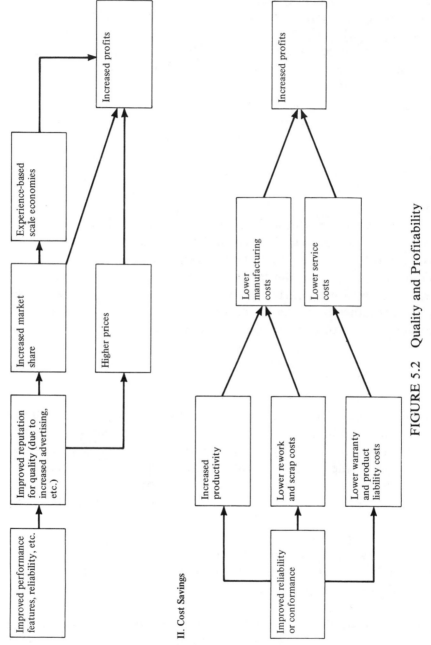

**I. Market Gains**

**II. Cost Savings**

FIGURE 5.2   Quality and Profitability

90

TABLE 5.4  *Effect of Market Share and Product Quality on Return on Investment (ROI)*

| | Return on investment | | |
| --- | --- | --- | --- |
| | *Inferior Quality* | *Average Quality* | *Superior Quality* |
| Market share: | | | |
| Under 12% | 4.5% | 10.4% | 17.4% |
| 12–26% | 11.0 | 18.1 | 18.1 |
| Over 26% | 19.5 | 21.9 | 28.3 |

SOURCE: Reprinted by permission of the *Harvard Business Review*. An exhibit from "Impact of Strategic Planning on Profit Performance," by Sidney Schoeffler, Robert D. Buzzell, and Donald F. Heany (March/April 1974), page 141. Copyright © 1974 by the President and Fellows of Harvard College; all rights reserved.

ever the market share. More sophisticated statistical studies have reached similar conclusions. They have also shown that quality improvements, by increasing share, lead to experience-based cost savings and further gains in profitability.[69]

The market-based link between quality and profitability is thus supported by evidence from the PIMS studies. The second linkage described in Figure 5.2 is less firmly established. As an earlier discussion has shown, the relationship between quality and cost depends on how the terms are defined. Studies that have equated quality with conformance and cost with total quality costs have found an inverse relationship between the two, but they have not carried the analysis a step further to find if profitability was similarly affected. Nor have the studies focusing on the connection between quality and direct cost taken into account differences in investment levels or capital costs, which would clearly affect the relationship between quality and ROI.

## THE BOTTOM LINE

The empirical research on quality has produced mixed results, with few clear directions for managers. The relationship between quality and such variables as price, advertising, and direct cost is both complex and difficult to predict. Few unambiguous results are found in the literature. Even where the expected relationships have emerged, further work is required because of the highly aggregated nature of the PIMS and *Consumer Reports* quality measures that have been employed.

Nevertheless, a number of tentative generalizations can be made. The studies reviewed in this chapter suggest the following:

- Quality and price lack a consistent association, although positive correlations are common in hedonic studies that equate quality with performance and features.
- Quality and advertising are positively correlated in some product categories and uncorrelated in others, with nationally advertised brands generally ranking ahead of regional or miscellaneous brands.
- Quality and market share are positively correlated when the PIMS measure of relative quality is used but are negatively related when other measures of quality are used.
- Quality and cost are negatively correlated when quality is defined as conformance/reliability and cost is defined as total quality cost; when measures of direct cost are used, the results vary by industry.
- Quality and productivity are positively correlated when quality is defined as conformance/reliability and productivity is defined as labor productivity or total factor productivity.
- Quality and profitability are positively correlated when the PIMS measure of relative quality is used.

The tentative and inconsistent nature of the findings suggests that further research is required. The book's concluding chapter contains a number of recommendations. The greatest need is for studies that recognize the multiple dimensions of quality, examine them empirically, and then relate them to cost, market share, profitability, and other measures of business performance. More refined research is vital; otherwise, managers will continue to lack the hard evidence linking quality with the bottom line.

# Part
# II

An
Industry
Example

Chapter

# 6

# Quality in the U.S. Room Air Conditioning Industry I: Subjective Ratings

Thus far, quality has been discussed in general terms. Previous chapters have examined the history and meaning of quality with little attention, other than illustrative examples, to specific industries or applications. A broad conceptual framework has been the goal. How that framework translates into the day-to-day realities of marketing and manufacturing has been sketched only briefly.

For these reasons, this chapter and the next three are devoted to a single industry example. Focusing on one industry provides the raw material for fleshing out the concepts introduced earlier. By limiting discussion to a single product and market, the dimensions of quality can be further refined. Customer preferences can be put under a microscope, and each dimension of quality can be translated into its own concrete terms. Individual brands can be ranked by their standing on the dimensions of quality and the results compared. Different user groups can be surveyed. And perhaps most revealing of all, objective measures of quality can be contrasted with more subjective evaluations.

Industry-level analysis has other virtues as well. Because firms differ in their quality practices and performance, and because focus on a single industry ensures that firms can be compared without the risk of mixing apples with oranges, the determinants of superior quality can be precisely identified. The relative importance of such factors as design practices, inspection and testing, and the nature of the production process can be weighed by noting differences between companies with high and low quality. Even such hard-to-measure influences as management attitudes can be studied using this approach.

Of course, success requires a well-chosen industry. (Even then, care must be taken when generalizing research findings, because no single industry is completely representative). Enough firms must be available to ensure a reasonable degree of variation; otherwise, there will be no basis for analysis. But products should not vary so much that interfirm comparisons are suspect. Some degree of standardization is therefore required, as is some degree of product maturity. The latter ensures that both producers and consumers have had sufficient experience with products to judge them accurately. Simple, straightforward manufacturing processes and technical designs are also desirable in order to keep the number of possible explanations for quality variation within the practical limits of research.

The room air conditioning industry, on which this study focuses, meets all these criteria. It provides evidence for Chapters 6, 7, 8, and 9, as well as for the discussion of Japanese quality management in Chapter 11. Room air conditioners are relatively simple, well-understood products; like refrigerators, they employ compressors, motors, and coils of tubing to transfer heat from one part of a closed system to another.[1] Designs have changed little since air conditioners were first introduced on a large scale in the 1950s. Nor has output varied appreciably in recent years. After reaching a high of nearly 6 million units in 1970, annual production volumes have held steady at between 3 and 4 million units for most of the late 1970s and early 1980s. Today, ten firms account for virtually all U.S. output.[2]

Chapters 6 through 9 use this setting to provide a case study of quality management. The present chapter begins by exploring the meaning of quality in room air conditioners as it is perceived by customers, companies, and servicemen and -women, as well as by such third parties as *Consumer Reports*. Much of the analysis rests on a comparison of brand quality rankings generated by the different groups. More objective quality measures are introduced in Chapter 7, drawing on data collected from individual firms. Few companies track each dimension of quality separately; most rely instead on composite measures that have become standard practice in the industry. These measures fall into two distinct categories: measures reflecting field quality and those reflecting in-plant quality. After a discussion of the meaning and significance of these measures, firms are compared on their performance, and trends over time are reviewed. Chapters 8 and 9 complete the story, exploring the connection between quality performance and management practice. They identify the prime determinants of the quality variations reported in Chapters 6 and 7 and answer the question, What makes for effective quality management?

## THE DIMENSIONS OF QUALITY APPLIED: CONSUMERS' VIEWS

Even simple products may involve complex evaluations of quality. Room air conditioners are no exception. Their primary purpose is obvious enough: to lower inside air temperature and humidity when outside levels are uncomfortably high. Product performance, however, can be assessed in many ways: how well units operate under normal temperature and humidity conditions, how well they operate under extreme conditions (for example, temperatures above 110° or low electrical power because of brownouts), or how well they operate on automatic rather than manual settings.[3] Energy efficiency—the ratio of an air conditioner's cooling capacity to the power required to run it—is another valued aspect of performance. Features may vary as well. Among the most popular offerings are fans with multiple speeds, built-in timers and other electronic controls, and slide-out chassis for ease of mounting and repair. On performance and features alone, quality comparisons in this industry involve a large number of separate elements.

Because room air conditioners are capital goods designed to be used over time, quality assessments are further complicated by issues of reliability, durability, and serviceability. Each has a large subjective component. For example, in its simplest form reliability reflects an air conditioner's failure rate per unit of time. This measure implicitly gives equal weight to all failures. Consumers, however, are unlikely to see every breakdown in the same light. Problems that arise during peak periods, when temperatures have reached summer highs and sleep without an air conditioner is difficult, are likely to be weighed more heavily than interruptions during other periods. A related problem concerns breakdowns due to customer misuse or ignorance. Sometimes a product will have been installed improperly;

at other times, controls may have been misset. A service call is recorded, yet no real failure is found. Has there been a problem with reliability? From the manufacturer's standpoint, no, but customers may still conclude that the unit has performed badly. Here again, quality perceptions are very much in the eyes of the beholder.

The same can be said of durability and serviceability. Especially when design changes are few, consumers may find an air conditioner with a twelve-year life indistinguishable from one that lasts two years longer. Moreover, physical obsolescence may be less of a concern than the cost and convenience of repair. Some units are easily maintained at home and can be disengaged with ease from the window; others require expensive and time-consuming service calls. The availability of repair parts and local service is also likely to play a role in evaluations of quality, for its affects the amount of time units are inoperable during periods of highest need.

In such evaluations, aesthetic judgments are the most subjective of all. Yet they are of obvious importance in assessments of room air conditioner quality, if only because installed units are always on display. Quietness is an especially valued trait, because many consumers apparently feel that room air conditioners are meant to be seen but not heard. Company advertising brochures frequently play up that quality characteristic. Other aesthetic elements include the appearance of a unit's casing (whether it is scratched or dented), the attractiveness of the front cover (whether the lettering is clear and the design appealing), and the condition of the interior (whether the aluminum fins are bent or uniform). And, of course, quality judgment may also be influenced by brand names and companies' reputations in related product lines.

### From Product Characteristics to Quality Perceptions

Together, these traits combine to produce an air conditioner's quality image. The precise mechanics of the process—how quality perceptions emerge from such raw materials as published data, word-of-mouth publicity, and customer experience—are only dimly understood. A telling example comes from recent consumer surveys examining the purchase and use of household appliances. The surveys found that approximately 80 percent of respondents received the quality they expected from their room air conditioners.[4] Most purchases were based on comparison shopping rather than brand preferences; of those relying on comparisons, slightly over half said they chose their model based on price, 26 percent cited features, 31 percent cited perceived quality, and 4 percent cited sales persuasion. But in spite of the apparent care with which purchases were made, the high proportion of expectations that were fulfilled, and the degree of satisfaction with the product information available prior to sale (85 percent deemed it "adequate or more than adequate"), a remarkable statistic emerged from the surveys: More than half the owners of major brands of room air conditioners claimed they would not repurchase the same brand.[5] Apparently, they were deeply dissatisfied with some aspect of the product. Prior expectations ultimately proved to be of less importance than later practical experience.

But if experience matters, how is such information processed and combined? Quality assessments involve multiple attributes; these must somehow be integrated into an overall quality image. In the process, do certain dimensions of quality receive more weight than others?

Table 6.1 provides a partial answer. It shows that among owners of

TABLE 6.1    *Consumer Rankings of the Dimensions of Quality, Room Air Conditioners*

| Dimension of Quality | Percentage of Respondents Who Rated This Dimension as: | | | Overall Score (Weighted Mean) |
| --- | --- | --- | --- | --- |
| | *Most Important* | *2d Most Important* | *3d Most Important* | |
| Performance | 59% | 25% | 9% | 5.3 |
| Dependability | 22 | 40 | 26 | 4.6 |
| Longevity | 12 | 21 | 28 | 3.8 |
| Ease of use | 6 | 9 | 19 | 3.1 |
| Ease of service | 1 | 3 | 11 | 2.3 |
| Cleanability | 2 | 3 | 7 | 2.0 |

*Note:* Each dimension was ranked separately on a 1 to 6 scale, ranging from least to most important. Percentages are based on the number of respondents actually ranking each dimension (that is, nonresponses are excluded). Columns may not add to 100 percent due to rounding.

SOURCE: Computed from *Appliance Manufacturer,* "The American Consumer: A Market for Quality—Room Air Conditioners" (Chicago: Cahners Publishing Company, 1980).

room air conditioners, a clear ordering of quality preferences exists. Performance was the key quality dimension, followed by dependability (reliability) and longevity (durability). Such traits as ease of use, ease of service, and cleanability were all secondary concerns.[6]

That performance should head the list of desired quality characteristics—at least among owners of room air conditioners—is hardly surprising. Consumers frequently purchase products to fulfill specific needs and then judge them by how well those needs have been met. Product performance is also easily monitored; of all the dimensions of quality, it is the one for which experience is the surest guide. On sweltering days, for example, an air conditioner either has cooled a room or has not. Because product performance is continuously on display, judgments in this area are for the most part firmly grounded.

Dependability (reliability) is a different story. While it is clearly important to consumers—in one of the surveys cited above, 86 percent of respondents claimed that poor reliability would cause them to change brands on their next purchase of a home comfort appliance like an air conditioner—it is difficult to judge accurately. Not only do consumers often lack familiarity with multiple brands, which is required for sound comparisons, but they even draw inaccurate conclusions from their own personal experience. A 1978 study found that owners of air conditioners, color televisions, washers, ranges, and refrigerators all had expectations of repair incidence that were significantly higher than the repair rates they actually experienced. Nonowners had expectations of repair incidence that were still more inflated.[7]

Surprisingly, assessments of product life have been closer to the mark. According to a 1980 survey, owners of room air conditioners expected their units to last an average of 11.5 years, a figure that corresponds well with the twelve-year life estimated by more objective research.[8] The variance in owners' expectations, however, was wide. Nearly one-fifth of respondents expected their units to last five years or less; almost the same proportion expected them to last at least twenty years. Do these differences mean that a large percentage of owners were in error? Do they imply that deterioration rates vary widely among brands? Or do they reflect a more complex phenomenon, blending objective product characteristics with personal preferences?

According to Chapter 4, the life expectancy of repairable products like room air conditioners is only partially explained by such objective criteria as component durability and conservative design. An element of consumer choice is also involved. Whenever units break down, owners must decide if further repair makes economic sense. If not, units are scrapped and their operating lives end; otherwise, they continue to function. Table 6.2 shows that consumers vary in the cutoffs they use when making this decision. For home comfort appliances, more than half of all owners used a cutoff of 50 percent of replacement price. Whenever the cost of a single repair reached this level, units were left unfixed. Similar percentages were reported by owners of other types of appliances. Within each category, however, there was considerable dispersion. Some owners were unwilling to fix units once service costs reached 10 percent of replacement price, while others were more accepting and held off until service costs reached 75 percent of replacement price. These differences suggest an explanation for the varying estimates of expected life reported earlier. Two individuals, each owning the same air conditioner and facing the identical service problem, might not reach the same conclusions about the desirability of repair. Their choices would reflect personal economics or, more precisely, where each individual fell among the categories of Table 6.2. To the extent that

TABLE 6.2   *Repair Costs and the Decision Not to Repair*

| | Percentage of Owners Who Decide Not to Fix Units When Service Calls Are: | | | |
|---|---|---|---|---|
| Category of Appliances | 10% of Replacement Purchase Price | 25% of Replacement Purchase Price | 50% of Replacement Purchase Price | 75% of Replacement Purchase Price |
| Home comfort | 3% | 33% | 57% | 8% |
| Majors | 2 | 33 | 59 | 7 |
| Portable electrics | 14 | 38 | 44 | 5 |
| Consumer electronics | 5 | 37 | 52 | 6 |

*Note:* Rows may not add to 100 percent due to rounding.

SOURCE: "The American Consumer Rates Appliance Reliability and Service," *Appliance Manufacturer*, April 1981, p. 62. Reprinted with permission, *Appliance Manufacturer,* © Corcoran Communications, Inc.

durability is governed by such idiosyncratic factors, estimated product lives are likely to vary as well. Reported estimates of appliance durability would then say as much about the predilections of users as they say about embedded product characteristics.

Of course, estimates may also vary because of differing degrees of product knowledge. Not all consumers are fully informed; in some cases, the necessary data are unavailable. For example, there is no obvious way of discriminating in advance between long- and short-lived products. *Ex ante* predictions of durability therefore involve considerable guesswork. Personal experience is often the only sure test. The same is true of interbrand comparisons, but because durable goods are used for long periods, familiarity with multiple products is seldom widespread. Few owners of room air conditioners, for example, have had contact with more than two or three brands. For that reason, it is instructive to contrast consumers' quality rankings with the rankings of more knowledgeable groups.

## BRAND QUALITY RANKINGS

Quality rankings were collected from four sources: consumers, *Consumer Reports,* appliance servicemen and -women, and first-line production supervisors. The last three groups qualify as expert panels, for each has an objective basis for rating quality. But the groups are likely to bring differing perspectives to the evaluations, because each has its own skills and competencies and observes products in different stages of completion and repair.

### Consumer Reports

*Consumer Reports* bases its ratings on objective product tests of items newly purchased from stores. Different size classes of products are rated separately. In room air conditioners, the broadest study has involved popular midsized units with capacities of 7,800 to 8,800 British thermal units (Btu) per hour. Units were first mounted in environmental test chambers; their ability to cool and dehumidify was then monitored by instruments. Tests included thermostat sensitivity (the ability to hold a designated temperature) under normal and extreme operating conditions, the effectiveness of automatic controls, and the uniformity of cooling. Quietness—both indoors and outdoors, and at high and low settings—received special attention. Ease of installation, maintenance, and features were also evaluated.

*Consumer Reports'* rankings have several obvious strengths. Performance characteristics are objectively measured, ensuring accurate comparisons among brands. Product testers are all experienced professionals, unlikely to have hidden biases. And models are assessed on a number of quality dimensions, each of considerable importance to users.

But there are deficiencies as well. Such critical elements of quality as reliability and durability are not included in the tests (although they do appear in the reports for such products as automobiles). Nor is the weighting scheme used to create overall rankings from the scores on individual quality attributes ever made explicit. Thus, there is no way of knowing whether the weights that have been used actually accord with consumer preferences. There is also no assurance that the ranking of brands in any one size class—for example, 7,800–8,800 Btu per hour—is representative of their ranking in other size classes as well.[9]

### Servicemen and -Women

Appliance servicemen and -women are likely to have a different perspective on quality. They too have had contact with multiple brands and have a basis for making informed judgments. But unlike *Consumer Reports,* the rankings of servicemen and -women are not derived from performance tests carried out under controlled conditions. Rather, they reflect direct, personal experience—a history of repairing units with operating problems.

That perspective also has both pluses and minuses. In certain areas, it guarantees a truly expert panel. For example, servicemen and -women are especially well positioned to comment on such dimensions of quality as reliability and durability. They regularly observe broken and malfunctioning units, see which models are repeatedly repaired rather than retired from active life, and observe the relative frequency with which different brands appear in the shop. Because of their wide exposure to multiple units, servicepeople are also likely to be reasonably informed judges of quietness, excellence in design, and other aspects of aesthetics or performance that do not require controlled laboratory tests for accurate comparisons.

Of course, servicepeople are not without bias. Those who sell units as well as repair them are likely to favor their own product lines. For that reason, the data reported here exclude servicemen and -women who also sell units. (For a description of the sample and the questionnaire used, see Appendix A.) Some servicemen and -women are likely to have broader experience than others; they will undoubtedly be more accurate judges of the full range of brands. Some degree of bias may arise because of differences in companies' policies and attitudes when dealing with independent servicemen and -women. In such cases, companies that cultivate the service network, communicating regularly and soliciting advice, may have the quality of their products ranked higher for that reason alone.

### First-Line Supervisors

First-line production supervisors form a third expert panel. Of all managers, they are the closest to day-to-day operations and the activities of the shop floor. Because they observe production practices at first hand, supervisors' judgments about workmanship, quality of materials, and attention to quality are likely to be especially well informed. Many are directly responsible for reducing defect rates and solving quality problems. Moreover, because of their unique organizational position, midway between management and labor, first-line supervisors are apt to be accurate judges of their companies' *true* commitment to quality—the messages that are communicated to the shop floor daily, both verbally and through the evaluation and control system, which sometimes conflict with management's more public pronouncements.[10]

Few supervisors, however, are likely to have had direct experience with multiple brands. Their expertise is based largely on in-plant observation: defect rates, internal production reports, design problems that have impeded manufacturing, and appearance or cosmetic flaws that are visible in the factory. For that reason, they are likely to be especially good judges of conformance but less knowledgeable about other dimensions of quality—unless those dimensions are strongly correlated with in-plant variables such as workmanship. Few first-line supervisors, for example, are likely to have direct access to field failure data or other measures of reliability. In these areas, their opinions are likely to reflect advertising, word-of-mouth publicity, and published brand comparisons to the same extent that consumers' rankings reflect such influences. Thus, supervisors' views on quality are likely to be more a litmus test of factory operations than a true comparison of competing products.

Because direct experience with multiple brands is usually lacking among first-line production supervisors, their quality rankings were compiled in a slightly different fashion from those of the other groups. All supervisors were asked to "rate the quality of their firm's products in relation to its major competitors" using a 1 to 7 scale. Possible responses ranged from "much worse" (1) to "much better" (7). Average scores were then compiled for each firm and placed in rank order, producing the rankings reported here.

### Comparing Quality Rankings

How, then, do the brand quality rankings of consumers match up with those of *Consumer Reports,* servicemen and -women, and first-line production supervisors? The basic data appear in Table 6.3, while the corresponding rank correlations appear in Appendix C.[11] They prompt several observations. First, with the single exception of the ratings of first-line supervisors and servicemen and -women, the quality rankings of different groups are not well correlated. Few brands scored consistently high or low across the board. For example, General Electric did well with consumers and first-line supervisors, less well with servicemen and -women, and poorly with *Consumer Reports.* Fedders was ranked highly by consumers but much lower by all other respondents. And Amana barely appeared in consumers' rankings yet was well received by supervisors, servicemen and -women, and *Consumer Reports.*

Only a few brands were ranked similarly by the three expert panels. These brands were usually in the middle of the pack, like Emerson Quiet Kool and Gibson, or close to the bottom, like Fedders and Kelvinator. Only two brands, Friedrich and Amana, were ranked in the top five by all three groups.

The differences in the rankings—especially the contrast between consumers and the three expert panels—are revealing. Consumers appear to lack comprehensive information on brand quality; with little else to go on, many cite their own brands as being the best.[12] Since the most widely owned brands are the ones that receive the

TABLE 6.3  *Brand Quality Rankings*

| Brand | Consumers[e] | | Consumer Reports | Servicemen and -Women | | First-Line Supervisors |
|---|---|---|---|---|---|---|
| | Best Quality | Brand They Would Buy | | Best Quality | Brand They Would Buy | |
| General Electric | 1 | 2 | 10 | 5 | 2 | 1, 4[d] |
| Fedders | 2 | 3 | 12 | 11 | 8 | 13 |
| Carrier | 3 | 4 | 2 | 6 | 6 | 6 |
| Whirlpool | 4 | 6 | 13 | 1 | 1 | 3 |
| Sears | 5 | 1 | 8 | 2 | 11 | N/A |
| White-Westinghouse | 6 | 5 | N/A | 12 | 11 | 8[c] |
| Frigidaire | 7 | 8 | N/A | 10 | 9 | 8[c] |
| Chrysler Airtemp | 8 | 9 | N/A | 14[f] | 11 | N/A |
| J. C. Penney | 8 | 13 | 5 | 13 | 11 | N/A |
| Emerson Quiet Kool | 10 | 6 | 6 | 7 | 5 | 7 |
| Gibson | 10 | 13 | 7 | 9 | 4 | 8[c] |
| Friedrich | 12 | 10 | 1 | 3 | 3 | 4 |

| | | | | | |
|---|---|---|---|---|---|
| Hotpoint | 12 | 10 | 9 | 14 | 11 | N/A |
| Wards | 12 | 10 | 3 | 14 | 11 | N/A |
| Amana | 15/16[a] | 16 | 4 | 4 | 6 | 2 |
| Kelvinator | 15/16[a] | 15 | 11 | 8 | 10 | 8[c] |
| Keeprite | N/A[b] | N/A | N/A | 14 | 11 | 12 |

[a]Because data for these brands were reported under the heading "other brands," it was impossible to determine which of the two brands ranked higher.

[b]N/A = not available.

[c]Gibson and Kelvinator brands are produced in the same factory, as are Frigidaire and White-Westinghouse. In each case, brands were assigned first-line supervisors' ratings for the factory as a whole.

[d]General Electric manufactures room air conditioners in two factories. The responses of supervisors at both factories are reported here.

[e]Consumers ranked a number of brands that the other three surveys did not. These brands are not included in the table; most are no longer manufactured. In no case was any of these brands ranked higher than thirteenth.

[f]Brands receiving no votes from servicemen or -women were all ranked last—fourteenth in the column "best quality" and eleventh in the column "brand they would buy."

SOURCE: Consumers: *Appliance Manufacturer*, "The American Consumer: A Market for Quality—Room Air Conditioners" (Chicago: Cahners Publishing Company, 1980), pp. 33–35 (best quality). *Appliance Manufacturer*, "The Buying Consumer: Room Air Conditioners" (Chicago: Cahners Publishing Company, 1979), pp. 47–49 (brand they would buy).
*Consumer Reports:* "Air Conditioners," *Consumer Reports*, July 1982, pp. 356–360.
Servicemen and -women: Questionnaires distributed by the author.
First-line supervisors: Questionnaires distributed by the author.

107

largest number of votes for best quality, consumers' quality rankings closely parallel existing patterns of brand ownership. That result, in turn, has two possible explanations: Either consumers are in fact buying the brands they feel to be the best—a conclusion supported by the close correlation between consumers' rankings of "best quality" and "brand they would buy"—or else the most popular brands received the largest number of votes as best quality simply because of their overwhelming dominance in the population. Sheer numbers, rather than a consensus about the superiority of best-selling brands, appears to be the primary explanation. A recent survey of owners of the five most popular brands of room air conditioners found that the proportion rating their own brand as "best quality" never exceeded 50 percent. By far the largest percentage of respondents answered by saying, "I don't know."[13]

The lack of correspondence between consumers' quality rankings and those of other groups is thus partially explained by consumers' limited experience. Brands such as Friedrich and Amana, which received high scores from the expert panels but low scores from consumers, probably did poorly for that reason alone. Neither has a dominant market share. The three expert panels, however, did not always agree among themselves. Their differences can be traced to varying conceptions of quality, as well as different sources of information.

*Consumer Reports,* for example, interprets quality strictly in terms of performance. Its rankings are based on relatively narrow, technically defined criteria and extremely small samples. Not surprisingly, its findings diverged the most from those of the other groups. *Consumer Reports* rankings were negatively (but insignificantly) correlated with all rankings but those of first-line supervisors.

By contrast, the rankings of servicemen and -women and first-line supervisors were closely matched. Brands that scored well with one group scored well with the other. Low rankings showed a similar pattern. Evidently, what supervisors observe in the factory bears some relationship to what servicemen and -women observe in the field. But despite the connection, which is discussed at length in Chapter 7, the two groups appear to be responding to different influences and forming their opinions on different criteria.

Table 6.4 sheds additional light on the perspectives of servicemen and -women. It shows how they ranked brands in six categories: overall quality, product life, ease of repair, cost of repair, quietness,

TABLE 6.4  *Rankings of Room Air Conditioners on Multiple Quality Characteristics, Servicemen and -Women*

| Brand | Overall Quality | | Product Life | | Ease of Repair | | Cost of Repair | | Quietness | | Engineering Design | |
|---|---|---|---|---|---|---|---|---|---|---|---|---|
| | *Rank* | *Score* | *Rank* | *Score* | *Rank* | *Score* | *Rank* | *Score* | *Rank* | *Score* | *Rank* | *Score* |
| Whirlpool | 1 | 2.8 | 1 | 2.6 | 1 | 2.1 | 1 | 2.6 | 1 | 3.2 | 1 | 2.8 |
| Friedrich | 2 | 4.3 | 3 | 4.0 | 5 | 5.0 | 7 | 5.6 | 4 | 4.1 | 7 | 4.8 |
| Amana | 3 | 4.4 | 4 | 4.3 | 9 | 6.2 | 8 | 6.1 | 5 | 4.3 | 2 | 4.2 |
| General Electric | 4 | 4.4 | 2 | 3.6 | 2 | 4.3 | 2 | 3.7 | 3 | 3.7 | 3 | 4.6 |
| Carrier | 5 | 4.5 | 5 | 4.6 | 7 | 5.5 | 6 | 5.4 | 6 | 4.7 | 4 | 4.6 |
| Emerson | 6 | 4.8 | 7 | 5.4 | 4 | 5.0 | 3 | 3.8 | 2 | 3.4 | 6 | 4.7 |
| Kelvinator | 7 | 4.9 | 8 | 5.7 | 6 | 5.1 | 4 | 4.3 | 7 | 5.4 | 8 | 4.9 |
| Gibson | 8 | 5.2 | 6 | 5.3 | 3 | 4.4 | 5 | 4.3 | 8 | 5.7 | 5 | 4.7 |
| Frigidaire | 9 | 6.5 | 10 | 6.6 | 10 | 6.5 | 11 | 7.0 | 9 | 6.1 | 10 | 6.3 |
| Fedders | 10 | 6.7 | 9 | 6.5 | 8 | 5.9 | 9 | 6.5 | 10 | 6.2 | 9 | 6.3 |
| White-Westinghouse | 11 | 6.9 | 11 | 6.7 | 11 | 6.6 | 10 | 7.0 | 11 | 6.3 | 11 | 6.6 |

*Note*: In each category, actual scores reflect the average (mean) ranking of the brand by respondents.

SOURCE: Questionnaires distributed by the author.

and engineering design. All rankings were closely correlated, suggesting tight links between overall quality perceptions and perceived performance in each of the narrower quality categories. The dominant influences, however, were product life and engineering design, for rankings in these two categories best matched the overall quality ratings assigned to brands.[14] For that reason, they represent the forms of excellence to which servicemen and -women are likely to be most closely attuned.

Further disaggregation is necessary, however, if the perspectives of servicemen and -women are to be better understood. Distinct subgroups coexist. For example, respondents vary in the amount of comparative information they possess; quality rankings might vary as a result. One measure of the amount of comparative information available to servicemen and -women is the number of brands serviced: the larger the number, the wider the frame of reference. As Table 6.5 indicates, when quality rankings are broken out in this fashion, with separate listings for respondents servicing one to five brands, six to eight brands, and so on, a clear pattern emerges.[15] As the number of brands serviced goes up, several popular brands receive lower ratings while several less popular brands show broader appeal. General Electric presents the most dramatic example. The proportion of servicemen and -women saying that they would buy the brand falls from 40 percent for those servicing five or fewer brands to zero for those servicing twelve brands or more. By contrast, the proportion of servicemen and -women saying they would buy Carrier rises from zero for those servicing five or fewer brands to 17 percent for those servicing twelve brands or more. Apparently, broader experience alters the perception of such brands by providing a larger pool of comparative data. A secondary influence may also be at work: shifting definitions of quality. As the number of brands serviced goes up, respondents tend to define quality increasingly in terms of ease of repair.[16] Brand rankings may simply have shifted to accommodate the new definition of quality.

First-line supervisors undoubtedly base their quality judgments on different criteria from those of servicemen and -women. Few have the technical backgrounds to compare products' engineering designs, component durability, or operating lives. Most supervisors have only limited knowledge of field performance. As a result, they are more sensitive to internal concerns—the principles governing day-to-day factory operations. Not surprisingly, the quality scores that supervi-

TABLE 6.5 *Rankings of Room Air Conditioners on Overall Quality and Willingness to Buy, Servicemen and -Women, by Number of Brands Serviced*

| | Number of Brands Serviced | | | | | | | | | | | |
| | 1–5 | | | 6–8 | | | 9–11 | | | 12–15 | | |
| | Overall Quality | | Brand They Would Buy (%)[a] | Overall Quality | | Brand They Would Buy (%)[a] | Overall Quality | | Brand They Would Buy (%)[a] | Overall Quality | | Brand They Would Buy (%)[a] |
| Brand | Rank | Score | | Rank | Score | | Rank | Score | | Rank | Score | |
|---|---|---|---|---|---|---|---|---|---|---|---|---|
| Whirlpool | 1 | 1.5 | 33 | 2 | 2.7 | 44 | 1 | 2.1 | 41 | 5 | 5.5 | 44 |
| Amana | 2 | 2.0 | 0 | 5 | 3.3 | 6 | 2 | 3.7 | 3 | 8 | 6.9 | 11 |
| Emerson | 2 | 2.0 | 0 | 9 | 4.3 | 3 | 5 | 4.9 | 10 | 4 | 5.4 | 11 |
| Friedrich | 2 | 2.0 | 13 | 1 | 2.0 | 3 | 6 | 5.5 | 17 | 1 | 4.5 | 11 |
| Frigidaire | 2 | 2.0 | 7 | 8 | 3.9 | 3 | 9 | 7.1 | 0 | 11 | 9.4 | 0 |
| General Electric | 6 | 2.4 | 40 | 6 | 3.5 | 9 | 4 | 4.8 | 21 | 7 | 6.4 | 0 |
| Kelvinator | 7 | 3.3 | 7 | 7 | 3.8 | 0 | 7 | 5.8 | 0 | 2 | 4.6 | 6 |
| Fedders | 8 | 3.7 | 0 | 10 | 4.5 | 6 | 11 | 7.8 | 3 | 10 | 7.9 | 0 |
| White-Westing-house | 9 | 4.0 | 0 | 11 | 6.0 | 0 | 10 | 7.4 | 0 | 9 | 7.4 | 0 |
| Carrier | 10 | 5.0 | 0 | 3 | 2.9 | 3 | 3 | 4.2 | 3 | 6 | 6.3 | 17 |
| Gibson | NR[b] | NR | 0 | 4 | 3.3 | 22 | 8 | 6.4 | 0 | 3 | 5.3 | 0 |

[a]Columns indicate the percentage of all brands listed by respondents in the category. Some respondents indicated more than one brand. Figures may not total 100 percent due to rounding.
[b]NR = not ranked.

SOURCE: Questionnaires distributed by the author.

sors assign to their firms' products closely match their judgments about manufacturing priorities: the weight their management attaches to producing high-quality (defect-free) products and the stage they feel their company has reached in understanding its quality problems.[17] Such product characteristics as appearance, workmanship, and conformance, which can all be judged with some assurance within the factory, appear to be equally important in shaping supervisors' perceptions of quality.[18]

## QUALITY IN THEORY AND PRACTICE

Even when applied to a product as simple as a room air conditioner, quality remains a complex and elusive concept. Multiple attributes must be weighed, often with limited information. Users employ different definitions of quality; the resulting product assessments depend heavily on the breadth of their experience. Disagreements are common, even among acknowledged experts. Yet despite these difficulties, the data reviewed in this chapter support several strong conclusions.

For one thing, they show the danger of treating quality as a single, simple idea. Even products as straightforward as room air conditioners involve multiple dimensions of quality; as the chapter's discussion of performance makes clear, these dimensions frequently involve subcategories of their own. Without such refinement, quality remains an amorphous and inaccessible concept.

Analysis along multiple dimensions also provides greater insight into how judgments about quality are formed. For example, in the room air conditioning industry consumer preferences show a clear rank ordering: Performance is the most desired quality attribute, followed by dependability (reliability), longevity (durability), ease of use, ease of service, and cleanability. This finding has obvious implications for product positioning. Nevertheless, in a number of these areas consumers lacked the information necessary for forming accurate judgments. Assessments of reliability were especially suspect because of consumers' inability to draw comparisons among brands and to predict correctly based on their own experience.

Even so, personal experience with products remained the source of most quality judgments in the industry. Such experience varied widely among the three expert panels: *Consumer Reports,* service-men and -women, and first-line supervisors. Not surprisingly, their brand quality rankings differed as well. Few brands were universally applauded or condemned. Only servicemen and -women and first-line supervisors produced similar results. For the most part, the disparities reflect differences in the comparative data that groups have available and differences in their implicit definitions of quality. The poor correspondence between consumers' quality rankings and those of the expert panels, for example, is best explained by the limited data that consumers have available for forming judgments in this area, while the lack of fit between *Consumer Reports* rankings and those of the other three groups can be traced to the narrow, performance-based definition of quality that the magazine uses.

There is an important methodological point here as well. Expert panels can be a powerful research tool, especially when topics are subjective and ill-defined. When coupled with consumer surveys, they provide insight into the way judgments are formed, the amount of comparative information that users have available, and the role played by personal experience. But they come with built-in limitations. Every expert panel has biases of its own, reflecting its position in the production and use chain. Service technicians, for example, will seldom have the same views as product designers, because their perspectives and experiences are so different. Even within categories opinions may vary, suggesting the need for further disaggregation and even narrower categories. The fact that sharp differences appeared in the quality rankings of servicemen and -women who serviced large and small numbers of brands shows the need to be sensitive both to the sources of a panel's expertise and to possible disparities within groups.

Even with these precautions, the ratings of expert panels are still likely to contain subjective elements. Few outside observers are completely disinterested. Even those who are, like *Consumer Reports,* combine product attributes into a single quality ranking using their own preferred weighting schemes. More objective measures of quality might therefore lead to conclusions quite different from those reported in this chapter. In fact, there is clear evidence of such a gap in the room air conditioning industry. None of the quality rankings reported in Table 6.3 is significantly correlated with the ranking of brands by first-year service call rates, which count the number of service calls incurred for all types of quality problems in a unit's first year of life.[19] Most room air conditioner manufacturers track their quality performance through such measures, rather than through consumer surveys or expert panels. As the next chapter will show, comparing these measures across companies and over time permits an unusually detailed portrait of industry quality performance.

# Chapter

# 7

# Quality in the U.S. Room Air Conditioning Industry II: Objective Measures

Objective measures of quality normally fall into two categories: measures of field quality, which reflect the quality of products that have reached customers' hands, and measures of in-plant quality, which reflect the quality of parts, subassemblies, and products that are still within the factory. In the room air conditioning industry, the primary measure of field quality is the first-year service call rate, and the primary measures of in-plant quality are defect rates.

## SERVICE CALLS AND FIELD QUALITY

Service calls are trips made by servicemen and -women to customers' homes or by customers to service shops to repair their appliances. Units may be inoperative or otherwise performing poorly. A service call for a room air conditioner, for example, might result from a unit's failure to work when first plugged in, uneven and intermittent cooling, or excessive noise because internal parts are misaligned. To use the terminology of Chapter 4, service calls are largely measures of reliability and conformance.

Not all service calls, however, are of equal interest to appliance makers, for repairmen are reimbursed only for calls incurred while products are covered by warranty.[1] In the room air conditioning industry, the most comprehensive warranty coverage—reimbursement

115

for all parts and labor—extends over the first year of ownership. Virtually all manufacturers offer such coverage and have done so for some time.

Service call rates under first-year warranty coverage are thus a widely used guide to quality performance, but they are not without drawbacks. Some companies compute service call rates from a proportion of all units sold; others base their calculations on a year's entire population of units. Some companies calculate service incidence by dividing the number of service calls incurred in a year by the number of units sold in the same period; others divide by an average of the number of units sold in current and preceding years. These calculations are not strictly comparable. Moreover, service calls remain accurate reflections of reliability and conformance only if all repairs are quickly and completely reported to manufacturers. Improper or late filing of warranty claims means that service call rates will be imperfect measures of problem incidence.[2]

Most of these failings are relatively minor. Comparisons of the different techniques suggest that, in practice, they induce only small errors. A more serious problem is definitional: how to classify service calls that are due to customer failings rather than product deficiencies. Poor design, construction, or materials are not the only reasons why products fail to work. Sometimes units are inoperative because they have been installed improperly, their controls have been misset, or they have not been plugged in. Service calls of this sort do not involve quality problems in the conventional sense; for that reason, they are known within the industry as "customer instruction calls." The problem created by such calls is that they are easy to identify in theory but, because of varying company policies, hard to classify in practice. They are therefore likely to vary among companies for definitional reasons alone.[3] But because customer instruction calls appear to be a relatively small proportion of all service calls—especially in recent years—any resulting biases are likely to be small.[4]

### Service Call Rates over Time

Industry service call rates were tracked over a ten-year period using two sources of data: trade association reports and service call rates collected from individual plants. The results for 1972–75 and 1976–81 are therefore presented separately. Service call rates for the earlier years appear in Table 7.1, and those for the later years in Figure 7.1.

TABLE 7.1    *Service Call Rates (SCR) per 100 Units Under First-Year*
*Warranty Coverage, Room Air Conditioning*
*Industry, 1972-75*

|  | 1972 | 1973 | 1974 | 1975 |
|---|---|---|---|---|
| All service calls |  |  |  |  |
| Average | 15 | 13 | 12 | 11 |
| Range | 6-27 | 7-18 | 6-17 | 5-18 |
| "Valid" service calls (manufacturers' responsibility) |  |  |  |  |
| Average | 12 | 11 | 11 | 9 |
| Range | 5-26 | 4-17 | 4-15 | 4-16 |

*Notes:* All figures have been rounded.

All figures are for the period of twelve months ending December 31, except for 1975, which is for the twelve months ending June 30.

The category "valid" service calls excludes service calls for customer education and installation correction.

The number of firms reporting all service calls was seven in all years except 1974, when it was eight. The number of firms reporting "valid" service calls was eight in all years except 1975, when it was seven.

SOURCE: Association of Home Appliance Manufacturers (AHAM) surveys.

Table 7.1 is based on annual surveys conducted by the Association of Home Appliance Manufacturers (AHAM). All surveys were accompanied by detailed instructions for companies to follow in computing service call rates, including minimum sample sizes, appropriate model mix, and the definition of service calls to be used. With one exception, the same firms participated in every survey. Data are limited to 1972-75, because surveys were discontinued the next year after several companies withdrew from the program.

By contrast, Figure 7.1 is based on data collected by the author on an individual basis from companies (for reasons of confidentiality, data are not reported by company name). Conventions for reporting service call rates therefore differed to some degree, although attempts were made to keep the data as comparable as possible. All data were collected at the plant level. Complete industry statistics are reported only for 1981; in earlier years the necessary records were not always available.

With these descriptions in mind, what conclusions emerge from the two sets of data? First, there appears to have been a steady decline in service call rates (that is, an improvement in quality) between

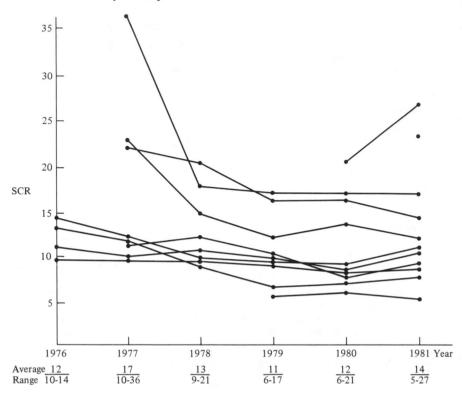

| | 1976 | 1977 | 1978 | 1979 | 1980 | 1981 Year |
|---|---|---|---|---|---|---|
| Average | 12 | 17 | 13 | 11 | 12 | 14 |
| Range | 10-14 | 10-36 | 9-21 | 6-17 | 6-21 | 5-27 |

*Notes:*
All figures have been rounded.

The number of plants reporting service call rates was: 1976, four; 1977, eight; 1978, eight; 1979, nine; 1980, ten; 1981, eleven.

FIGURE 7.1    Service Calls Rates (SCR) per 100 Units Under First-Year Warranty Coverage, by Plant, Room Air Conditioning Industry, 1976–81

SOURCE: Company records and questionnaires distributed by the author.

1972 and 1975.[5] Overall, the improvement was 25 percent. Yet at the end of the period, quality problems were still widespread: During the first year of warranty coverage there was one service call for every nine units in the field.[6]

No trend is visible in more recent years. Between 1977 and 1979 service call rates generally declined, but in the following two years they rose slightly.[7] Overall, quality improved during the period, but largely because of two plants that reported big gains.[8] No plant reduced its service call rate year after year.

A similar lack of progress emerges from a comparison of the two sets of data.[9] Service call rates appear to have changed little between 1972 and 1981, with marginal improvements at best.[10] Nor has the spread between the best and worst producers narrowed appreciably.

If anything, the data show a widening gap. In 1972, the poorest firms had service call rates four to five times higher than those of the best firms. In 1978 the spread had narrowed to a factor of two, but in 1981 it had risen again to above five.

On balance, there appear to have been few dramatic shifts in the field quality of room air conditioners between 1972 and 1981. First-year service call rates remained stubbornly high, with the best and worst producers still separated by a wide margin.

### The Impact of Product Mix

One possible explanation for the separation between producers would be differences among firms in product mix. Larger units, for example, are often subject to more demanding use than smaller models, because they are run continuously rather than intermittently. Designs seldom compensate for the increased use. According to engineers in the industry, larger units are often built from components that have been stressed for use at lower capacities. Not surprisingly, the result is service call rates that vary appreciably by unit size. Table 7.2 shows that on average the service call rates of 17,000–34,000 Btu units were more than 75 percent higher than those of 4,000–10,000 Btu units. Intermediate sizes generally had service call rates between the two poles.

At first glance, the figures suggest that differences in product mix can explain much of the spread in aggregate service call rates. Firms having the highest call rates might simply be selling more of the largest units. That interpretation, however, conflicts with two other pieces of evidence: the wide dispersion of service call rates *within* size classes—with the rankings of firms within each category corresponding closely to rankings based on overall service call rates—and the comparatively small number of units that most firms sell in the largest size classes. For these reasons, differences in the service call rates of different brands of room air conditioners are unlikely to result from differences in product mix alone.

### Perceptions of Reliability

Surprisingly, these differences have attracted little attention in the industry. One leading executive has observed that "the quality spread from best to worst is very narrow in major appliances."[11] Others in the industry shared his ignorance. In the course of this research, managers at every company were asked, "Which firm has

TABLE 7.2 *Service Call Rates by Size of Units, Room Air Conditioning Industry, 1981*

| | Size of Units (Btu Capacity) | | | | | |
|---|---|---|---|---|---|---|
| | 4,000–10,000 | 6,000–16,000 | 9,000–18,700 | 13,000–27,000 | 17,000–34,000 |
| Service call rate per 100 units under first-year warranty coverage | | | | | |
| Average | 8 | 10 | 13 | 16 | 15 |
| Range | 2–11 | 3–20 | 4–23 | 5–24 | 8–26 |

*Notes*: All averages are unweighted means.
All figures have been rounded.
All size classes are composite categories, formed by combining the classifications used by different firms. For example, the 4,000–10,000 Btu category includes one firm's 4,000–8,000 Btu units, a second firm's 5,000–10,000 Btu units, and a third firm's 6,000–9,000 Btu units. The lack of a standard reporting scheme made the use of such categories necessary.
Because data on service call rates by size classes were not available from all firms in the industry, this table and Figure 7.1 are not directly comparable.

SOURCE: Company records and questionnaires distributed by the author.

120

the best quality (lowest service call rate) in the room air conditioning industry?'' The answer was the same each time: "We do.'' When managers were later asked, "Which firm has the second-best quality?'' their responses included at least half of the firms in the industry. No single company dominated the list, nor did the responses bear much relationship to actual service call rates.

Such comments appear to reflect the limited comparative information now available about appliance reliability. Published data are especially weak, but even servicemen and -women, who are able to draw on firsthand experience, are frequently in error. According to Table 7.3, their brand reliability rankings are only approximations

TABLE 7.3   *Brand Reliability Rankings, Room Air Conditioners, 1981*

| Brand | Consumers | Servicemen and -Women |
|-------|-----------|----------------------|
| Sears | 1 | 11 |
| General Electric | 2 | 10 |
| Fedders | 3 | 15 |
| Carrier | 4 | 5 |
| Whirlpool | 4 | 3 |
| Norge | 4 | 17[b] |
| Friedrich | 7 | 4 |
| White-Westinghouse | 8 | 14 |
| J.C. Penney | 9 | 13[c] |
| Field Crest | 9 | 17 |
| Frigidaire | 11 | 9 |
| Chrysler Airtemp | 11 | 12[c] |
| Hotpoint | 11 | 1[c] |
| Philco | 11 | 17 |
| Wards | 15 | 16[c] |
| Emerson Quiet Kool | 16 | 8 |
| Gibson | 17 | 7 |
| Kelvinator | 17 | 6 |
| Amana | N/A[a] | 2 |

[a]N/A = not available
[b]Brands receiving no votes were all ranked seventeenth (last).
[c]These brands were ranked by five or fewer servicemen and -women. For that reason, the ranks may be less representative than those of other brands.

SOURCE: Consumers: *Appliance Manufacturer,* "The American Consumer Rates Reliability and Service: Room Air Conditioners" (Chicago: Cahners Publishing Company, 1981), pp. 18–20.
   Servicemen and -women: Questionnaires distributed by the author.

of more objective rankings based on first-year service call rates.[12] Consumers fared even worse: Their reliability rankings were inversely related to first-year service call rates.[13] With few exceptions, consumers' reliability rankings paralleled patterns of brand ownership, as they did in the overall quality rankings of Table 6.3.

Taken together, the data in this section paint a disturbing picture of field quality in the room air conditioning industry. Reliability and conformance have improved little during the 1970s. At both the beginning and end of the period, at least one service call was incurred in the first year for every seven or eight units produced. The spread between the best and worst performers has remained large, as has the gap between the failure rates of large and small units. Yet none of the groups—consumers, managers, or servicemen and -women— have been especially knowledgeable about reliability differences among brands.

## DEFECTS AND IN-PLANT QUALITY

Typically, multiple measures are used to judge a plant's quality. Most involve defect rates of some sort, defined as the proportion of parts, subassemblies, or finished units that fail to meet specifications. Such measures are widely used to monitor manufacturing. Little attention has been paid, however, to the precise meaning of defect rates and the degree to which they are truly objective measures.

### Reported Versus Actual Defects

At the broadest level, defective units are those that fail to match preestablished standards.[14] They may function improperly (if at all), display obvious deficiencies in workmanship, or perform poorly in mandated safety tests. Both functional and cosmetic problems are involved: parts that have been attached incorrectly, loose screws, blotchy or uneven paint, misaligned labels, mechanical and electrical problems. In the language of Chapter 4, these are largely deficiencies in conformance, although aspects of performance and aesthetics are involved as well.

Defect rates thus cover a wide sweep. Because problems vary in seriousness, classification schemes have emerged for grouping defects into categories by their expected impact.[15] Most schemes use some variant of an A-B-C system, distinguishing "critical" from "major" and "minor" defects and then assigning demerit points by category. Such systems serve a valuable purpose by showing that not all defects are alike, but they overlook a more crucial point: Defect rates are seldom recorded with complete accuracy.

From a control standpoint, defects "exist" only when they have been recognized and counted. They have no independent identity; only after discovery are they traceable and known. If inspection were perfectly accurate and objective, that would present few problems. Reported and actual defects would be one and the same. Even if inspection errors existed, they would be of little concern if they were purely random or if all companies faced them in equal measure. There are two reasons, however, why systematic errors might exist: differences in the way companies classify defects and differences in the rigor and intensity of inspection.

Not all defects are equally easy to catch. Some, like wiring problems, are unmistakable: Units on the assembly line reach designated test stations and are plugged in but fail to function. Other defects, however, involve elements of discretion; for them, the dividing line between acceptable and unacceptable products is hazy and ill-defined. Proper noise levels are a good example, as are fits and finishes. In both cases, inspector judgment determines whether product imperfections are serious enough to be called defects. The most difficult decisions involve judgments of an even higher order—a process that one manufacturing manager has called "calibrating the eyes." Particularly where subtle technical distinctions must be made, inspectors tend to see only what they have been trained to see.[16] Parts misalignment, for example, is seldom obvious; unless inspectors know precisely what to look for and where their attention should be focused, problems will remain undetected. In the absence of clear direction, reported defects would be lower than actual defects.

Inspection accuracy might be related to other variables as well. For example, thorough inspection of newly assembled units takes time, for defects in hard-to-reach places are easily overlooked. Often inspection tasks are divided among several individuals, so that each sees units for only a brief period as they move by on the assembly line. The larger the number of inspectors, the greater the oversight provided, and the more likely that a defect missed by one inspector will be caught by another. Similarly, the more time devoted to inspection, the less cursory will be the investigation, and the more likely that defects will be found. The underlying principle here is simple but compelling: More careful inspection is likely to mean higher *reported* defect rates.

For these reasons, reported and actual defect rates may diverge to differing degrees among companies in the same industry. The extent of the differences is an empirical question; unfortunately, the analysis that follows, because of its exploratory nature, supports few conclusions. Using data from the room air conditioning industry, assembly-line defect rates were collected and correlated with various measures of inspection accuracy and inspection intensity.[17] One measure of special interest was compiled from the defect check sheets used by inspectors at each company. These sheets list all defects inspectors should be searching for at their work stations as units pass by on the assembly line. Surprisingly, the sheets varied widely among companies in specificity and detail. Some companies confined themselves to broad categories of defects and allowed inspectors considerable discretion, while others provided long lists of carefully delineated problems. For each company, a figure was computed showing the total number of items appearing on all defect check sheets used by inspectors stationed on the assembly line; it reflects the degree to which companies tried to "calibrate the eyes" of their inspectors.[18] In the same spirit, three additional variables were developed to measure inspection intensity: the total number of assembly-line inspectors, the total number of inspectors divided by daily output, and the time available for inspection per unit. The last variable was itself measured in two ways: by total inspection time—the number of inspectors on the line multiplied by the cycle time—and by the average amount of inspection time available for each item listed on a company's defect check sheets.

Correlations based on these data are suggestive but lack statistical significance. Assembly-line defect rates were positively related to the total number of inspectors divided by daily output, total inspection time, and inspection time per defect check sheet item; unrelated to the number of inspectors; and negatively related to the number of defect check sheet items.[19] The first three findings fit well with earlier speculations; the latter two do not. Overall the results are inconclusive, although they do suggest that reported defect rates should be treated with care, because they may reflect the amount of time that inspectors have to search for and identify problems.

Defect Rates by Plant

Table 7.4 reports defect rates in four categories: incoming parts and materials, subassembly, final assembly (assembly line), and quality audit. Each represents a different point in the production chain. Incoming parts and materials are goods that have been received from suppliers but have not yet been processed. Subassembly involves the brazing (soldering) of metal parts and small-scale assembly. Final assembly combines subsystems into completed units; it takes place on a moving assembly line and involves the largest range of activities. Firms put inspection stations at strategic points along the line—after refrigeration systems have been pressurized and sealed, for example, or after all electrical connections have been made—and then tally up the defects found at all inspection points. Dividing by the number of units produced yields a figure for the defect rate. Because of their importance, assembly-line defects are reported here in several categories: total defects, defects requiring off-line repair (which are likely to involve more serious problems than defects that can be fixed without removing units from the flow of production), leaks, and electrical problems. Finally, quality audit, the last category in Table 7.4, is a comprehensive inspection of completed units before they are shipped to warehouses or to customers. Because audits are unusually time-consuming, only a small proportion of total production is normally involved.

In all these categories, defect rates varied widely among plants. On most measures, the best and worst performers were separated by a vast amount—normally, a factor of twenty. Assembly-line defects, for example, ranged from 8 per hundred units to 165, while defect rates at incoming inspection ranged from 0.8 percent to 16 percent. Whether defects were measured broadly to include both cosmetic and functional problems, as at incoming inspection and quality audit, or more narrowly, as in leaks and electrical problems, the distance between plants remained large.

Defect rates also tended to move together. According to the correlations of Appendix C, most defect rates were positively and significantly related; a high score on one measure meant a high score on another. There were two notable exceptions: quality audit rates, which were unrelated to the other defect measures, and incoming and assembly-line defect rates, which were unrelated to one another.

TABLE 7.4  *Defect Rates by Plant, Room Air Conditioning Industry, 1981*

| Plant | Incoming Parts and Materials (% defective) | Subassembly (coil leaks per 100 units) | Assembly-line (defects per 100 units) | | | | Quality Audit (% defective) |
|---|---|---|---|---|---|---|---|
| | | | Total | Requiring Off-Line Repair | Leaks | Electrical | |
| 1 | .8 | 1.0 | 26 | 7 | 3.1 | .9 | N/A[c] |
| 2 | 2 | 6.0[b] | 150 | 34 | 3.0[a] | 5.0 | 5.0 |
| 3 | 2 | 5.0 | N/A | N/A | >3.5[a] | N/A | 12.6 |
| 4 | 2 | .5 | 18 | 11 | 2.3 | 1.0 | 1.0 |
| 5 | 2 | .1 | 10 | 10 | 1.3 | 3.3 | 6.6 |
| 6 | 3 | N/A | >100[a] | >30[a] | 2.0 | 2.0 | N/A |
| 7 | 3.3 | N/A | 165 | 165 | 1.6 | 25.4 | N/A |
| 8 | 10 | 4.4 | 8 | 8 | 3.5 | 2.9 | N/A |
| 9 | 10 | 3.0 | 70 | 67 | 7.7 | 14.0 | 21.7[a] |
| 10 | 13.5 | 9.0 | 57 | 47 | 6.6 | N/A | 15.7 |
| 11 | 16 | 7.8 | 135 | >68[a] | 34.0[a] | 34.0[a] | 2.0 |

[a]Company estimates.
[b]Reflects an unknown percentage of central air conditioner coils assembled on the same line as room air conditioner coils.
[c]N/A = not available

SOURCE: Company records and questionnaires distributed by the author.

126

The former result reflects the peculiar statistical properties of quality audit measures, discussed later in the chapter, while the latter result probably reflects the wide discretion firms have in choosing the type and rigor of quality tests performed during incoming and assembly-line inspections. Such flexibility means that inspection standards at the two points do not always move in parallel.

Even with these weaknesses, the data in Table 7.4 are robust. They show consistently high defect rates and wide variations among plants. Neither has changed much in recent years. Five room air conditioning manufacturers provided historical data on defect rates; according to Figure 7.2, these rates declined between 1977 and 1981, but by only a small amount. No plant put more than two years of improvement back to back, and one actually lost ground.

Combining these results with the results for service call rates prompts several summary observations. Companies in the room air conditioning industry varied enormously on measures of both in-plant and field quality. On defect rates, the best and worst per-

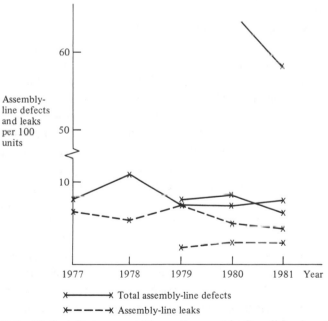

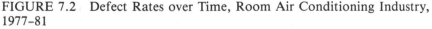

FIGURE 7.2   Defect Rates over Time, Room Air Conditioning Industry, 1977–81

SOURCE: Company records and questionnaires distributed by the author.

formers were separated by a factor of twenty; on service call rates, they were separated by a factor of five. Most differences were of long standing. Between 1977 and 1981, only three firms lowered their defect or service call rates by more than 25 percent. Improvements that leapfrogged competitors were even rarer. Superior performers therefore retained their edge, while poor performers remained far behind. Chapters 8 and 9, which focus on the sources of quality, provide an explanation for these persistent differences. But a related issue must first be addressed: the connection between in-plant and field quality.

## LINKING IN-PLANT AND FIELD QUALITY

That in-plant and field quality might be linked is hardly surprising. Such in-plant activities as assembly, inspection, and testing have an impact on performance in both the factory and the field. The real question concerns the direction of the relationship: Do the two move inversely or together? The answer depends on how quality problems are classified.

At one extreme is the view that field problems and in-plant defects are identical, even though they are observed in different places. In this interpretation, most service calls would involve units that were already flawed by the time they left the factory. Field problems would result from imperfect inspection—leaks that went undetected in pressure tests, wiring errors that were overlooked at electrical tests, or mechanical flaws that slipped by quality audit—and categories of in-plant and field problems would correspond perfectly.[20] Moreover, because of the mediating role of inspection, in-plant and field quality would be inversely related.[21] Tight inspection would mean that problems were confined to the factory and field problems were few; ineffective inspection would couple a high level of field problems with low (reported) in-plant defect rates.

At the other extreme is the view that field problems and in-plant defects are fundamentally different. Because many types of field problems cannot be traced to inspection errors, other causes must be at work. One obvious example is damage incurred during shipment. Wiring or welding that was attached firmly enough to pass in-plant inspection might still come undone during transit between the warehouse and retailers. Because of rough handling, units might have electrical problems in the field even though they were previously deemed trouble-free. Similarly, some field problems might be time-related, involving slow processes of deterioration and decay. These would be difficult to identify in the factory, because initial product performance would have been unaffected. During final assembly, for example, excess moisture might seep into a unit's refrigeration system; over time, corrosion would increase, eventually causing the compressor to fail. Yet in-plant performance tests would seldom pick up the problem. As long as initial performance was satisfactory—and most units are run in the factory for less than forty-five minutes—units would normally be given a clean bill of health.

Field problems of this sort will not usually be caught by in-plant inspection.[22] In such settings, a high defect rate does not guarantee an absence of field problems. Even though inspection is screening out defects and ensuring that they are repaired within the factory, field problems may still emerge, but from different sources. By this reasoning, levels of in-plant and field quality would be uncorrelated.

Suppose, however, that performance in both areas is driven by the same underlying forces: management attitudes, rewards for quality improvement, the sophistication of information and control systems, and levels of training. Then, companies that are successful on one form of quality would be likely to succeed on others as well; weaknesses would also be shared. Because of common roots, in-plant and field quality would vary together, even though they involved different *specific* problems and remedies.

Correlations support this last interpretation, for they show that the two forms of quality move together rather than separately. First-year service call rates, for example, are positively and significantly correlated with assembly-line defect rates.[23] Appendix B, which ranks plants on in-plant and field quality using a broader combination of measures, reaches a similar conclusion. These findings therefore suggest that common influences lie behind a company's success on in-plant and field quality. Excellence in one area is normally associated with excellence in another; weaknesses are also shared. Chapters 8 and 9 will have more to say on the subject, but for the moment it is important to recognize that across-the-board success is seldom automatic. Often, the specific factors determining in-plant and field quality are quite different. Yet in the room air conditioning industry, most companies monitored the two forms of quality by the same yardstick: defect rates at quality audit. Unfortunately, their approach reflects a basic misunderstanding of audit activities and the misapplication of a valuable technique.

The Role of Quality Audit

Quality audits normally take place after final assembly is completed. They involve thorough assessments of units from the customer's point of view, focusing on whether manufacturing and assembly have been performed satisfactorily.[24] Typically, a small number of units—five or ten per day—is chosen randomly from those awaiting shipment; they are then carted to a separate work area and inspected by auditors, who are guided by long lists of potential problems. Defect rates are computed based on the number and type of problems found. The process is normally thoroughgoing and time-consuming, far more so than the cursory inspections performed while units are moving along the assembly line. Because of the care required—it sometimes takes as long as an hour to audit a single room air conditioner—only a small proportion of each day's production is reviewed.

Audit results thus differ from other in-plant quality measures in two ways: the small number of units involved and the comprehensiveness of inspection. The latter explains why companies rely so heavily on audits when assessing their overall quality performance; the former, why these assessments are so frequently incorrect. In the room air conditioning industry, audit results were regularly misused. They were often employed as predictors of field performance or substitutes for less demanding measures of in-plant quality. Because of their peculiar statistical properties, they are misleading on both counts. Audits are best used instead for a narrower purpose: determining whether production processes have fallen out of control.[25] The reason is that audit samples are seldom large enough to be accurate predictors of levels of in-plant or field quality. At best they are rough approximations, true within broad limits. Even small samples, however, are capable of identifying changes in the status quo, *if problems are found*. Thus, audits that fail to turn up defects say little about the quality of total output and are therefore poor predictors of overall quality levels, because the odds of finding problems in unaudited units remain high. But audits that uncover defects send a clearer message: Processes are likely to have fallen out of control, and problems are likely to be widespread; otherwise, the probability of finding defects in such small samples would be low.[26]

These arguments are generally supported by statistical analysis. According to the correlations of Appendix C, defect rates at quality audit are positively but insignificantly related to other measures of in-plant quality. They are negatively but insignificantly related to first-year service call rates.[27] Audits thus serve a screening function, alerting companies to systematic and widespread problems within the factory and keeping them from the field. But because of the small samples involved, they fail to catch many in-plant problems—which explains, in part, why the correlations lack statistical significance even though they are in the expected direction.

The same conclusion emerges from an analysis of audit rates over time. Despite companies' use of these measures as predictors of field performance, they are poorly related to first-year service call rates.[28] Five manufacturers of room air conditioners provided at least three years of audit data; in no case did the numbers consistently track changes in direction in service call rates. Nor is the tracking ability of audit rates improved by comparing them with in-plant quality measures. The experience of one manufacturer, which briefly compiled audit results and assembly-line defect rates on a monthly basis, is representative. It provided complete data for a three-year period extending from February 1971 to April 1974. Statistical analysis of the data showed no association between defect rates at quality audit and defect rates on the assembly line.[29]

As predictors, then, quality audit measures leave much to be desired. Companies that use them for this purpose are certain to be disappointed. Yet audits still serve a vital role. Chapter 9 will show that one factor distinguishing superior quality plants from plants with poorer performance is the rigor and frequency of their quality audits. Thorough and careful inspection of a small number of units ensures that production processes are kept under control and common problems do not escape the factory undetected. In that respect, quality audits represent a court of last resort for defects—the final, critical link tying together in-plant and field quality.


## AN INDUSTRY PORTRAIT

This chapter has reviewed a host of measures used to monitor quality in the room air conditioning industry. Each measure has deficiencies of some sort: limited scope, small samples, reporting biases, or coverage confined to a single year. But each also has a large objective component that legitimizes interfirm comparisons. Quantifiable criteria are usually involved, and defects are frequently reported in common categories. Moreover, the data typically point in a single direction. On both in-plant and field quality, there are wide spreads between the best and worst performers in the industry. These differences persist over time. And companies that score high on one set of measures normally score high on others as well.

When compared with the subjective quality ratings of the previous chapter, quantitative data tell a clearer, more consistent story. The overall findings are difficult to dispute: Some members of the industry consistently are quality leaders, while others invariably lag behind. Common technology has not produced a uniform quality level, nor has competition led to a narrowing quality gap. Mere chance is unlikely to explain the differences. As the next two chapters will show, a variety of influences, all tied to management action, are responsible.

# Chapter

# 8

# The Sources of Quality: From Design to Production

There is no shortage of theories to explain superior quality performance. Almost every company has a list of its own. Typically, the theories are narrow, idiosyncratic, and highly particular: They single out specific individuals or equipment, unique to the firm, and deem them the primary contributors to quality. Occasionally, however, common explanations appear. Over time, these theories gain strong support; today many of them are routinely—and often unthinkingly—cited by managers as the sources of superior quality.

In the room air conditioning industry, for example, managers at several firms were quick to claim that "we build in quality, we don't inspect it in." Other companies were equally insistent that their quality advantage came from "conservative engineering" or from a purchasing department that was "tough on vendors." Such claims are almost impossible to verify, because they involve broad generalizations. Common explanations could easily mask distinctive practices and behaviors. Moreover, companies normally lack the data required to construct sound theories about the sources of quality. Their evidence is usually anecdotal and piecemeal, a series of highly visible examples rather than comparative or longitudinal data. Little can be concluded from such evidence.

The same is true of most academic research on the subject, but for different reasons. Few scholars have taken the time to examine prevailing quality practices. Descriptive studies—especially ones employing controlled, comparative samples—have been rare. Rather, prescription has been the norm, and the primary tools have been statistical methods and mathematical proofs.[1] But since researchers

133

have spent little time examining actual quality levels or quality variations among firms, what works in practice has remained in doubt.

This chapter and the next one take a different approach. By focusing on a single American industry and isolating specific practices and behaviors that are associated with superior quality performance, they avoid the problems listed above. The approach has limitations of its own, however, since no single industry is completely representative. Moreover, it can only identify patterns of behavior. With a sample of eleven manufacturing plants, independent variation among the several hundred possible contributors to quality is certain to be limited, and the impact of any single variable is almost impossible to determine.

To aid in interpreting the results, plants have been grouped into four categories of quality performance: best, better, fair, and poor. Two plants fell in the best category, and three in each of the other categories. Several measures were used to ensure consistency, for as Chapter 7 has shown, companies did not always employ identical practices in recording information about quality. The classification scheme is described at length in Appendix B; it includes measures of both in-plant and field quality. To organize the discussion, explanations for superior quality have also been grouped into categories, moving generally from early to later stages in the production chain. Chapter 8 explores the impact on quality of product design, vendor selection and management, and production and work force management, while Chapter 9 focuses on the softer and more embracing themes of quality policies and management attitudes.

## PRODUCT DESIGN

For obvious reasons, design practices provide the ideal starting point for a study of quality performance. At this stage, all is in flux. Product requirements are still on paper, components have yet to be determined, and vendors are unspecified. A wide range of possible choices exists. Moreover, changes are still relatively simple and inexpensive to make. Once designs are final, however, the character and functioning of new products is largely set—and with them, several crucial elements affecting final product quality.

The Design Process

Surprisingly, the basic steps in the design process were quite similar at all plants in the industry, whatever their level of quality performance. New products typically progressed through four stages: concept development, engineering prototypes, pilot runs, and production units. Along the way, signoffs were obtained from marketing, quality control, manufacturing, purchasing, and service.[2] At both the best and worst quality performers, prototypes were subject to the same engineering tests. In part, the similarity reflects the influence of trade associations, such as the American Refrigeration Institute (ARI) and the Association of Home Appliance Manufacturers (AHAM), whose test standards were recognized throughout the industry. But even when managers claimed uniqueness, pointing to tests more rigorous than the norm, identical procedures were observed at competitors. For example, plants in several quality categories claimed that their reliability was enhanced by testing new products at temperatures above recommended standards. Yet in practice the same cutoff was being applied by each plant: 125°–130°F.

The same was true of another often-repeated claim about the design process. Several plants reported that their defect rates were low because "our engineers sit down with manufacturing beforehand [while designs were still in flux] and strive for manufacturability." Yet at virtually every plant, manufacturing's earliest involvement in the design process came at the same point: after prototypes had been constructed.[3] Pilot runs were equally universal.[4] At only one plant—which boasted the highest defect rate in the industry—was resistance reported. There, engineers claimed that manufacturing managers, under pressure to control costs, sometimes resisted pilot runs to avoid being charged for the set-up of new tooling.

Because they were so widely shared, such practices as pilot runs and tests at high ambient temperatures cannot explain variations in quality performance. They were common denominators, not differentiators. Managers in this industry were therefore mistaken in their belief that these practices distinguished good quality from bad. In one area, however—the use of reliability engineering—pronounced differences were found among plants. Despite the long history of these techniques and their proven record in enhancing reliability, only the best and better quality performers showed any inclination to use them. At these plants, failure mode and effects analysis (FMEA), which assesses likely failure points and tries to design around them, was widespread, especially for new products. The other reliability techniques described in Chapter 1 were employed to lesser degrees. At only one plant, however, was there a comprehensive attempt to manage product reliability, and it was associated with one of the best quality records in the industry.

At this plant, all stages of the design process included explicit discussions of reliability. For both new products and major product revisions, marketing was required to state quantitative reliability goals up front. The objective of the process was clear. According to the company's reliability and quality policy, managers were expected to "use reliability and quality standards above the average of what constitutes good industry practice." Formal, multifunctional reviews followed; only after goals had been approved were materials, components, and manufacturing processes selected. A large quality engineering staff was then empowered to conduct FMEAs, hazard and safety checks, and other formal assessments of reliability. Product performance was predicted using such measures as first-year failure rates, mean time between failures, and mean time between maintenance. Eventually, the results of these analyses were summarized in a Management Visualization Document; its purpose was to advise top management of potential product risks that might result in "the loss of product availability, loss of company reputation, or the incurrence of warranty expenses that may exceed planned reserve levels." Signoffs on this document were required before pilot runs could begin; it was updated again before initiating full production. Finally, equipment and components were qualified to ensure that they were capable of meeting reliability requirements. Test procedures were stipulated, and a choice was made between in-house testing and field trials. Because of its technical complexity, the choice process was directed by a special committee, the Program Qualification Board, comprising experts from product engineering, development engineering, reliability engineering, quality control, service engineering, and marketing.

Such a comprehensive approach to reliability was unique in the industry. Its link to subsequent quality performance—particularly to lower service call rates—should be obvious (although the approach is not without weaknesses).[5] In fact, several other manufacturers also recognized up-front engineering and design as key contributors to superior quality, but they emphasized a very different approach: conservative engineering.


### Conservative Engineering

In theory, conservative engineering is straightforward. It requires that products be designed with ample safety margins. Components might be used below designated stress levels; units might be tested in conditions more demanding than normal operation; or exceptionally durable parts might be specified for critical subsystems. In each case, the underlying motivation remains the same: to avoid problems, especially those that are unanticipated. Designers can seldom predict all conceivable failures. Among engineers this is known as the "ignorance factor"; because of it, large safety margins are frequently built into products to compensate for "unknown stresses that might occur, variability in the strength of the materials used, [and] variability due to workmanship."[6]

Conservative engineering, then, rests on well-established principles. But in the room air conditioning industry, there was considerable confusion about their application and impact. Several manufacturers claimed to be practicing conservative engineering, but when pressed, many had difficulty citing specific actions or behaviors as evidence. One chief engineer was blunt. After noting that his plant tore down and analyzed only three to four competitive models per year, he admitted: "We like to think we're conservative in engineering, but we really don't know by comparison with the industry."

At best, managers were able to cite two or three practices that they felt were indicative of conservative engineering. One, the testing of new models under especially stressful conditions, such as high ambient temperatures, has already been discussed; it was found at plants of both high and low quality performance. Another, involving average compression ratios (which quantify differences in pressure between condensor and evaporator coils, and thus measure the strain put on compressors), produced similarly undifferentiated results. In fact, there was little agreement within the industry on what constituted a low (that is, desirable) compression ratio in the first place. A dramatic example was provided by two plants that claimed the same numerical compression ratio for their product lines. One regarded the figure as average for the industry, while the other insisted it was low.[7]

A final practice that managers associated with conservative engineering was choice of components.[8] For marketing and cost reasons, designers frequently used different parts to perform the same function; occasionally they justified their choices by citing superior reliability or ruggedness. This was true of both thermostats and fan motors. The former were available in bulb and bimetallic versions, the latter in models that were open and sealed. Bimetallic thermostats were generally considered simpler and less prone to breakage (although less accurate). Sealed fan motors were normally viewed as better protected and more reliable. But were these assumptions correct? One can get a rough idea by breaking out first-year service call rates by component, and then searching for differences in failure rates by types of parts. Lower failure rates should be associated with more reliable parts. But in this case, no statistically significant differences were found.[9] Bulb and bimetallic thermostats had comparable failure rates, as did open and sealed fan motors. Thus, the evidence in this section suggests that conservative engineering explained few quality variations in the room air conditioning industry, despite its theoretical appeal.

## Product Line Breadth

Design choices, of course, involve more than components and test methods. Features, sizes, energy efficiencies, and the amount of customization across models must also be considered. These decisions might be linked to a company's overall quality performance in a number of ways. For example, some models are inherently complex, and a company that chooses to manufacture them exclusively might have an unusually high failure rate. Proliferating features might lead to the same result. Occasionally, variety alone might cause quality problems because of the difficulties it creates for manufacturing. Is there any evidence linking these characteristics with quality levels in the room air conditioning industry?

In terms of two critical variables that managers thought were related to quality performance—energy efficiency and Btu capacity—the answer is no. Models with energy efficiency ratings (EERs) above the industry average were found at all levels of quality performance. Nor did the results change when EERs were averaged by plant. Even then, high overall EER scores were reported by plants in the best and worst quality categories.[10]

The same was true of Btu capacity, which measures an air conditioner's cooling power and also serves as a proxy for size. Virtually every plant in the industry manufactured at least one simple, no-frills 4,000–5,000 Btu unit. Most indicated that 30 to 40 percent of their sales came from models of less than 9,000 Btu, which Chapter 7 has shown to have lower than average service call rates. While there was some evidence linking the poorest quality performers with the very highest Btu units—suggesting that in terms of size and capacity, they had the widest range of offerings—the differences were small and the production volumes insignificant.

A number of other measures might be used to examine product variety. The most commonly cited was the total number of models produced, for in most cases the larger the number of models, the greater the variety. Some models, however, are closely related—so much so that shifting from one to another causes hardly any disruption in manufacturing or design. In such cases, a better measure of variety is the number of chassis sizes produced. Each chassis size represents a distinct model family, a collection of units built around shared characteristics. Because components and subsystems are normally tailored to a family, models within these groupings are usually more similar than different.

Using these criteria, the best quality performers were offering narrower product lines and less variety than their competitors. As Table 8.1 shows, they manufactured an average of three chassis sizes and fifty-six models; by contrast, plants with the poorest quality offered

TABLE 8.1   *Product Line Variety and Quality Performance*

| Grouping of Companies by Quality Performance | Number of Chassis Sizes | Number of Models |
|---|---|---|
| Best U.S. plants | 3 | 56 |
| Better U.S. plants | 5 | 66 |
| Fair U.S. plants | 6 | 104 |
| Poor U.S. plants | 8 | 89 |

*Note:* All figures are averages (means) for the category.
SOURCE: Company records and questionnaires distributed by the author.

eight chassis sizes and eighty-nine models. When measured by the number of chassis sizes, these differences were statistically significant across all quality categories. But the relationship was not significant when variety was measured by differences in the number of models—largely because of high variations within categories—even though the best and better plants generally offered narrower product lines than the fair and poor plants.[11]

These relationships make good sense. A simple, narrow product line has the advantage of focus.[12] In both design and manufacturing, each model receives ample attention. Fewer parts must be handled, fewer blueprints developed, fewer assembly operations mastered, and fewer disruptions overcome. Purchasing, production control, and work force management are greatly simplified, and higher productivity is the frequent result.[13] As Table 8.1 indicates, high levels of quality are likely as well.

Overall, the evidence in this section has been mixed. While superior quality was associated with narrow product lines and careful reliability engineering, few other relationships were found. Neither conservative engineering nor sophisticated test procedures had much explanatory power. High EERs and a broad range of Btu capacities were equally common at plants of widely varying quality performance. Of course, design differences might still be responsible for significant quality variation, but in that case they would have to involve practices other than those examined here.

## VENDOR SELECTION AND MANAGEMENT

Once designs have been determined, the next step in the production chain is the selection of vendors and the monitoring of incoming parts and materials. The link between these practices and final product quality is a recurrent theme in the literature on quality. As far back as 1968, a leading quality expert was arguing that "to an extent far beyond anything in earlier industrial history, the performance of modern complex systems depends on the qualities of our subsystems."[14] Or, to use the more colorful language of computer experts, "garbage in means garbage out."

For ease of analysis, the process of assuring acceptable parts and materials has been divided here into three stages: the initial choice of vendors, management of vendors over time, and receiving inspection. Each is examined separately for links to subsequent quality performance.

### Vendor Selection

Plants in this industry reported that most supply relationships were cordial and longstanding. A typical relationship was estimated at twelve years. In the same spirit, few vendors were dropped for quality reasons—a median of less than three per year.[15] Such stability is easily explained. In this industry, neither products nor components have changed appreciably in recent years. A mature technology is involved, and also a mature supplier base. Choices are quite limited, especially for major components; according to industry sources, there were three primary suppliers of compressors, three of thermostats, six of fan motors, and one of switches. With the exception of compressors, where the Japanese have emerged recently as a new source of supply, pairings between manufacturers and vendors were expected to continue for many years.

For these reasons, traditional approaches to vendor selection were of limited value in explaining quality variation in the industry. Most changes of suppliers involved secondary components; even then, they were few in number. Nevertheless, plants' policies in this area were still examined to see if approaches differed by categories of quality performance. No significant differences were found. Practices were either common to all plants, absent at most, or visible at both ends of the quality spectrum. For example, all plants involved members of the engineering department in vendor selection, but hardly any required visits to all potential suppliers before they were accepted as vendors.[16] At both the best and worst quality performers, members of the quality department were actively involved in vendor selection. Overall, there was little or no evidence in the industry of an association between a plant's quality performance and its approaches to vendor selection.

### Vendor Management

Approaches to vendor management, on the other hand, were clearly linked to categories of quality performance. Vendor management refers to the ongoing process of monitoring suppliers, responding to quality problems, and improving incoming parts and materials. In each of these areas, the best and better quality performers were employing practices quite different from their competitors'.

All of the best and better plants, for example, had formal programs to prevent degradation of supplier quality. Typically, the programs involved some type of "hit list" or "Ten Most Wanted List," identifying problem vendors on the basis of high incoming rejection rates. Most lists were compiled annually and served as the basis for remedial action. Vendors on the list were first contacted by the purchasing department and their shipment history was reviewed; frequently, members of the engineering and quality departments were then called upon to assist in problem-solving. Rapid improvement was expected, backed by an implicit threat: Too many years on the hit list, and business would be lost. To underline the connection, shipments from problem vendors were monitored especially carefully.[17]

No such practices were found at plants with fair or poor quality. Remedial programs were *ad hoc,* if they existed at all. Even when problem vendors were identified, follow-up was partial and ineffective. Recurrent problems were the norm. In part, such behavior reflects low expectations and an unwillingness to confront vendors. For example, the quality control manager at the plant reporting the highest incoming rejection rate in the industry (16 percent) noted that in his three and a half years at the plant he could recall "only ten instances perhaps of leaning on vendors; and only one was changed after trying everything we could."

Such accepting attitudes go a long way toward explaining vendor quality performance. A common tenet among managers is that "you get what you expect." But attitudes are only part of the story. A number of specific practices were also observed at the best and better quality performers but not at other plants. These practices all revolved around the role of the purchasing department and the extent of its involvement in quality management.

Historically, U.S. companies have assigned a narrow role to purchasing departments. Technical skills have often been weak. As one manufacturing manager observed, his purchasing agents were qualified to do little but "shop for sources."[18] Technical assessments of vendors have usually been assigned to members of the engineering and quality control departments. In the room air conditioning industry, that was the typical pattern at fair and poor quality performers. But at the best and better plants, purchasing agents took a more active role. Many had been trained in quality analysis and other technical skills, often in courses created by their companies. The purchasing department was far more than a buyer; it was an essential link in ongoing vendor management. Thus, at these plants members of the purchasing department received regular reports (usually monthly) on field failure rates; no such data came to purchasing agents at lesser quality performers. Using these reports, quantitative goals were set for vendor quality—another practice lacking at lesser performers. Three of the best and better plants had gone even farther, creating special purchasing positions devoted to quality management. The individuals in these positions were responsible for monitoring suppliers and taking the lead in initiating improvement programs. Perhaps the clearest indication of purchasing's role at superior performers was its involvement in new product development.[19] At the best and better plants, members of the purchasing department were expected to attend design reviews and to keep suppliers informed of new demands. Neither practice was observed at plants with fair or poor quality.

The cumulative impact of these vendor management practices is likely to be enormous. A simple index developed to measure a plant's overall approach to supplier quality was strongly related to quality performance; it appears in Appendix C. The index illustrates a crucial point: To achieve high levels of quality, superior performers usually relied on a combination of mutually reinforcing practices, rather than one or two practices in isolation. The whole was expected to be greater than the sum of its parts. Vendor management is but one example of this approach; several others are described in Chapter 9.

Yet surprisingly, expectations of vendors were low even at the most successful performers. Few managers thought that incoming quality could be greatly improved. At one of the better plants, the quality control manager observed that his goal was simply to keep incoming rejections below 2 percent—a number he had "dreamed up" because in his experience it was the best that American manufacturers could do. Yet in the same industry, drawing from a similar set of suppliers, one plant had achieved an incoming rejection rate of 0.82 percent. Five years earlier the rate had been nearly three times higher. Forty-five percent of incoming parts and materials were now sent directly to the assembly line without receiving inspection, and the number of receiving inspectors had fallen by a third.

At this plant, improvements in supplier quality were pursued aggressively. Programs were proactive as well as remedial, and the status quo was never accepted as "the best our vendors can do." For example, letters were sent from the plant's vice president for procurement to the presidents and chief executive officers of all suppliers, informing them of the need to improve their quality and announcing several new assistance programs. Buyers were trained in such technical areas as design review, failure mode and effects analysis, and cost of quality calculations. With these tools in hand, they were trying to help suppliers design quality into their manufacturing systems instead of relying on end-of-the-line inspections. Suppliers were also held accountable for results. Each had to meet a number of quantitative goals, including cost per lot, permissible number of defects, and quality audit problems due to defective parts. To ensure proper oversight, the receiving plant's purchasing manager was evaluated each year on nearly identical measures: the number of unacceptable suppliers, incoming lot rejections, stock and assembly line rejections, and the percentage of quality audit problems and field failures due to defective parts.

The experience of this plant is revealing, for it shows that supplier quality can be improved even without intensive inspection. Most other plants in the industry, however, were less advanced and reported fewer direct contacts with vendors. For that reason, their receiving inspection practices played a more central role in explaining variations in quality performance.

Receiving Inspection

Receiving inspection involves the review of incoming parts and materials before they are combined into subassemblies and final products. Reviews can be cursory or careful: at one extreme, they may provide for detailed oversight; at the other, their looseness may encourage permissiveness and lax standards. Assessing the degree of oversight is essential when comparing companies' approaches to receiving inspection. In this analysis, the degree of oversight has been measured by two simple variables: the incoming inspection plan and a list of the criteria used to test incoming parts and materials.

Because of its high cost, few plants today rely on 100 percent inspection. Rather, small samples of incoming goods are checked, usually on a lot-by-lot basis; should defects be found, inspection then expands to a larger number of items. This is a time-honored practice. As noted in Chapter 1, it can be traced back to work conducted at Bell Laboratories in the 1930s and 1940s. Yet despite the long history, in this industry only the best and better quality performers were sampling according to accepted statistical techniques. Most were using some variant of Military Standard 105D (MIL-STD-105D), a well-known sampling plan. By contrast, the fair and poor plants were using unscientific, *ad hoc* approaches. In some cases, only the first item in a lot was checked; in others, the number of items to be checked was without any clear rationale. Round numbers—for example, "check half a dozen"—were common. Even more disturbing, at several plants production pressures were so great that entire lots were sometimes diverted around receiving inspection and sent directly to the assembly line.[20] The roots of this problem varied. At one plant, production schedules and orders from suppliers were poorly synchronized, leaving little slack; at another plant, receiving inspection was grossly understaffed, with two workers responsible for reviewing 14,000 incoming shipments per year; at a third plant, the receiver at the shipping dock had long worked for the materials control department rather than the quality department, so his overriding loyalty was to keeping the assembly line moving. Whatever their roots, these practices had a similar impact: They shifted the discovery of defective parts and materials to later (and more expensive) stages of the production process. In many cases, problems were not discovered until after units were in customers' hands.

Approaches to sampling, then, were closely related to plants' overall quality performance. They provide an obvious clue to the rigor of receiving inspection. By contrast, another measure of supplier oversight, the criteria used for testing incoming parts and materials, had little explanatory power. Plants at all levels of quality claimed to be conducting both functional and dimensional tests. All plants, for example, checked parts for conformance to blueprints and specifications; most also tested some aspects of performance. Comparable tests were cited for major components such as compressors, fan motors, and thermostats. Overall, incoming test procedures were little differentiated.

Nevertheless, in a small number of cases improvements in quality could be traced directly to changes in test procedures. One of the better plants, for example, had resolved its problems with capacitors by insisting that they be checked electronically on arrival in the receiving laboratory. It had also curbed fan problems by introducing dynamic (that is, in-motion) testing of fan blades. Improvements in vendor performance had quickly followed, and for the simplest of reasons: Faulty parts were now immediately visible. As the plant's quality control manager noted: "Once the vendors found out they were being measured, they got better."

Unlike design practices, then, approaches to vendor management were clearly linked to levels of quality performance. Superior performers monitored incoming shipments through statistical sampling plans, identified problem vendors, insisted on remedial action, set quantitative goals for supplier quality, and allowed purchasing departments to play an active role in product design and vendor evaluation. Such activities were lacking or attenuated at plants with lower quality. There, vendor monitoring was *ad hoc* or nonexistent, receiving inspection was frequently bypassed, feedback to vendors was limited and unsystematic, and purchasing departments lacked the technical skills to do much more than shop for sources. Approaches to vendor selection, however, were less varied among plants and explained little of the difference in overall quality performance.

## PRODUCTION AND WORK FORCE MANAGEMENT

Once designs have been set and components purchased, production at the factory can begin. A variety of processes are normally involved. For convenience they can be grouped into two broad categories: subassembly and final assembly operations. The former includes the fabrication and brazing (soldering) of coils and the wiring of control panels; the latter involves the attachment of parts and the combining of subassemblies into working units. In this industry, neither stage is particularly complex. The technology has been stable for many years, and products are standardized and mature. One would therefore expect to see great commonality among plants in both subassembly and final assembly operations. And, in fact, most plants had divided tasks similarly between the two stages. Subassembly activities normally took place off the assembly line and were worker-paced, while final assembly operations invariably employed a moving line set to operate at a predetermined speed.

Despite these similarities, manufacturing processes were not identical. Factories employed different layouts and used equipment of different vintages. Manufacturing tasks varied in sequence and duration. Assembly lines were sometimes short and sometimes long; companies differed as well in their reliance on feeder lines. All these variables can be combined into a single, overarching category: process design, or the choice of methods, equipment, and approaches to manufacturing.[21] Within that category are included activities as diverse as the selection of production technology and the routing of parts between work stations.

Process design is not the only basis for manufacturing differences. In this industry, plants also differed in how they chose to operate their production processes. Some tried to keep the level of output smooth and unvarying over the course of the year, while others allowed pronounced peaks and valleys. Capacity utilization was tight at some plants but loose at others. Changeovers, second shifts, engineering change orders, and other disruptive influences were present to greater or lesser degrees. And managers had distinctly different ideas about work force training and supervision.

### Process Design

Most plants in the industry employed comparable production processes. Technologies were basic and unsophisticated: the brazing of tubing, the handwiring of electrical connections, and the use of simple tools to mount mechanical parts. There was only one significant exception, but it was found at one of the best plants in the industry. At this plant, managers observed that "the factory was designed around the product." A plastic molding technology had been specially developed for the air conditioner's casing and base pan; the resulting one-piece construction sharply reduced the number of required parts and attachments. Simple assembly errors were eliminated by having screw holes prealigned. Most tubing was sealed by epoxy joints cured in an oven rather than by brazing; the resulting leak rates were only one-tenth of competitors'. Modern equipment was in place throughout the factory, including company-designed test equipment and a decoupled assembly line that allowed earlier and later stages of final assembly to be paced at different speeds.

The connection between such advanced manufacturing processes and overall quality performance is obvious. Superior technology limits the opportunity for errors, simplifies the product, substitutes more reliable methods for those that are less certain, and builds flexibility into assembly-line management. Yet, despite these advantages, no other plant in the industry had committed comparable resources to the development of new techniques. Most plants were using processes that had changed little in the past five years, and most had settled on a surprisingly similar sequence of operations. Figure 8.1

| Step Number | Description |
|:---:|:---|
| 1 | base pan placed on assembly line |
| 2 | partitions and barriers added |
| 3 | insulation attached |
| 4 | compressor mounted and bolted in place |
| 5 | evaporator and condenser coils mounted |
| 6 | brazing of tubing to seal refrigeration system |
| 7 | initial leak test |
| 8 | evacuation and charging of refrigeration system |
| 9 | fan motor mounted |
| 10 | fan and blower wheels attached |
| 11 | miscellaneous wiring and electrical connections |
| 12 | initial electrical test |
| 13 | final assembly |
| 14 | performance and run test |
| 15 | packaging and preparation for shipment |

FIGURE 8.1   Typical Sequence of Final Assembly Operations, Room Air Conditioning Industry

illustrates the typical pattern for final assembly, showing the progression from refrigeration components to electrical components and mechanical parts.[22] Typically, the sequence was traced to a concern for efficiency—the need to balance tasks along the assembly line with a minimum of idle time—or else to technical requirements.

Choosing an assembly sequence for these reasons is hardly unusual. Industrial engineering criteria normally govern such decisions.[23] But process flows are likely to affect quality as well as productivity. For example, parts that are attached earlier may be mounted more securely because workers find themselves less hampered by other components that are in the way. For the same reason, inspections may be easier when subsystems are completed and tested before moving on to the next stage of assembly. Errors may be reduced by ensuring that critical tasks like wiring are performed before units have become clogged with other parts.

The connection between production sequences and quality performance can be tested empirically. While most plants followed the sequence of operations described in Figure 8.1, there were several notable exceptions. At two plants, fan motors were mounted much earlier in the process; at three plants, fans and associated parts were attached earlier; and at two plants, compressors were mounted much later. Since first-year service call rates were collected at the level of individual components, failure rates can be compared to see if different production sequences were associated with differences in component reliability. The results of the analysis were mixed. Early attachment of fans made little difference in the incidence of service calls due to fans and associated parts. But the time at which such major components as fan motors and compressors were mounted was far more significant. The two plants that attached fan motors early had the lowest fan motor failure rates in the industry, and the two that attached compressors late had the highest compressor failure rates in the industry (excluding those plants that manufactured their own compressors).[24]

Of course, production sequencing is only one element of process design. Other elements that might affect quality performance include the age of plant and equipment, layout, and the configuration and speed of assembly lines. In this industry, age of facilities was not a significant factor.[25] Of the best quality performers, one had the newest plant in the industry and the other the second oldest. The poorest quality performers included the oldest plant in the industry as well as the second newest. In terms of layout, virtually all companies had constructed feeder lines for building subassemblies; they were invariably worker-paced or else moving lines run at extremely slow speeds. Most final assembly lines were arranged in a semicircular or twisting flow; there was no obvious connection, however, between line configuration and such variables as ease of assembly or the spacing of workers along the line.[26]

Further analysis of the connection between assembly line characteristics and quality performance in the industry yielded mixed results. According to Table 8.2, the best quality performers generally had short assembly lines and long cycle times. They therefore imposed only a limited division of labor.[27] But the same was true of the poorest performers, who not only ran their assembly lines slower than other groups in the industry but also used relatively short lines (although they were more than twice the length of the assembly lines at the best plants). There was also high variance within quality categories, and the results for intermediate quality performers were without obvious pattern. Few firm conclusions can be drawn from such data.[28]

In three other areas, however—each linked in some way to the intensity with which facilities were used—differences among plants were more systematic, although not always statistically significant. Superior quality performers left less space between workers on the line, had lower capacity utilization rates, and ran production with less variation across the year. The first of these findings fits well with the literature on just-in-time (JIT) production methods, which argues that eliminating the buffers between manufacturing processes

TABLE 8.2 *Assembly-Line Characteristics and Quality Performance*[a]

| Grouping of Companies by Quality Performance | Assembly-Line Design | | | Assembly-Line Operation | | |
|---|---|---|---|---|---|---|
| | Number of Assembly Lines | Assembly Line Length (feet) | Assembly Line Feet Per Direct Laborer | Cycle Time (minutes) | Capacity Utilization Rate (%) | Percent That Peak Production Exceeded Low Production[b] |
| Best U.S. plants | 2 | 250 | 5 | .70 | 63 | 27 |
| Better U.S. plants | 2 | 987 | 7 | .56 | 57 | 63 |
| Fair U.S. plants | 2 | 1,085 | 9 | .39 | 80 | 67 |
| Poor U.S. plants | 2 | 657 | 11 | .89 | 77 | 167 |

[a]All figures are averages (means) for the category.
[b]Derived by dividing each plant's largest daily output for the year by its smallest (non-zero) output for the year.
SOURCE: Company records and questionnaires distributed by the author.

leads to improvements in both quality and productivity.[29] The other findings reflect the pressure put on production facilities and the amount of change introduced into manufacturing. In most cases, greater variation and pressure were associated with lower quality.[30]

In summary, a limited set of process characteristics varied directly with overall quality performance. Most plants employed comparable technologies and equipment. Assembly-line length, layout, and speed were poorly related to quality. Production sequencing, however, was linked to component failure rates. Investments in major process changes were important as well, for the only plant in the industry that had invested heavily in new production methods had defect and field failure rates among the lowest observed. How facilities were operated was less significant, although most relationships were in the expected direction. Both slack capacity and stable production were associated with superior quality, but only the former relationship was statistically significant. Such findings are tantalizing. They suggest a host of areas for further study, all centered on the details of manufacturing management.


## CONFUSION AND CHANGE

It is virtually an iron law among production managers that change is the enemy of quality. In their eyes, variability and confusion go hand in hand. Shifts in skills and requirements impose new demands; they make control difficult and consistent output hard to obtain. New products, employees, and manufacturing methods often disrupt established operations and reduce quality. Change—especially when it is unanticipated or discontinuous—is frequently at the heart of the problem.[31]

Manufacturing disruptions take a variety of forms. Most, however, can be grouped into three categories: changes in labor force, production, and product. Labor force changes include absenteeism, turnover, layoffs, overtime, and bumping—anything, in fact, that alters the level of employee experience or reduces skills because of fatigue or lost knowledge. Production changes are closely related. They involve disruptions of manufacturing know-how or product familiarity that result from such production decisions as run length and the frequency of changeovers.[32] Finally, product changes include the rate of new product introductions, the frequency of engineering change orders, and related variables tied to the stability of designs.

Labor Force Changes

Surprisingly, there was little relationship between overall quality performance and most traditional measures of labor force stability. Absenteeism, turnover, average overtime, new hires as a percentage of direct labor, and layoffs as a percentage of direct labor did not vary systematically with levels of quality.[33] The variance within quality categories was large. And the same was true of the tenure of managers and supervisors. Long-term relationships were observed at both the best and the poorest plants.

These findings are difficult to explain, for labor force changes were cited frequently as a leading cause of quality problems. At one of the better plants, for example, the director of quality claimed that "manpower moves [were] the single biggest deterrent to quality" that he faced. In other industries, excessive overtime has been linked with reduced quality.[34] Thus, these results should be treated with caution. Labor force changes might well have an important impact on quality even though they did not discriminate among plants in different quality categories.

The same was clearly true of bumping. Bumping occurs when several of a company's factories, all in a tight geographical area, are covered by the same union and seniority ladder. Layoffs at one location then trigger multiple job changes; workers will be "bumped" from one factory to another as the least senior people are removed from the system. Of course, bumping also occurs within factories as layoffs trigger job changes. But in this industry, managers claimed that bumping within factories had little impact on quality. By contrast, managers of plants at all quality levels cited bumping between factories as an important cause of quality problems, and one whose impact persisted for days. Two reasons were usually given: changing cycle times and the skill required for key jobs. In most cases, workers were bumped from operations with slow assembly speeds (long cycle times) to operations that were run much faster. For example, one company was forced to move workers from its commercial refrigeration plant, with cycle times of 20–25 minutes, to its room air conditioner plant, with cycle times of 40–45 seconds. Workers who had previously regarded themselves as craftsmen were suddenly assigned to narrow, tightly defined tasks. The results were predictable: a high degree of "emotional upset" and mushrooming quality problems. By contrast, the one company reporting little difficulty with bumping was able to transfer workers between plants with comparable cycle times: .32–.37 minutes at the high-seniority plant and .26–.33 minutes at the room air conditioner plant.

Bumping problems were also associated with changes in key jobs. Because these jobs went unprotected (by either certification or contractual agreement), untrained employees could be bumped into positions that were critical to subsequent quality performance. The impact was usually an immediate increase in defect rates until the new skills were mastered. All plants cited brazing as the job most often affected by bumping moves and high leak rates as the most visible result.

Bumping had a pronounced impact on other aspects of performance as well. At one plant, line speeds were slowed so much after bumping that two and one-half days of volume were lost. Another plant estimated that defect rates increased 25–50 percent after bumping and stayed at that level for three to four days. Most plants also reported a short-term increase in the number of inspectors and supervisors required to manage the assembly line. Thus, bumping provides a classic example of productivity and quality moving hand in hand.

### Production Changes

The same is true of manufacturing experience. Greater output brings increased product familiarity, refined methods, and new skills and techniques; these, in turn, are expected to improve efficiency and lower costs. A large literature has grown up around these principles and the associated mathematics—learning curves, experience curves, and progress functions.[35] Surprisingly little, however, has been written about the relationship between manufacturing experience and quality.

Yet managers often see a clear connection between the two. In the room air conditioning industry, for example, changeovers were cited frequently as a source of quality problems. Changeovers occur when a company shifts from making one model to making another and must "change over" the assembly line so that necessary parts, equipment, and staffing are available and in position. In the process, learning is frequently disrupted and the benefits of experience are lost.[36]

Not all changeovers, however, have the same impact. Some are readily accommodated, with few adjustments; others require sharp changes in assembly line operation. Managers claimed to have few problems with changeovers within model families, because the sizing

of products remained roughly the same and changes in job requirements were few. Changeovers across model families (chassis sizes),
however, were more burdensome. A different size product was usually involved; with it came changes in line balancing, new mixes of
tasks and skills, different welding and wiring configurations, and
different parts requirements. All of these imposed new demands on
the production system and disrupted past learning. Managers reported that defect rates remained abnormally high for several hours
after these changeovers. Estimates ranged from a 3–5 percent increase in defect rates to a 50 percent increase when especially complex units were involved. A 10–15 percent increase was cited most
frequently.[37] Moreover, such problems were equally common at superior and inferior performers, since there was no statistically significant difference in the frequency of changeovers at plants in different
quality categories.[38]

### Run Length

A closely related measure of production experience is run length—
the number of units produced each time a model is manufactured.
Few plants meet their annual quantities through one production run.
Rather, they build models in smaller volumes and separate lots at
different times of the year. The precise size and timing of the runs is
a scheduling decision, which all plants in the industry said was governed by sales and inventory targets. Quality seldom entered into
the equation.[39] Yet at the same time, several managers pointed to a
connection between run length and defect rates. Long runs, they
noted, provided a stable environment—the opportunity to master
required skills through repetition. As techniques improved, defect
rates normally fell, up to a point. Eventually, diminishing returns set
in as technical limits were reached and opportunities for learning
were exhausted. Most managers therefore predicted that the relationship between run length and defect rates would be that shown in
Figure 8.2.

The relationship was strongly supported by statistical analysis. All
equations appear in Appendix C.[40] Differences in average run length
were enormously important; they alone explained more than 30 percent of the variance in defect rates among plants in the industry.
Even better results were obtained when the analysis was limited to a
single plant. One producer provided data on leak rates and run
lengths for three different models that it manufactured. Depending

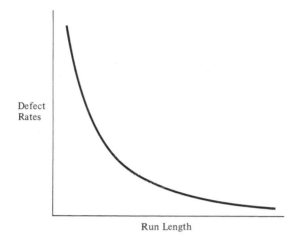

FIGURE 8.2    The Predicted Relationship Between Run Length and
Defect Rates

on the model, differences in run length explained a remarkable 50 to
70 percent of the variance in leak rates.[41]

These findings can be combined with the findings in the preceding
two sections to draw a powerful conclusion: From a quality standpoint, the worst manufacturing environment is one with bumping,
short runs, and frequent changeovers.[42] Each changeover is likely to
cause defects to rise abnormally for a brief period. Because changing
work assignments and short runs mean that workers never reap the
full benefits of experience, defect rates will fall only a small amount
between changeovers. The net result will be persistently high defect
rates. It is no coincidence that the room air conditioning plant with
the highest defect rate had frequent bumping and both the shortest
average run length and the largest number of changeovers in the industry.

### Product Changes

On the product side, engineering change orders (ECOs) are the
counterparts of bumping, changeovers, and short-run lengths. They
too introduce new elements into manufacturing—in this case, modifications in design—often without suitable training or explanation.
At one plant, for example, ECOs were never circulated to the quality
department for prior comment or approval. Most other plants also
reported problems in introducing ECOs smoothly into manufacturing. The disruptive potential of such changes is obvious. But even

though the best quality plants processed far fewer ECOs than the poorest plants—forty-two per year, as opposed to 131—the differences across quality categories were not statistically significant.[43] The primary reason was high variance within one quality category. Plants with fair quality reported both the largest (660) and smallest (10) number of ECOs in the industry. For that reason, the data on ECOs support only limited statistical conclusions, although they suggest an association between superior quality and a small number of ECOs.


## THE SOURCES OF QUALITY

This chapter has examined a number of possible contributors to successful quality performance. In some cases conventional wisdom has been undercut; in other cases it has been soundly supported. Overall, the following conclusions emerge:

- Design practices differed little at plants of varying quality performance, with one notable exception: Only the best and better quality plants used reliability engineering.
- The best and better quality plants generally offered narrower product lines than their competitors.
- Approaches to vendor selection differed little at plants of varying quality performance.
- The best and better quality plants all had formal programs to prevent degradation of supplier quality; the fair and poor plants did not.
- Receiving inspection procedures were based on statistical methods at the best and better quality plants but were *ad hoc* or ignored at fair and poor plants.
- Manufacturing processes differed little at plants of varying quality performance, with one notable exception: One of the best plants had invested heavily in innovative processes and equipment.
- Component failure rates were related to the sequence of assembly operations but to few other aspects of assembly line operation or design.
- Plants at all levels of quality performance experienced problems with bumping, changeovers, short production runs, and engineering change orders.

Together, these findings convey an imporant message: Superior quality is associated with well-defined management practices and not simply a supportive corporate culture. Design, purchasing, and manufacturing activities all play a role, but they must be accompanied by the right policies and attitudes. As the next chapter will show, a plant's perspective on quality is intimately related to its overall quality performance.

# Chapter
# 9

# Quality Policies and Attitudes

In traditional organizations, the quality department has primary responsibility for quality.[1] Tasks are assigned along functional lines, and specialization is the rule. Quality is treated no differently from marketing or sales: A separate department, staffed by its own experts, makes most of the critical decisions. In such settings, designers, purchasing agents, and production managers are considered peripheral to quality management, for their responsibilities lie elsewhere.

This approach to quality has serious flaws. As the previous chapter has shown, defect and field failure rates are strongly affected by design, vendor management, and production practices. In these areas, the quality department cannot proceed alone. But in other areas its mandate is clearer. Most quality departments house special skills in testing, inspection, and statistical analysis, and most are unusually well positioned to serve as clearinghouses for quality information, sources of feedback and advice, and counterweights to forces wishing to compromise quality to meet deadlines.

For these reasons, few companies are without quality departments. Their role and impact, however, remain unclear. Little is known about their day-to-day responsibilities or about their precise contributions to quality. For example, some quality departments are more effective than others. What accounts for their success? Which practices are critical and which are peripheral? Do superior quality performers differ from lesser performers in the tasks they assign to their quality departments?

In this chapter, as in the previous one, evidence from the U.S. room air conditioning industry is brought to bear on such questions.

The analysis follows the same basic pattern as before, with plants assigned to the same four categories of quality performance: best, better, fair, and poor. The first section examines the structure and operation of quality departments at plants in each quality category. Among the variables investigated are organizational form, reporting relationships, authority of the quality control manager, inspection and test procedures, quality audit activities, and quality information systems. Many of the most powerful conclusions are negative. A number of commonly cited explanations for superior quality—all related in some way to the activities of quality departments—prove to be of little importance in this industry. By contrast, management attitudes toward quality and a company's overall quality commitment are found to be strongly associated with quality; both are discussed at length in a separate section. The chapter then concludes with a series of quality profiles, summarizing the findings of Chapters 8 and 9 and sketching, with broad brush strokes, differences among the best, better, fair, and poor quality plants.

## QUALITY DEPARTMENTS

All plants in this industry had quality departments of some sort. Most were traditional quality control groups, but a few had broader responsibilities, holding sway over quality assurance or customer assurance. Reporting relationships were diverse. In some cases, quality had its own line of authority, reporting directly to the plant or division manager; in others, it reported through a separate function such as engineering or manufacturing. Several companies had appointed vice presidents or directors of quality, assigning them positions at the same level as the heads of engineering and manufacturing. Two plants, owned by the same company, had split quality control from quality assurance. The former reported to manufacturing and the latter to engineering. At these plants, quality control oversaw defect rates and manufacturing conformance, while quality assurance was in charge of audits and engineering tests.

None of these choices was related systematically to plants' quality performance. Vice presidents and directors of quality were found at both ends of the quality spectrum. At the best and better plants, no single reporting relationship was dominant. Broad, customer-related responsibilities were equally well distributed among the best and poorest plants. The same was true of department size. In this industry, bigger was not necessarily better. The number of people in a plant's quality department, measured in total or as a percentage of the plant labor force (direct plus indirect labor) was without clear pattern and failed to vary systematically with overall quality performance.[2]

But these choices were not without impact. In at least two cases, biases and miscommunication were introduced by having the quality department report through intermediaries. At one plant, the manager of quality audit observed that his boss, the vice president of engineering, did not like hearing that quality problems resulted from faulty designs. Faced with this pressure, he occasionally slanted his reports—especially in uncertain or gray areas where manufacturing was as likely to be responsible for problems as engineering—to make them more palatable. At another plant, where assembly line inspectors reported directly to the manufacturing department, the inspection supervisor was the only supervisor not invited to the department's daily production meetings, even though the plant's manufacturing manager claimed to be as concerned about quality as he was about cost and efficiency.

In both cases, a more powerful quality department might have been able to redress the balance in favor of quality. In such efforts, quality managers have normally had two tools at their disposal: hold orders and line shutdowns. Hold orders are issued only after end-of-the-line audits have uncovered serious deficiencies in units selected for review. Other units from the same production run are then impounded and "hold" tags attached; they cannot be shipped until the quality department is satisfied that they are free of defects. Additional inspection is usually necessary to prove that the impounded units are in compliance and the required remedial work has been performed. Line shutdowns are similar in philosophy but more drastic in impact. They occur when defects have risen so dramatically that quality managers insist on stopping the assembly line and idling workers so that problems can be identified and solved. Because they bring operations to a dead halt, line shutdowns are often actively resisted by manufacturing managers.

In the room air conditioning industry, all quality departments had the authority to issue hold orders. They exercised that power to varying degrees—four times per year at the best quality plant and 750 times per year at the worst. Yet even when holds were used rarely, quality managers cited their symbolic importance.[3] The right to halt shipments, they felt, provided both credibility and leverage: the ability to deal with recalcitrant departments from a position of strength.

Because hold orders were such a visible enforcement tool, few quality managers could imagine doing without them.

Manufacturing managers were often less enthusiastic. Some treated hold orders as grounds for immediate change, but many did their best to ignore or work around them. At two of the fair quality plants, manufacturing's usual reponse to a hold order was immediately to change over production to another model—"shuffling the problem," as a quality manager put it, "rather than solving it." Occasionally, quality departments were themselves responsible for the reduced impact of product holds. At two of the poorest plants, corrective action plans were nonexistent. Hold orders temporarily delayed shipments but had little other effect, because no attempt was made to uncover the source of problems or prevent their recurrence. According to the manufacturing manager at one of these plants: "The quality department seems to feel that 'if we catch the error, we've done our job.'"

Hold orders, then, were widely used in the room air conditioning industry but varied in effectiveness. Line shutdowns were less frequently used, although quality departments had the authority at eight of the eleven plants studied. The exceptions included one of the best and one of the better plants, where plant managers alone had the authority to stop production. At all of the plants studied, however, line shutdowns were rare. Five of the eight quality departments empowered to stop assembly lines had not done so in the previous year. In the same period, no plant had stopped its assembly lines for quality reasons more than eight times. Nor was there any association between the number of shutdowns and plants' overall quality performance.

In sum, the evidence in this section has provided little basis for distinguishing among levels of quality performance. The reporting relationship, responsibility, and authority of a company's quality department were unrelated to either defect or field failure rates. The only obvious link to quality performance was manufacturing's response to hold orders—whether it ignored or resisted them, as it did at the fair and poor plants, or initiated remedial action, as at the superior performers.


Inspection and Test Procedures

Traditionally, inspection and testing have been the raison d'être of quality professionals. The entire discipline is steeped in their history. Even today, many companies regard inspection and testing as the foundations of their quality programs, because they confine problems to the factory, reduce field failures, and provide information on design, vendor, and manufacturing problems that can be used to trigger remedial action. These attitudes were widespread in the room air conditioning industry and were reported, with few variations, by managers at all plants.

Inspection and test procedures, however, are not all alike. They differ in many of the same ways as manufacturing processes. Even when mature products are involved, managers have a range of approaches from which to choose. Capital can be substituted for labor, resulting in a more sophisticated test technology; large numbers of inspectors can be assigned to a fast-moving assembly line or smaller numbers to a slow one; and product performance can be monitored with a limited or lengthy list of criteria. For simplicity of analysis, all such differences in inspection and testing are reduced here to three elements: frequency, rigor, and sophistication. Frequency refers to how often an inspection or test is performed, rigor to how carefully the practice is conducted, and sophistication to the nature of the test and the associated equpment.

For the most part, similar tests were observed throughout the industry. All plants tested units for leaks in the course of production, and all checked product performance after final assembly. Calorimeter tests (to assess Btu capacity) were universal, largely because of a capacity certification program run by the industry's chief trade association. Shake and impact tests (to assess the resistance of units to handling damage) were also widespread. Only life tests (in which selected units were run in a test chamber for thousands of hours to assess their performance over time) were confined to a small number of plants.[4]

The frequency of these tests, however, differed among plants, but there was no clear pattern. Table 9.1 shows that the best quality performers did not always conduct the most tests. Calorimeter tests were most frequent at the best plants, but the average number of on-line leak tests was stable across quality categories. Shake and impact tests were most frequent at the better and fair plants.[5] Overall, the frequency of quality tests did not vary systematically with categories of quality performance.

A low frequency of tests, however, might be counterbalanced by more rigorous procedures. Frequency alone would then be an imperfect measure of test precision. For example, a plant with a large number of inspectors might be doing a more careful job than one with

TABLE 9.1  *Frequency of Quality Tests*

| Grouping of Companies by Quality Performance | Number of Leak Tests Along the Assembly Line | Number of Shake and Impact Tests per Day | | Number of Calorimeter Tests per Day | |
| --- | --- | --- | --- | --- | --- |
| | | Total | As Percentage of Daily Production | Total | As Percentage of Daily Production |
| Best U.S. plants | 2 | <1 | .02 | 8 | .8 |
| Better U.S. plants | 2 | 3 | .1 | 3 | .2 |
| Fair U.S. plants | 2 | 3 | .2 | 4 | .2 |
| Poor U.S. plants | 2 | 0 | 0 | 1 | .2 |

*Note:* All figures are averages (means) for the category.

SOURCE: Company records and questionnaires distributed by the author.

fewer inspectors, even though both conduct the same tests. In assessing product performance, plants might be observing a wide or narrow range of variables; their test results would convey different information. And on-line leak tests might be conducted with instruments of varying sensitivity, set according to perceptions of problem seriousness.[6]

None of these variables was of much help in distinguishing among categories of quality performance. For example, the smallest number of inspectors was found at both the best and poorest plants. As Table 9.2 indicates, that was true at all points on the production chain: receiving (incoming) inspection, subassembly (coil) inspection, and final assembly (assembly line) inspection.[7] Similarly, while plants employed a wide range of end-of-the-line performance tests, most differences were unrelated to quality levels. Tests varied in several ways: units were run from two to forty-five minutes before being checked; were tested in both open rooms and environments controlled for temperature and humidity; were run continuously at some plants but cycled on and off at others; and were checked for varying combinations of wattage, amperage, and fan speeds. There was no relationship between these variables and overall quality performance. Tests of short duration and controlled environments were observed at both the best and poorest plants; amperage and fan speeds were checked at most plants, but not at several of the best and better performers; and units were cycled on and off during tests at only two plants—one of the fair and one of the poorest performers. Based on this evidence, plants that claimed superior quality because they ran tests for longer periods or because they tested for a larger number of variables were simply in error.

TABLE 9.2   *Inspection Intensity*

| Grouping of Companies by Quality Performance | Number of Receiving Inspectors | Number of Coil Inspectors | Number of Assembly Line Inspectors |
|---|---|---|---|
| Best U.S. plants | 2 | 1 | 6 |
| Better U.S. plants | 5 | 3 | 9 |
| Fair U.S. plants | 4 | 8 | 16 |
| Poor U.S. plants | 2 | 3 | 8 |

*Note:* All figures are averages (means) for the category.

SOURCE: Company records and questionnaires distributed by the author.

In fact, the opposite was often true: The shortest tests were conducted by the best and better plants. They were usually the most sophisticated tests as well. Three plants had designed their own test equipment, using innovative approaches rather than off-the-shelf equipment. Both of the best plants had assigned process engineers to their quality departments, with responsibility for test equipment design and development. Their presence, according to one quality manager, gave his department "control over its own destiny." In addition, computerized or automatic test equipment was used whenever possible at the best and better plants, to minimize mistakes. Consistency was considered to be as important in test procedures as it was in manufacturing; and the less human judgment involved, the better the expected results. Sophisticated equipment also enabled these plants to test for variables ignored by lesser performers, such as the temperature differential between air going in and coming out of the system and the amount of air being delivered by the fan and blower wheel. Differences in test sophistication carried over to other points in the assembly process as well. The most primitive assembly-line leak tests, for example—dipping a unit in water and checking for air bubbles—were found only at the three poorest plants, while the most sophisticated technique—helium mass spectrometry—was limited to one of the best and one of the better plants.

Overall, this section has observed few links between quality performance and the traditional role and activities of quality departments. Neither the number of quality tests, the number of variables checked, nor the frequency of inspections varied systematically by quality categories. More sophisticated test equipment, however, was observed at the best and better plants, as well as process engineers dedicated to test equipment design and development.

## Quality Audits

Quality audits normally occur after final assembly is complete and involve the careful inspection of a small number of units. In Chapter 7 they were found to be of great help in determining whether production processes were out of control but of little use in predicting defect or field failure rates. Every plant in the industry relied on audits to some extent. Most employed similar approaches: a rating scheme for classifying audit problems by seriousness and a combination of visual, dimensional, and performance tests for reviewing units.

There were pronounced differences among plants, however, in the care and sophistication of audit procedures. Practices at the best and better plants were clearly superior. At one of these plants, audit problems triggered an educational process in which line workers were brought to the audit area to review units and discuss ways of avoiding future problems; at another, the audit area was called the "customer assurance laboratory," and tests, including one in which units were mounted in makeshift windows before testing, were carefully designed to simulate conditions of actual use; at a third, units that the audit group found to be "dead on arrival" (that is, unable to operate) were mounted prominently in a display area outside the cafeteria, accompanied by explanations of the problems found. These efforts shared a common goal, despite their apparent diversity: They sought to increase employees' sensitivity to quality and to avoid repeated mistakes.[8]

By contrast, audit activities at the poorest plants were limited in scope. Their primary goal was to keep faulty units from escaping the factory, not to control production processes. At one plant, the quality manager described his audit activities as "final, last-gasp inspection." Procedures were informal and loosely defined. Two plants, for example, were without seriousness rating schemes, and simply tallied up the number of daily problems. Their reports gave little insight into the composition and impact of problems and were of little use in monitoring quality performance over time. Two plants relied primarily on visual inspections, with few performance tests; in one case units were not even checked against engineering drawings. Moreover, all of the poor plants conducted audits infrequently or with little planning. At one plant audits were scheduled for only eight units per week. One unit per day was examined visually, while one every other day was tested operationally. At another plant, the quality manager explained that, because he had only a single auditor, not every assembly line could be audited with the same care. He decided on the number of units to be audited per line using informal, *ad hoc* procedures: "It's done by ear. If you know who the roving inspector is, and who the lead man is, you can almost smell the problems before they happen."

Overall, approaches to quality audits were closely related to levels of quality performance. The best and better plants employed a variety of innovative techniques for feeding audit results back to the work force and developing sensitivity to quality. Poor plants audited units less frequently, assigned fewer employees to the task, and relied on less rigorous tests, inspections, and reporting schemes. Fair plants fell between the two extremes.

Quality Information Systems

Without accurate and timely information, quality control is impossible. Remedial action requires an understanding of problems and their causes, just as improvement programs require a baseline for measuring progress. Timeliness is important as well, for if information is provided quickly enough, problems can be recognized and corrected before they recur a second or third time. Data must also be in the right hands; otherwise, an acknowledged problem may not be solved because authority is lacking or communication is inadequate.

Quality information systems can therefore be judged on multiple criteria: the specificity and detail of their data, the rapidity of feedback, and the level in the organization at which information is reported.[9] Equally important is the distinction between in-plant and field quality. The two will not necessarily be governed by the same information system. One deals with factory matters, and the other involves customers. In the room air conditioning industry, defect and service call rates (SCRs) were, for this reason, handled by different groups, with separate lines of authority, employing their own sets of data.

*Service Call Rates.* Data on service calls, the industry's primary measure of field performance, were reported at much higher levels and in much greater detail at plants with superior quality. At the poorest plants, such information was seldom available. SCRs were not tracked on a regular basis, but only through special studies conducted every few years.[10] By then, small problems had often become "epidemics," common to a large proportion of all units. Design flaws remained undetected. At one plant nearly a quarter of all 1979–81 warranty expenses came from problems with a single type of compressor. In such circumstances, to quote the German philosopher Hegel, "Hell is truth seen too late."

Other plants reported more extensive quality information, but with varying degrees of detail. Among fair performers, reports were quite general. Data on field failures were usually reported for entire product lines rather than for individual models. Without further refinement, such data are of limited use, for they fail to isolate quality problems. As engineers at several plants pointed out, a 10 percent failure rate for a product line can mean any number of things: that all models in the line fail to perform 10 percent of the time, with no single problem standing out; that several models have a 5 percent failure rate and one a 30 percent rate, suggesting a single problem of epidemic proportions; or anything in between. There is no way of distinguishing such cases from aggregate data alone.

But if the problem was recognized by engineers, why was it not addressed? Largely, it turns out, because of organizational barriers: the separation of service activities from engineering and manufacturing. Two of the fair performers, for example, were manufacturers alone. Sales and service were handled by separate organizations, with their own staffs and facilities. Interactions between the groups were rare. Moreover, SCRs were reported to manufacturers with a considerable lag—as long as twelve to fourteen months—and early figures, based on projections, suffered from constant revision. In that environment, most engineers preferred to judge quality by in-plant measures, such as audit results, rather than by SCRs, in which they had little faith. According to one vice president of engineering: "If you're asking why we're not [pushing for modifications in the SCR reporting system], it's probably because we don't think it's that important."

By contrast, the best and better plants generally had sophisticated computer systems that tracked field failures by individual models and components.[11] To ensure rapid feedback, several plants had developed early warning systems that projected SCRs from limited data, sometimes using elaborate statistical methods. "Red flags" were raised whenever early returns suggested that problems might be widespread—in one case, when failure rates were as low as 0.5 percent. Supplementary information was collected from telephone hot lines, distributors, service engineers, and warranty files that listed by type the total number of parts replaced under warranty. Even more important, failure data did not languish at low levels of these organizations, as it often did at lesser performers. Rather, SCR reports were sent directly to the top, where they were reviewed by presidents, division managers, and plant managers.

*Defect Rates.* Information on defect rates was collected and discussed by all plants in the industry. Reporting systems were quite similar, with most plants aggregating the results of individual inspection stations into daily or weekly summaries covering the entire assembly line. The poorest performers, however, were again lacking. One of them saw no reason to compute total defect rates and was monitoring production by audit results alone, while another had been tallying defect totals for only a few months. Neither plant scheduled regular meetings of manufacturing or quality managers to review defect results. At most other plants, meetings were held at least once a week, and sometimes daily. Most plants also sent defect reports to the same level in the organization: the vice president of operations, manufacturing, quality, or engineering. In only two cases were they also reported regularly to division or plant managers, but these were the two best plants in the industry.

Quality information systems, then, varied closely with levels of quality performance. A composite index summarizing the key elements of these systems was strongly related to a plant's level of quality; it appears in Appendix C. As with vendor management, a series of mutually reinforcing practices provided the best results. Superior performers collected more detailed data, reported it at higher levels of the organization, and employed more sophisticated methods, especially for SCRs, where early warning systems ensured rapid feedback. Poor plants, by contrast, were ill-informed about quality. They often lacked critical data and failed to summarize it in a useful fashion.

Together, the evidence in this section and the preceding ones permits a portrait of effective quality departments. In this industry, quality departments at the best and better plants were not distinguished by such traditional variables as large size, a large number of inspectors, a particular organizational form, the power to issue hold orders or stop the assembly line, or the range of performance tests. Rather, they were notable for their effectiveness in managing and monitoring information about quality. At the superior performers, in-line test equipment, quality audits, and quality information systems were sophisticated and innovative. Data were tracked in fine detail. And information was fed back quickly to interested parties, including designers, shop floor employees, and high-level managers. As the next section will show, the involvement of high-level managers was especially critical to long-term success. For it is they—and they alone—who have the power to shape continuing commitments to quality and sustain them in difficult times.

## MANAGEMENT ATTITUDES

By now it is almost an article of faith among quality experts: Successful quality performance requires a management dedicated to that goal.[12] Without commitment at the highest levels, such objectives as delivery and cost are thought to take precedence. All too often, the result is an "us versus them" attitude that pits quality control against production.

But if top management embraces quality, these tensions are thought to be reduced. Little empirical work, however, has been done to confirm this view. Nor have the specifics of management communication and direction-setting been studied carefully. Some messages about quality are more effective than others, yet little is known about how employees distinguish among them. Are policy statements, for example, enough to demonstrate management's seriousness? Will slogans and banners suffice? Or are tangible actions and personal participation required if quality is to improve?

### Setting Direction

In the room air conditioning industry, most successful quality initiatives were driven from above. Often a major event, such as sharply rising costs or a new plant opening, was the trigger. Top management then stepped in and seized control. At the best and better plants, it sent signals that were clear and unambiguous. For example, at one company service costs had been rising steadily for a number of years while managers had been doing little to improve the situation. Action came only after the chairman, faced with another set of depressing projections, had exploded: "I've been talking about quality, but it obviously hasn't gotten anywhere. Now we'll tell people what to do." A new program was in place within months, and service call rates quickly began to fall. At another firm, a group executive was the first to recognize the side effects of mushrooming volume: deteriorating quality and a progressive loss of control. His response was to create a new position, the vice president of quality and reliability systems, reporting directly to him, and to staff it with a manager experienced in the more demanding world of aerospace. Together the two developed an elaborate quality system, supported by policy statements from the president's office, that sharply reduced field problems.

Such highly visible efforts were not always necessary. At one of the best plants, the importance of quality had been signaled unmistakably, but with little fanfare, even before the factory was opened—when the plant manager was hired. His background spoke volumes about the new plant's priorities: In a previous job he had been a quality control manager.[13]

Of course, starting a quality program on the right foot does not guarantee its long-term success. Sustained commitment is required as well. For that purpose, slogans and banners are not enough; they were used extensively only at one of the fair plants and played a minor role elsewhere. Nor were exhortations and speeches of much benefit. Plants at all levels of quality claimed to have spoken with their employees about improved performance. Rather, at the best and better plants success was associated with visible demonstrations of management commitment and activities that took time from busy schedules.[14] At one company, weekly quality meetings were attended by the president; the vice presidents of manufacturing, materials, quality, and service; product planners; and the chief engineer. Their purpose was to identify critical field problems and ensure that they received immediate attention. At another company, monthly quality meetings were held for the same purpose; they were chaired by the division general manager. At a third firm, top managers were cycled through the company's telephone hot lines, where they logged calls from customers and spent hours discussing reliability and service; service call reports were also sent each month directly to the president. His interest was highly visible. When the reports were returned to the director of service, they had been covered with annotations and questions.

These examples all show active quality leadership by top management. Responsibility for quality was not delegated to lower levels, nor was it expected to take care of itself without monitoring and proper incentives. In fact, in most cases top management insisted on supplementary measures to heighten their organizations' sensitivity to quality. The most important of these measures was goal-setting: the development of annual, quantitative goals for defect and field failure rates.[15] Only the best and better plants had developed systematic goals and evaluated managers against them.[16] Because of their link to personal performance, the goals ensured a deep and continuing commitment to quality improvement. By contrast, managers at many of the lesser performers were uninterested in quality, and at times actively hostile. Such behavior was perfectly consistent with the incentives they faced. Two of the three poorest plants, for example, paid workers on the basis of total output, not defect-free output. Managers had similar goals. Is it any wonder that they viewed defects as being of little consequence?

### Manufacturing Versus Quality

The last example highlights a pervasive organizational problem: the tension between manufacturing and quality departments. Manufacturing managers have historically been driven by cost and output goals; for them, "making the [production] numbers" has been the name of the game. The room air conditioning industry clearly fits the pattern. Table 9.3 shows that first-line supervisors in this industry felt that a single goal, meeting the production schedule, predominated over all other manufacturing objectives.[17] The same perspective was acknowledged by middle managers. One observed that in his organization the manager of operations had long been first among equals; he could say "don't worry about the problem; let's run it" without fear of being overruled by the quality manager. Another noted that production managers at his plant were concerned primarily with line efficiency; as a result, "the pressure for quality came from the director of quality and his staff." A third commented that his manufacturing managers usually looked the other way when

TABLE 9.3   *Quality Attitudes as Perceived by First-Line Supervisors*

| | Weight that Management Attaches to the Manufacturing Objective of: | | | |
|---|---|---|---|---|
| | *Meeting the Production Schedule* | *Producing High-Quality (Defect-Free) Products* | *Low-Cost Production* | *Improving Worker Productivity* |
| Best U.S. plants | 6.5 | 6.2 | 6.4 | 6.3 |
| Better U.S. plants | 6.5 | 6.1 | 5.8 | 5.9 |
| Fair U.S. plants | 6.5 | 5.7 | 5.5 | 5.4 |
| Poor U.S. plants | 6.4 | 5.4 | 6.0 | 5.5 |
| All U.S. plants | 6.5 | 5.9 | 5.9 | 5.8 |

*Note:* Items were scored by supervisors on a 1 to 7 scale, with 1 indicating the least weight or concern and 7 indicating the most. All scores are averages (means) for the category.

SOURCE: Questionnaires distributed by the author.

quality problems came up. Action came only when it was unavoidable: "It's only when defective units have to go on the floor [because repair holds had already been filled with defective units] that something gets done."

In each of these cases, intense production pressures were the norm.[18] Manufacturing managers were not opposed to quality *per se;* rather, they were responding rationally to incentives pointing in another direction. That was true at all plants in the industry, for tensions between manufacturing and quality were common even at superior performers.[19] They too acknowledged the critical role of the production schedule and its perennial conflict with defect-free operation. But if the same conflicts were observed at both superior and poor plants, an obvious question arises: Were their attitudes toward quality really all that different?

According to Table 9.3, the answer is yes. The strength of management's (perceived) quality commitment was closely tied to plants' overall quality performance.[20] Even though conflicts between manufacturing and quality were as likely at superior performers as at lesser plants, the former's commitment to quality was perceived to be significantly higher. At the best and better plants, meeting the production schedule remained the primary goal, but because of the backing of top managers, quality had established its own secure beachhead.

## PROFILES IN QUALITY

To round out the room air conditioning study, a summing up is now required: a way of consolidating earlier findings and distinguishing plants from one another. A series of quality profiles serves that pur pose. Each focuses on one or two categories of quality performance and outlines the policies, practices, and attitudes that have accounted for success or failure.

### Best and Better Plants

Plants in the top two categories had similar approaches to quality. Their managements were strongly committed to the subject and had often initiated improvement programs. Commitment was equally evident at lower levels, supported by policies such as the annual setting of quality goals. Selected quality practices were also superior to those of the rest of the industry. Quality information systems were more detailed and responsive and reported to higher levels; test equipment was more advanced; and quality audits were more innovative and complete. But in other respects, quality departments at these companies were little different from the norm. Rather, these plants succeeded in quality largely because of their approaches to the day-to-day details of design, purchasing, and production. A focus on reliability engineering encouraged careful designs; hit lists for problem vendors, statistical sampling at receiving inspection, and active purchasing departments ensured tight control of suppliers; and narrow product lines and long production runs reduced the number of shop-floor errors. Together, these efforts provided tangible support for management's commitment to quality.

In most of these areas, best and better plants were much alike. Differences were largely matters of intensity or degree—for example, slightly stronger commitment or slightly narrower product lines. In combination, these incremental differences yielded substantial gains. The best plants, however, stood out in another respect as well: their unswerving devotion to a single concept, pursued with great intensity. Each tried to do one thing unusually well. In one case, it was reliability engineering, and in the other, it was superior process design and innovative technology and equipment. In these areas, the best plants were leagues ahead of their competitors.

Yet, despite their superiority in this industry, neither of the best plants was a full-fledged practitioner of strategic quality management. While several elements of the strategic approach were evident—for example, top management involvement and the setting of quality goals—others were weak or nonexistent. In particular, neither of the best plants approached quality from the customer's point of view. They were interested primarily in cost reduction and problem-solving, rather than increased customer satisfaction. Market research on quality was rare. And because there were pockets of resistance in both organizations, wholesale commitment to quality had not yet been attained. Thus, even though they were leaders in their own industry, these plants did not represent the very best American practice. They lagged behind such companies as Hewlett-Packard, Xerox, and Corning Glass, whose approaches to quality, described in Chapter 2, were more comprehensive and strategic.

## Fair Plants

In most respects, the fair plants fell in the middle of the pack. Their managers and workers, for example, were only moderately committed to quality. Formal quality goals were lacking, and decision-making was driven primarily by the production schedule. Other policies did little to elevate the importance of quality. Quality information systems were slow and highly aggregated; in several cases they were actively resisted. Quality audits provided only limited oversight. Designs failed to include reliability engineering, and purchasing practices were often loosely organized. Hit lists were not used to track problem vendors, nor was receiving inspection based on statistical sampling. Production and test equipment were standard for the industry. At these plants, quality was not ignored, but compared to the best and better plants, it was much less of a concern.

## Poor Plants

At the poor plants, quality was a very low priority. Neither management nor workers gave it much attention. Incentives, in fact, often pointed in the opposite direction, encouraging volume production and rapid shipments at the expense of quality. Remedial action was limited because quality information was often nonexistent. Service call rates, for example, were not tracked on a regular basis, nor were quality audits frequent enough to provide tight control. Problem vendors were dealt with *ad hoc,* if at all; receiving inspection was thinly staffed and without statistical rationale; and testing methods were often unsophisticated. Quality was seldom managed in a structured way. In most cases, it became important only after problems had reached epidemic proportions. As a manager at one of these plants observed: "If nobody has complained about our quality, we assume it's okay." Yet even after problems were uncovered, quality initiatives often met great resistance. Change was slow, because engineers and manufacturing managers had other priorities. Quality was not high on their lists, even though the issues they faced, like short production runs, frequent changeovers, and proliferating product lines, were intimately related to it. At the poor plants, quality improvement was limited as much by imperfect knowledge as it was by lack of interest.

Together, these four profiles paint a clear picture of quality management in the U.S. room air conditioning industry. They show how practices, policies, and attitudes varied systematically from the best to the poorest plants. But for all their value, the profiles are limited in an important respect: They are confined to U.S plants. A fifth category, Japanese plants, must now be introduced, for it represents even higher levels of quality. To provide some background, the next chapter reviews the history of the Japanese quality movement and contrasts it with the American quality movement described in Chapter 1. Chapter 11 then considers the contributors to Japanese quality in more detail, drawing again on data collected from the room air conditioning industry.

# Part III

# Japanese Quality Management

# Chapter
## 10

# The Japanese Quality Movement

Today the Japanese seem to have cornered the market on product quality. Names like Nikon, Sony, and Toyota have become synonymous with superior quality and reliability, and "made in Japan" is now a mark of distinction. But these developments are relatively recent. In the early postwar period, Japanese manufacturers were known primarily for inferior quality. One Japanese expert recalls those days as "the age of 'cheap and poor' products."[1] Since that time, however, a remarkable transformation has taken place—to the point where quality has become a national obsession in Japan. How that transformation was accomplished, and especially how the Japanese quality movement differed from its U.S. counterpart, are the subjects of this chapter.

## PREWAR QUALITY CONTROL

Before 1945 Japan's quality efforts were limited primarily to inspection. Statistical quality control techniques were known but seldom applied. Control charts, for example, were used as early as 1929 at the electric light bulb factory of Shibaura Electric Ltd.; four years later they were used to develop the standard specification for the incandescent bulb.[2] But there were few other early applications. For the most part, statistical quality control remained a technical oddity in the 1930s and 1940s, of interest to only a small circle of experts.[3]

The same was true of early efforts to develop quality standards. The standardization movement began in Japan about 1910, and Japanese Engineering Standards were first established in 1921. A number of British and American quality standards were later studied by Japanese scholars; a few were then translated for wider use during World War II. But they had only slight impact.[4] Japanese quality remained poor, and most design, production, and quality control practices were haphazard and uncoordinated. It was only after the war that real changes began, stimulated in large part by U.S. advisers.

## THE AMERICAN ROLE

Quality control techniques have been one of America's most successful exports. They have been warmly received around the world, and no more so than in Japan, where they have been carried by a succession of American statisticians, engineers, anad management theorists. W. Edwards Deming is the most famous of the group, but he is far from the only one. The earliest such counsel, in fact, was provided by a little-known group within the Allied command, the Civil Communications Section (CCS).

### The Civil Communications Section

Within a month of Japan's surrender, the CCS was established within General Headquarters, the Supreme Commander for the Allied Forces.[5] A small part of it, the Industrial Division, was soon assigned the task of working with Japanese manufacturers of communications equipment to improve production methods. Quality control quickly became a principal concern, and for obvious reasons: the poor reliability of the national communications network. But the Industrial Division's key engineers—W. S. Magil, Frank Polkinghorn, Charles Protzman, and Homer Sarasohn—were also unusually sensitive to the issue. Each had worked previously at Western Electric or Bell Laboratories, the birthplaces of American quality control. (Magil, in fact, is sometimes regarded as the father of statistical quality control in Japan. He first advocated its use in a lecture in 1945–46 and successfully applied its techniques to vacuum tube production at NEC in 1946.)[6]

Between 1945 and 1949 these engineers pursued such varied activities as upgrading Japanese working environments, establishing the Electrical Testing Laboratory to certify that quality standards were being met, and advising Japanese business leaders on questions of production management. This last need was especially acute, and in 1949–50 it led to the famous CCS seminars. These were courses on industrial management, lasting eight weeks, to which only (newly appointed) top executives in the communications industry were invited. They were offered by the CCS twice—once in Tokyo and once in Osaka—but proved so popular that they were reinstituted under Japanese leadership when the Allied command was disbanded and continued for twenty-four more years.

The CCS seminars were comprehensive in scope but had a single, dominant theme: the principles of Scientific Management. Factory operations received the greatest attention, for it was there that CCS engineers felt the most improvement was necessary. Quality was emphasized throughout the course. The seminar began, for example, by citing the need for statements of company philosophy, and then referred pointedly to the philosophy of Newport News Shipyard:

> We shall build good ships here
> At a profit if we can
> At a loss if we must
> But, always good ships.[7]

The course manual then continued: "The primary objective of the company is to put the quality of the product ahead of any other consideration. A profit or loss notwithstanding, the emphasis will always be on quality."[8] This message was reinforced by lengthy discussions of quality control practices and techniques throughout the seminar.

Other sections of the course introduced concepts that are now routinely cited as Japanese. Leadership, for example, was defined in soft, nondirective terms: "A leader's main obligation is to secure the faith and respect of those under him."[9] Participative approaches were encouraged: "If we who are paying these people for working with us could foster that desire to participate, what a profitable undertaking it would be."[10] Bottom-up management, with responsibility assigned to lower levels, was endorsed enthusiastically: "The people at lower levels who should be responsible and accountable for . . . these detailed functions are confused by the lack of proper definition of their job . . . any initiative and interest they may have in trying to do a job is often destroyed by the interference and meddling of higher management."[11]

The CCS seminars had a powerful impact on Japan's postwar approach to manufacturing. A number of quality control pioneers attended the earliest seminars; they continued to cite them decades later as sources of inspiration and support. The Japanese Industrial and Vocational Training Association has for years listed the course in its number one place of honor, even though it has not been offered since 1974. Moreover, because of purges by the Allies, new Japanese executives had only recently gained control of their companies when the course was first offered. Many were therefore open to immediate advice. The seminars were also unusually well attuned to Japanese interests and concerns. Such CCS themes as participative management and attentiveness to quality have become part of the fabric of Japanese industry. There are echoes of CCS principles in such Japanese innovations as quality control circles. Much the same is true of the quality initiatives introduced a short time later by three other Americans: W. Edwards Deming, Joseph M. Juran, and Armand V. Feigenbaum.

### Deming, Juran, and Feigenbaum

Deming was the first of the three to arrive in Japan. At the invitation of the Union of Japanese Scientists and Engineers (JUSE), he presented an eight-day seminar on quality control in 1950; it was so well received that he returned again in 1951 and 1952. Today Deming is regarded as a national hero in Japan. Not only has he been awarded the Second Order of the Sacred Treasure, Japan's premier Imperial honor, but the Deming Prize for quality, which carries his name (and was originally funded by royalties from the book based on his 1950 lectures), has become one of the country's highest industrial honors.[12]

Deming's message to the Japanese was primarily statistical: a rigorous and systematic approach to solving quality problems. That was in keeping with his professional background and training. Deming's Ph.D. was in physics, but his special expertise was in sampling techniques, which he had applied at both the U.S. Department of Agriculture and the Bureau of the Census. Moreover, Deming was a leading disciple of W. A. Shewhart, the Bell Laboratories statistician introduced in Chapter 1, whose book, *Economic Control of Quality of Manufactured Product,* had revolutionized the field of quality control. In 1934 Deming had expanded on Shewhart's ideas in a paper of his own, "On the Statistical Theory of Errors," which later became an integral part of his lectures to the Japanese.[13]

Like Shewhart, Deming urged managers to focus on problems of variability and their causes. He was especially concerned with separating "special causes," assignable to individual operators or machines, from "common causes," like faulty raw materials, that were shared by various operations and were management's responsibility. Statistical techniques—primarily, process control charts—were proposed for distinguishing between the two.[14] But Deming's lectures extended beyond mere statistics. He encouraged the Japanese to adopt a systematic approach to problem-solving—what later became known as as the Plan, Do, Check, Action (PDCA) or Deming cycle. He pushed top managers to become actively involved in their companies' quality improvement programs. And he introduced the Japanese to modern methods of consumer research, combining door-to-door surveys by participants in his courses with exposure to rigorous sampling techniques.[15]

From Deming, Japanese engineers and managers learned the rudiments of statistical quality control. They responded with enormous enthusiasm, especially at the factory level. Applications spread rapidly, encouraged by well-publicized success stories. But soon problems arose: employee resistance, lack of technical standards, and insufficient data.[16] Even more serious, not all managers understood the roles they had to play in quality improvement. The theories of two other American quality experts, Joseph Juran and Armand Feigenbaum, proved to be instrumental in combating these problems.

Like Deming, Juran was invited to Japan by the Union of Japanese Scientists and Engineers. He arrived in 1954 and conducted seminars for top- and mid-level executives.[17] His lectures had a strong managerial flavor and focused on planning, organizational issues, management's responsibility for quality, and the need to set goals and targets for improvement.[18] About the same time, the work of Armand Feigenbaum was discovered by the Japanese. First in his role as head of quality at General Electric, where he had extensive contacts with such companies as Hitachi and Toshiba, and then in translations of his books (*Quality Control: Principles, Practices, and Administration,* 1954) and articles ("Total Quality Control," 1956), Feigenbaum argued for a systemic or total approach to quality.[19] As Chapter 1 has indicated, that approach required the involvement of all functions in the quality process, and not simply manufacturing. Otherwise, quality would be inspected and controlled after the fact and not built in at an early stage.

Together, Juran and Feigenbaum awakened the Japanese to the

less statistical aspects of quality management. They were the last of a small but influential breed: U.S. management experts who personally shaped Japan's postwar approach to quality. With Deming and the engineers of the Civil Communications Section, they introduced advanced American methods and techniques, communicated their importance to managers and workers, and assisted in their implementation. Their impact was both profound and long-lasting. According to several scholars, even today "Japanese businessmen may well understand American management theory better, and implement it more faithfully, than almost anyone else."[20]

Nevertheless, the role of these experts should not be exaggerated. They alone do not explain Japan's quality revolution, for their ideas, while powerful, were preached elsewhere to little effect. Juran, for example, has commented:

> A segment of the Western press has come up with the conclusion that the Japanese miracle was not Japanese at all. Instead it was due to two Americans, Deming and Juran, who lectured to the Japanese soon after World War II. Deming will have to speak for himself. As for Juran, I am agreeably flattered but I regard the conclusion as ludicrous. I did indeed lecture in Japan as reported, and I did bring something new to them—a structured approach to quality. I also did the same thing for a great many other countries, yet none of these attained the results achieved by the Japanese. So who performed the miracle?[21]

Americans may have been the catalyst, as Juran notes, but the Japanese ultimately developed a quality movement that was uniquely their own. Several of the most important innovations came in the late 1950s and early 1960s; the seeds, however, were planted a decade before.

## CONSOLIDATION AND DIFFUSION

One of the most distinctive features of the Japanese quality movement has been its national focus. New ideas have diffused rapidly throughout the country. Success stories have been quickly publicized; the latest techniques have been translated almost immediately into training programs; and the same philosophy and approaches have emerged in industries as diverse as electronics and steel. The overwhelming impression is one of unity and purpose, with the entire nation moving en masse toward the goal of improved quality. Much of that unity can be traced to two sources: Japanese Industrial Standards and the Union of Japanese Scientists and Engineers.

### Japanese Industrial Standards

Japan's standardization movement began in earnest immediately after World War II. During the war, a number of temporary standards had emerged under the auspices of the Japanese Engineering Standards Committee (JESC), but they were simple in procedure and content, and had only slight impact. In 1945 the Japanese Standards Association was formed; it was joined the following year by a new governmental body, the Japanese Industrial Standards Committee, which replaced the JESC. The monthly journal *Standards and Norms* (*Kikaku to Hyojun*) was also first published in 1946. In 1949 the Industrial Standardization Law was passed; it led, a year later, to the first Japanese Industrial Standards (JIS). These proliferated rapidly, and by 1952 about 2,500 were in place. By 1980 their number had risen to more than 7,600.[22]

Standardization was a key vehicle for consolidating the Japanese quality movement. It provided uniformity and guidance, centered on a common pool of knowledge. As one Japanese expert has noted, "Standards constitute . . . the systematic accumulation of know-how which technology has built up."[23] In this respect, the Japanese approach differed little from standardization programs elsewhere.[24] Standards were first established through the cooperative efforts of government and industry, and compliance was voluntary. Most Japanese firms, however—especially in the 1950s and 1960s—felt compelled to obtain JIS certification in order to gain consumers' confidence.[25] It was the accompanying certification process that gave Japan's standardization movement its uniqueness and special force.

The entire process was coordinated by a department within the Ministry of International Trade and Industry (MITI). To verify compliance, production methods were assessed in addition to product characteristics. Moreover, an explicit objective of the program was to ensure that effective quality control systems were in place:

> [The] JIS Mark certification system . . . provides an effective means of promoting the use of industrial standards, as well as [a] way to promote the introduction of effective quality control methods at the factory level. The use of [the] JIS Mark shall be approved by the competent Minister only to the manufacturers or processors who are

> proven to have [a] high level of quality control practices to produce
> a designated commodity stably and regularly in conformity with the
> respective standards.[26]

Thus, JIS certification was contingent on a firm's possessing acceptable quality control procedures. These were assessed by auditing teams from MITI or other competent ministries, which conducted in-plant inspections after factories requested certification. Among other things, the teams evaluated a firm's quality control organization, its testing and inspection procedures, the condition of its production equipment, its maintenance procedures, and its education and training programs in the area of quality.[27] Because the application of statistical quality control techniques was considered critical, it received special attention.[28]

These efforts ensured the rapid spread of modern quality control methods within Japan. The JIS Mark quickly gained respect, and by 1981 more than 14,600 factories had been approved to display it.[29] JIS brought unity to Japan's quality movement and an increase in both legitimacy and coordination. A similar role was played by the Union of Japanese Scientists and Engineers (JUSE), a nongovernmental organization founded shortly after World War II.

### The Union of Japanese Scientists and Engineers

JUSE was established in 1946 as a nonprofit foundation, bringing together scientists and engineers from universities, government agencies, and business. Many of its members had previously belonged to the Greater Japan Engineering Association, which was dissolved by the Allies immediately after World War II. Originally, JUSE planned to study foreign technology and promote its use in Japan; its focus, however, soon narrowed to the themes of quality and reliability. It pursued these subjects through a combination of research, technical consulting, education and training programs, and promotional activities.[30]

In 1948, for example, JUSE launched one of Japan's earliest studies of statistical quality control. A year later it created a Quality Control Research Group and began offering a basic course in quality control techniques. The course met three days a month for an entire year and was aimed primarily at practicing engineers. An original text, written by the Quality Control Research Group, was later developed. In 1950 JUSE began publishing its own journal, *Statistical*

*Quality Control* (*Hinshitsu Kanri*), focusing on the same issues. Between 1950 and 1954 it was actively involved in promoting and arranging the lectures of Deming and Juran.[31]

These efforts were enormously successful. JUSE's Quality Control Research Group, for example, quickly gained prominence as the nation's leading authority on quality control methods and techniques. Its programs were well attended, and its advice was eagerly sought. The Deming Prize, which JUSE administered, won national acclaim. On matters of quality, the organization was soon accepted as the chief link among Japan's public, private, and university sectors.

Such early—and continuing—effectiveness reflected JUSE's stature within the business community. A small number of influential leaders were chiefly responsible. JUSE's founder and first chairman, for example, was Ichiro Ishikawa, a distinguished industrialist who served from 1948 to 1956 as the chairman of Keidanren (Japanese Federation of Economic Organizations), the most powerful business association in Japan. Ishikawa mobilized support for JUSE's activities but, even more important, set a vital precedent: Since his tenure, the chairman of JUSE has always been either a current or former chairman of Keidanren.[32]

The links between JUSE and Japan's business establishment were thus formed early. Continued credibility was provided by Ishikawa's son, Kaoru, who for many years served as JUSE's secretary general and supplied much of its intellectual leadership. Kaoru was one of the founding members of the organization's Quality Control Research Group; a pioneer in statistical methods; the author of several leading texts on quality control; and a great believer in the need for broader quality education and training. In 1956 he arranged to have the Japan Shortwave Broadcasting Corporation air a QC correspondence course for foremen; it proved so successful that the Japan National Broadcasting Corporation (NHK) began offering a QC series on its educational television channel the next year. Eventually 110,000 copies of the accompanying text were sold.[33]

Through such efforts, JUSE was instrumental in popularizing the concepts of quality control. It tackled the problem on many fronts: collecting company success stories and publicizing them at national and regional conferences; publishing a wide range of journals and books; promoting and administering Japan's national Quality Month; and coordinating international study missions to review best practices abroad.[34] Because of its tight links to the business establishment and the credibility of its independent professional staff, JUSE was highly visible and its activities were well regarded. It was thus able to serve as a focal point for change. In fact, JUSE's leaders played an important role in the development of both quality control circles (QCCs or QC circles) and company-wide quality control (CWQC), two of Japan's chief innovations in quality management.

## JAPANESE INNOVATIONS

The 1940s and 1950s were periods of rebuilding and consolidation for Japanese quality control. New techniques were imported from the United States, studied carefully, and then applied in a wide range of settings. Statistical tools received the primary emphasis; they produced great improvements in factory operations. In fact, the Deming Prize at the time was based almost exclusively on excellence in process control. Most early approaches to quality were therefore confined to manufacturing, guided by engineers or managers with a technical bent. Neither low-level employees nor managers outside of manufacturing had much involvement.[35] That problem was soon recognized. In response, JUSE promoted Juran's lectures and developed its own publicly broadcast lectures on quality control. Pronounced change, however, came only a decade later, when quality control circles and company-wide quality control finally took hold in Japan.

### Quality Control Circles

JUSE's efforts to educate foremen and shop-floor employees in the basics of quality control were a first step in creating quality control circles. They dovetailed neatly with the philosophy of the CCS seminars and the recommendations of a 1957 MITI report recounting the problems of supervisors in Japan. The report included the following observations:

- There is hardly any contact between top management and supervisors below the B class [foreman] level.
- No purposeful education and training is being carried out to equip supervisors with professional ability, production techniques, and human relations skills that are needed to accomplish their present as well as future job responsibilities.
- The upward communication is very poor. Ideas, proposals, and suggestions that are based on actual operations of the shop are

not reported to the top management in such a manner that management can reflect on its own activity and make corrections.[36]

These concerns led to extensive discussions within JUSE about ways to involve foremen more actively in factory operations, especially in quality control. Panel discussions and conferences were held to stimulate interest, and in 1962 the first edition of *Genba-To-QC* (*Quality Control for the Foreman,* later renamed *FQC*) was published. Its editorial committee proposed the following goals:

1. To facilitate education, training and propagation of QC techniques, and to help first-line supervisors and foremen improve their QC ability
2. To encourage foremen and workers to subscribe to the magazine on their own account
3. To organize at the workshop level a group called "QC Circle" headed by a foreman and participated in by his subordinate workers; to encourage them to study QC using the magazine as a textbook; and to make such a group function as a core of QC in each workshop[37]

Initially, then, QC circles were conceived as study groups. Problem-solving was encouraged, but primarily because it gave circle members experience in applying the statistical methods they had learned. Employees were expected to participate voluntarily in the groups, and their self-development was an explicit goal. Other principles suggested by JUSE included cooperation among circles and the eventual participation of all employees.[38]

A month after these ideas appeared in *Genba-To-QC,* the first quality control circle was registered by the Japan Telephone & Telegraph Corporation. In November 1962 JUSE sponsored a QC conference for foremen to publicize further QC circles; it was well attended and subsequently became an annual event. The first national QC conference was held in May 1963; it also proved extremely popular and has since been repeated many times. Regional conferences have been developed as well. In 1980, for example, 114 QC circle conferences were held throughout Japan, with more than 55,000 participants. The conferences gave circle members an opportunity to describe their projects before an audience of peers, and thus served two related goals: They helped to diffuse new ideas about quality control while providing recognition to especially successful and innovative circles.[39]

Today QC circles are widespread in Japan. A menu of simple statistical techniques—the so-called Seven Tools: Pareto charts, cause-and-effect diagrams, stratification, check sheets, histograms, scatter diagrams, and control charts—has been packaged and taught to countless factory workers.[40] Small groups of five to ten workers with problem-solving skills; trained in data collection, statistical analysis, and group processes; and rewarded with prizes, publicity, and nonmonetary awards, are now common at large Japanese companies. Many companies have developed their own elaborate infrastructures for promoting QC circle activities because of the large number of circles involved.[41] In 1984, for example, Toyota alone had more than 5,800 circles. At the national level, the number of registered circles has grown commensurately: from 215 QCCs in 1963 to more than 180,000 in 1984.[42]

These efforts have undoubtedly contributed to employees' familiarity with quality control techniques, more participative environments, and lower defect rates. They are frequently cited as *the* key to Japan's superior quality and reliability. An early study, for example, marveled at the success of QCCs in "harnessing the energy, ingenuity and enthusiasm of the work force," while a later study concluded that "the driving force behind [Japan's] productivity [and quality] movement came from millions of rank-and-file workers who have taken the initiative to suggest changes to their superiors."[43] Despite these sweeping claims, the precise contribution of QCCs has proved to be difficult to measure. Most evidence remains anecdotal and piecemeal.[44] Even Kaoru Ishikawa, a father of the QC circle movement, believes their influence is exaggerated. He regards QCCs as important, but as only a piece of company-wide quality control, the larger system that today guides most quality efforts in Japan.[45]

### Company-wide Quality Control

The Japanese approach to quality management has broadened with time to become sweeping in concept and philosophy. It now extends well beyond its earliest roots of improving manufacturing processes through the application of statistical methods. Today the guiding Japanese Industrial Standard (Z8101–1981) defines quality control as "a system of means to economically produce goods or services which satisfy customers' requirements." Effective implementation is expected to involve "the cooperation of all people in the company," including representatives of such diverse functions as marketing, research and development, procurement, manufacturing, and customer service. This approach to quality is known as company-wide or total quality control (CWQC or TQC).[46]

Japan's TQC movement dates originally to the mid-1950s, when the work of Armand Feigenbaum was first translated. Feigenbaum's total quality control, described earlier, served as the model for early Japanese efforts to integrate multiple functions into the quality process and to design quality into new products. The approach was subsequently expanded and refined, and in 1968 a new designation, company-wide quality control, was adopted to acknowledge Japan's unique contributions.[47] Today CWQC includes four principal elements: the involvement of functions other than manufacturing in quality activities; the participation of employees at all levels; the goal of continuous improvement; and careful attention to customers' definitions of quality. All four, it should be noted, are aspects of the strategic approach to quality described in Chapter 2.

The involvement of functions other than manufacturing in quality activities is an idea borrowed directly from Feigenbaum. He noted that horizontal linkages were critical if quality control was to be successful, especially when new products were designed and developed. The idea has been embraced enthusiastically by companies in Japan, which have often added twists of their own.[48] Fuji-Xerox, for example, in an effort to ensure close coordination among the members of a large multifunctional team designing a new copier, insisted that they all be located in a single enormous room.[49]

The second element of CWQC, the involvement of all employees, is uniquely Japanese. It is closely linked to the QC circle movement and to JUSE's efforts to broaden literacy in quality control through extensive education and training.[50] At most large Japanese companies, QC education now embraces all levels, from top executives to shop-floor employees. In-house training is supplemented by outside programs, and refresher and follow-up courses are the norm. The purpose of these efforts is to develop a shared concern for quality at all levels of the company—and in many cases a "quality first" mentality, which puts quality ahead of other objectives such as cost and delivery—coupled with a common set of problem-solving tools. Each and every employee is then expected to take responsibility for the quality of his or her work and actively to seek improvement. The result, according to one firm's quality control handbook, is that "the morality and morale of the working people are the practical basis of product quality."[51]

The third element of CWQC is a philosophy of continuous improvement.[52] Quality programs are expected to aim for perfection;

anything less is regarded as an interim goal, to be succeeded by progressively tighter standards. Improvements may be small or may require years of effort, but they will be pursued until defects can no longer be found.

The fourth element of CWQC is a strong customer orientation.[53] Quality is defined from the customer's point of view, and design and production processes are then focused accordingly. Careful market research on quality is a necessary first step—as the Japanese learned from Deming's earliest lectures. But more complex techniques, developed by the Japanese themselves, are also used. Known as quality analysis or quality function deployment (QFD), they use elaborate charts to translate perceptions of quality into product characteristics and product characteristics into fabrication and assembly requirements.[54] In this way the "voice of the customer" is deployed throughout the company. New designs incorporate customers' perspectives on quality and comparisons with competitors' products; these, in turn, dictate component characteristics and critical specifications and tolerances. Statistical plans for monitoring manufacturing are then developed. Thanks to the preceding analysis, they can be focused selectively on processes that heavily influence final product quality. All stages of design, purchasing, manufacturing, and quality control thus become linked to customers' definitions of quality.

Company-wide quality control represents the most recent step in Japan's quality evolution. It incorporates elements of each preceding era—statistical tools, broad education and training, top management involvement, leadership by JUSE, and quality control circles—while still forging new ground. By all accounts, it has been remarkably successful. Japan's quality record today is the envy of companies around the world. Yet the movement began with techniques that were readily available to American companies and were first practiced in the United States. An obvious question then arises: With similar roots, why did the U.S. and Japanese quality movements turn out so differently? Why did quality principles sink in so well—and so quickly—in Japan, but so much more slowly in the United States?

## EXPLAINING JAPAN'S SUCCESS

In the immediate postwar period, Japan's need and motivation for quality improvement were high. The Allied command was demanding improved quality from the communications and transportation industries; as a major customer, it received immediate attention.[55] Widespread labor shortages and high turnover prompted companies to seek ways of increasing employees' motivation and interest; one result was QC circles and the "quality first" philosophy.[56] Perhaps most important, after the war many Japanese companies found themselves facing the "grim reality" of products that could not be sold because of poor quality.[57]

These forces provided powerful motivation for the Japanese quality movement, but they alone do not explain its success. Other countries have suffered similar quality problems without later achieving Japan's gains. U.S. companies may have been complacent at the time—most, after all, faced a vast pent-up demand for their products—but they also had a fifteen- to twenty-year head start in applying quality control techniques. How, then, did the Japanese bridge the gap?

One critical element was the involvement of top executives.[58] From the very first CCS seminars through Deming's and Juran's lectures and into the present day, high-level Japanese executives have been personally involved in quality activities. They have attended and taught training programs; mastered the rudiments of statistical quality control; stressed the importance of quality in policy directives and statements of company philosophy; and set strong examples for their employees. The contrast with U.S. practices is stark. Chapter 1, for example, has described a series of wartime courses on statistical quality control offered by the U.S. Office of Production Research and Development. It was attended almost exclusively by engineers, technicians, and mid-level managers. By contrast, the CCS seminars in Japan were open only to top executives from the communications industry, and no substitutions or absences were allowed. Deming's early lectures were equally focused on top management.

In part, the heavy involvement of Japanese executives in quality activities can be traced to the role and impact of JUSE. Its links to Keidanren, Japan's powerful national business organization, ensured that a practical focus was maintained. Research and training activities were targeted to a broad audience, rather than to specialists alone. Moreover, JUSE's leaders had the credibility and connections to ensure that senior managers attended—or, at the very least, knew about—lectures by such experts as Deming and Juran. Through such activities, the organization provided a single national focal point for the development and diffusion of new ideas on quality control.[59]

Such leadership was lacking in the United States. According to Chapter 1, a national quality organization, the American Society for

Quality Control (ASQC), has existed in the United States since 1946—the very year JUSE was founded. But its orientation has been largely technical, and its focus has been primarily on the needs of QC specialists.[60] ASQC's prizes and awards, for example, have been directed at individuals who have made significant contributions to quality control, often through published technical articles. Its training and certification programs have focused on statistics, quality engineering, reliability, and other advanced techniques. Its links to top management have been few and far between. By contrast, JUSE has aimed at a far wider audience. Its Deming and All Japan Quality Control prizes (the latter, established in 1970, is open only to previous winners of the Deming Prize), have focused on companies rather than individuals.[61] Its training programs have targeted all points on the spectrum: top executives, quality control specialists, supervisors, and shop-floor employees. And it has worked closely with leading business organizations from its inception.

These differences go a long way toward explaining the success of the Japanese quality movement. An established national organization and well-defined infrastructure have given great unity to the Japanese approach. The same forces can be seen in Japan's standardization movement. Since 1949, standardization activities have been coordinated by a single group within MITI, in cooperation with JUSE and other ministries. In the United States, such activities have been far less centralized, and often far less effective. More than four hundred organizations are now responsible for standards development in the United States, including trade associations, professional societies, and specialized groups like the American National Standards Institute. Certification is performed primarily by private organizations such as Underwriters' Laboratory and the Factory Mutual Engineering Corporation, rather than by the government as in Japan. The National Bureau of Standards plays a secondary role, conducting research and providing coordination, but with much less power than MITI. Often, the result has been a patchwork of local and regional requirements, with delays in certification and a lack of national agreement.[62]

Of course, a unified national quality movement rests on more than organizations alone. It requires a common language and a shared understanding of problems, philosophies, and tools. The Japanese have acquired these through massive training programs, offered initially by CCS and JUSE and later by individual companies. No other nation has pursued quality education so vigorously, at upper and lower ranks, on an annual basis, with specially designed manuals and simple techniques. And none has achieved such impressive results: quality literacy on a national scale. In the eyes of at least one Japanese expert, "Quality control begins with education and ends with education."[63]

Such features of the Japanese quality movement distinguish it sharply from its U.S. counterpart. Motivation and the need to improve, top management involvement, a national organization and infrastructure, centralized leadership, and massive training programs were all elements of the Japanese effort but missing from the United States during the postwar period. They help to explain why the Japanese movement took hold while the U.S. movement did not. But there is another possible explanation for Japan's success that must also be considered, if only because it has been so frequently cited: the view that Japan's quality revolution was due not to specific actions or programs but to Japan's unique culture and national character.

## Culture and National Character

Of all the explanations for Japan's postwar industrial success, those rooted in culture and national character are the most controversial.[64] Typically, they include one of several elements, each in some way peculiar to Japan. Some analysts cite the legacy of Japanese craftsmanship and fine detail work, reflected in such arts as bonsai (miniature trees) and netsuke (carved or inlaid toggles used to fasten a purse or other articles to a kimono sash), as proof that the Japanese have always had unusual aptitude for precision work. Today, the argument runs, these skills are simply applied in such new directions as the assembly and testing of semiconductors, VCRs, and other complex electronic products.[65] In the same spirit, some analysts cite Japanese fastidiousness and perfectionism as sources of the Japanese quality advantage. Both have long ranked high in the country's value system; in factory environments, they are thought to take such forms as impeccable workplaces, attention to housekeeping, and pressures for continued improvement. Customers too set high standards for products and are unwilling to accept defects; for that reason, some analysts believe that defective products are matters of shame for employees, to be avoided because they reflect badly on one's company or one's honor. Such pressures are thought to make Japanese workers unusually sensitive to quality.[66] In much the same way, some scholars view a society built around groups and group processes as the primary explanation for Japan's success with QC circles.[67]

What is one to make of these claims? They undoubtedly contain elements of truth, for Japan's culture is indeed distinctive. Comparative studies of the U.S. and Japanese semiconductor industries, for example, have repeatedly cited Japan's superior dust control and clean rooms, linking them to Japanese habits of cleanliness and personal fastidiousness.[68] Even so, such arguments are easily overstated. They border on cultural determinism, confusing habits or tasks that support a particular end with more complete explanations. One recent study has put the issue bluntly:

> It may be that Japanese culture creates certain predispositions that are unusually supportive of efforts to establish exacting quality control standards . . . but that by no means guarantees that the Japanese will be successful in doing so, or that those who operate in another cultural context will fail.[69]

The cultural case for superior quality is further weakened by two additional pieces of evidence. First, if the Japanese are so naturally disposed toward quality and perfectionism, how is the immediate postwar period to be explained? Japanese products at the time suffered from poor construction and high failure rates, earning well-deserved reputations for poor quality. In 1957, for example, Toyota exported its first cars to the United States, and they quickly lost favor because of "their disturbing tendency to break down after only a few hours of freeway driving."[70] Quality problems of this sort are hardly consistent with the view that Japan's culture and national character lead inevitably to superior products.

Another point against the cultural argument arises from the success of Japanese subsidiaries abroad. In such diverse environments as Europe, Asia, Latin America, and the United States, Japanese factories, staffed by indigenous work forces and small teams of Japanese managers, have compiled outstanding quality records. They have regularly outperformed local companies and in several cases have attained parity with firms in Japan.[71] Bridgestone Tire's radial truck tire plant in LaVergne, Tennessee, for example, now claims scrap and defect rates comparable to its Japanese parent. Nissan's factory in Smyrna, Tennessee, appears to have reached the same goal. Both Matsushita and Sanyo have reduced defect and service call rates by as much as 90 percent at the color television plants they purchased in Illinois and Arkansas, while keeping work forces virtually intact.[72] In most cases, success was achieved by applying the principles of company-wide and statistical quality control, and then adapting them to local environments. The ability of these plants to achieve superior quality without Japanese workers—and thus, without their vaunted perfectionism or legacy of craftsmanship—suggests that culture and national character are at best partial explanations for Japan's quality successes.

## A MODEL FOR CHANGE

Since 1945, the Japanese have made enormous strides in quality management. They have gone from laggards to leaders and have done so by following a systematic and orderly progression. Table 10.1 recaps the principal events in Japan's postwar quality movement. It shows an interweaving of influences: the contributions of American experts, the rise of JUSE, the standardization movement, public education and outreach, and such new developments as QC circles and quality function deployment. These events were not separated into isolated periods but overlapped and cross-fertilized one another. All, however, were driven by the same powerful forces: centralized leadership and direction, top management involvement, and the desire to elevate quality to an issue of national importance. Together these forces produced change on a massive scale.

The U.S. quality movement, described in Chapters 1 and 2, has been far less successful. At many U.S. companies, the message has only recently taken hold. Yet there are striking historical parallels between the two movements. Each began with inspection and then proceeded to statistical quality control; was guided initially by a small number of experts; developed its own overseeing organization—JUSE in Japan and ASQC in the United States—and then focused heavily on education and training; and evolved toward strategic quality management.

The Japanese, however, made far swifter progress. More important, they reached their goal en masse. Company-wide quality control is now widely diffused throughout Japan, but strategic quality management is present at only a handful of leading U.S. companies. The Japanese approach thus qualifies as an organized movement, while the U.S. approach seems more fractionalized. American companies have generally launched their quality programs indepen-

TABLE 10.1   *Chronology of the Japanese Quality Movement*

| | |
|---|---|
| 1945 | Civil Communications Section is established within General Headquarters, Supreme Commander for the Allied Forces. |
| | Japanese Standards Association is established. |
| 1946 | Japanese Industrial Standards Committee is established. |
| | Union of Japanese Scientists and Engineers (JUSE) is established. |
| | The monthly journal *Standards and Norms* is first published. |
| 1949 | Quality Control Research Group is established within JUSE. First QC courses are offered. |
| | Industrial Standardization Law is passed. |
| | Civil Communications Section seminars are offered. |
| 1950 | JUSE publishes the magazine *Statistical Quality Control.* |
| | Japanese Industrial Standards are established under the Industrial Standardization Law. |
| | Deming offers seminars on quality. |
| 1951 | Deming Prize is established. |
| | First Quality Control Conference is held. |
| 1954 | Juran offers seminars on quality. |
| 1956 | Japan Shortwave Broadcasting Corporation broadcasts a QC correspondence course for foremen. |
| 1957 | Japan National Broadcasting Corporation (NHK) offers a QC series on its educational television channel. |
| 1960 | JUSE publishes a two-volume QC manual for foremen. |
| | The first "Quality Month" is introduced nationwide. |
| 1961 | A special supplement to *Statistical Quality Control* is published for foremen. |
| | The 11th Quality Control Conference is held, including panel discussions on "the role of foremen in quality assurance." |
| 1962 | *Genba-To-QC (Quality Control for the Foreman)* is published, including a proposal for QC circles. |
| | The first QC circle is registered with QC circle headquarters. |
| | The first annual QC conference for foremen is held. |
| 1968 | The term "company-wide quality control" (CWQC) is introduced. |
| 1969 | The International Conference for Quality Control is held in Tokyo. |
| 1970 | The All Japan Quality Control Prize is established. |
| | The Japanese Society for Quality Control is established. |
| 1972 | Quality Function Deployment is first practiced at Kobe Shipyard, Mitsubishi Heavy Industries, Ltd. |
| 1979 | The 100,000th QC circle is registered. |

dently, with little centralized control or guidance; by contrast, Japanese companies have enjoyed a well-developed infrastructure. Their quality programs have been supported by JUSE, MITI, and powerful business associations. The result has been a coordinated national effort, bringing success on multiple fronts.

# Chapter
# 11

# Contributors to Japanese Quality

In countless industries, Japanese firms have achieved vast improvements in defect rates, reliability levels, and product performance. The preceding chapter has examined one reason why: a coordinated national quality movement spanning four decades. That analysis was based primarily on aggregates and trends to highlight the environmental forces at work. In this chapter, a narrower lens is used to explore the sources of Japanese quality at the factory level.

Again, data from the room air conditioning industry are employed. Seven Japanese plants, accounting for 90 percent of Japanese industry shipments, are compared with eleven U.S. plants (the plants already discussed in Chapters 6 through 9), accounting for the same percentage of U.S. industry shipments. As Table 11.1 illustrates, the two groups had vastly different quality records. Japanese plants were superior across the board, whether quality was measured by incoming rejection rates, assembly line defect rates, or service call rates.[1] They averaged failure rates that were seventeen to sixty-seven times lower than their U.S. counterparts. Even more impressive, on all measures the poorest Japanese plant had a failure rate less than half that of the best U.S. manufacturer.

These findings confirm the wide gulf separating U.S. and Japanese quality performance. In this case, the roots of superiority are also clear, for every Japanese company traced its success to a system of company-wide quality control. The remainder of the chapter is devoted to fleshing out the details of these systems—their supporting practices and attitudes, including approaches to product design, vendor selection and management, and production and work force man-

200

TABLE 11.1   *Quality in the U.S. and Japanese Room Air Conditioning Industries, 1981–82*

| | Incoming Quality | In-Plant Quality | Field Quality |
|---|---|---|---|
| | *Incoming Parts and Materials (% defective)* | *Assembly-Line Defect Rate per 100 units* | *Service Call Rate per 100 Units under First-Year Warranty Coverage* |
| Median: | | | |
| U.S. | 3.3 | 63.5 | 10.5[a] |
| Japan | 0.15 | 0.95 | 0.6 |
| Range: | | | |
| U.S. | 0.82–16 | 8–165 | 5.3–26.5 |
| Japan | 0–.3 | 0.15–3 | .04–2.0 |

[a]Service call rates in the U.S. normally include calls where no product problems were found ("customer instruction calls"); those in Japan do not. For comparability, the U.S. median has been adjusted to exclude customer instruction calls. Without the adjustment, the median U.S. service call rate was 11.4 per 100 units. Figures for the range should be adjusted similarly, although the necessary data were not available from the U.S. plants with the highest and lowest service call rates.

SOURCE: Company records and questionnaires distributed by the author.

agement. Throughout the discussion, practices at the factory level are emphasized, to supplement Chapter 10's institutional and policy approach.

## ATTITUDES AND PHILOSOPHY

Perhaps the biggest difference between U.S. and Japanese plants in this industry was the depth of their commitment to quality. At Japanese plants, the commitment was deeply ingrained and clearly communicated. It was visible everywhere: in statements of company philosophy, policy manuals, and charts and banners on the wall. At Matsushita, for example, quality appeared prominently in the company's slogan: "Let us limitlessly supply good quality products to our society, and let us contribute to foster even richer electrified life to our people." An even stronger directive came from the company's quality manual: "Quality must be the first preference in the [work] group."[2]

Overall, quality was so important to the Japanese plants in this industry that a single principle appeared to govern their behavior: Anything worth doing in the area of quality is worth overdoing. That attitude, which migh be termed "overkill," took a variety of forms. Where product design was concerned, it led to "overengineering": A product that consumers typically used for ten years was constructed of materials designed to last fifteen years or longer. The testing of new models followed a similar approach, called "nasty testing" by the Japanese: A product whose normal operating environment was 90°F was required to perform effectively at much higher and lower temperatures.[3] In the same vein, several plants were "overinspecting" their units. Japanese plants in this industry employed an inspector for every 7.1 assembly line workers; the comparable U.S. ratio was 1:9.5.[4] The primary role of the inspectors was to monitor the production process for stability; they were less "gatekeepers," weeding out defective units before shipment, than providers of information. They also served an important symbolic role. At one plant, whose leak rate was 0.12 percent, there were six on-line leak testers; three of them were stationed back to back on the assembly line. As the plant's quality control manager pointed out, the last of these leak testers had very little to do. For all practical purposes, his job was unnecessary. The QC manager then added that the inspector could not possibly be removed for two very important reasons: To do so would signal the work force that quality was being deemphasized and, on the extremely rare occasion that leaks did get past the earlier inspectors, they would no longer be caught before shipment.

"Overtraining" was equally widespread in the industry. Assembly line workers at most plants were first trained for all jobs on the line, even though they were eventually assigned to a single work station. The process normally took six months to a year; comparable U.S. training periods were one to two days. Japanese workers were thus more likely to be able to track defects to their source and propose effective remedial action. Skilled employees like brazers, who welded together pieces of copper tubing and were largely responsible for whatever leak rates were experienced, were subject to even more rigorous training. At most plants, they were certified only after several months of practice; craftsmanship contests were then held on a regular basis, both within companies and among competitors, to ensure that skills did not atrophy. Training continued over time.[5] At one plant, brazers honed their skills by practicing on iron and brass, two of the most difficult materials to weld together. Having mastered these metals, they were expected to have few problems with copper.

Such practices indicate the great importance that Japanese plants in this industry attached to product quality. To ensure success, most efforts were incorporated within larger programs. Thus, all plants set formal quality goals, using a process that normally proceeded from highly general to highly specific targets.[6] From the corporate level came vague policy pronouncements ("this year, let the customer determine our quality"), which were further defined by division heads ("reduced service call rates are necessary if we are to lower costs") and by vice presidents of quality or manufacturing ("compressor failures are an especially serious problem that must be addressed"). Actual quantitative goals ("improve compressor reliability by 10 percent") were set by middle managers, or else by foremen or workers operating through quality control circles. The collaborative nature of the process distinguished it from U.S. approaches, as did the progressive narrowing of goals. Both ensured that targets were realistic and earned wide support.

The result of these efforts was an appreciation of quality at all levels of the plant, and in all functions. Tensions between quality and manufacturing departments were rare. In fact, the reverse was often true: The groups were mutually supportive. For example, the quality manager at one Japanese plant, where production workers were, as usual, performing inspection, argued that shifting such responsibility to his department would undoubtedly produce *inferior* results. Production workers, he explained, were likely to feel a stronger commitment to manufacturing improvement than QC specialists, and thus were more likely to feed back data rapidly and take immediate corrective action.

Even more revealing was the attitude of first-line supervisors. At four of the six Japanese plants surveyed, supervisors believed that high quality—not producing at low cost, meeting the production schedule, or improving worker productivity—was management's top manufacturing priority. At the other two plants, quality ranked a close second. By contrast, Chapter 9 has indicated that U.S. supervisors believed their managers were far more concerned with meeting the production schedule. At nine of the eleven U.S. plants, it was regarded as management's top manufacturing priority.[7]

## QUALITY PROGRAMS, POLICIES, AND SYSTEMS

Of course, attitudes and philosophy alone are seldom enough to improve quality. While they provide direction and emphasis—and thus play a critical role in shaping behavior—supporting structures are also necessary. A company's programs, policies, and systems are the practical embodiment of its attitudes toward quality. In each of these areas, Japanese room air conditioning manufacturers differed sharply from their U.S. counterparts.

As noted in Chapter 9, quality departments at most U.S. plants in the industry were viewed primarily as "policemen," enforcing standards that would otherwise be ignored. Their mission at Japanese plants was entirely different. Because final responsibility for quality was accepted by workers, quality departments served mainly as "coordinators," "consultants," and "information clearinghouses." Line organizations were clearly dominant. In only two cases were there corporate quality departments; each was small and had limited authority. At the plant level, quality departments were more active but still played a supporting role.[8] Their chief responsibilities were quality education and training, quality planning, and, especially, processing and interpreting quality data for other groups within the plant.

The emphasis on information was supported by exacting systems for generating, collecting, and reporting data. Failure data were especially detailed. At one Japanese plant, repairmen had to file written reports on every defective unit they fixed; at another, service call rates were coded into eighty different problem categories. In general, Japanese managers had far more precise information on quality than U.S. managers. It was not unusual for them to be able to identify the thirty different ways in which Switch X had failed on Model Y during the last several years or to have detailed figures on failure rates during the postwarranty period.[9] According to Chapter 9, such precision was the exception in the United States, where data were often highly aggregated and confined to the years covered by warranty. Reporting was also considerably slower.

Service call statistics in the United States took anywhere from one month to one year to make the trip from the field to the factory; in Japan, the elapsed time averaged between one week and one month. Elaborate systems were part of the explanation. For example, one Japanese company had developed a network of 1,100 "quality reporters"—most of them technically trained salesmen—located around the world. Each submitted reports on repairs, defective components, and other quality problems directly to the company's Quality Assurance Laboratory and received in return written confirmations of remedial action, as well as bonuses for all reports filed. Other companies also had sophisticated reporting systems, although few were as elaborate as this one. Such systems, however, were not the only reason that data were processed more rapidly in Japan than in the United States. Differences in attitude were important as well. As the director of quality at one Japanese company observed, information from the field reached his company's U.S. subsidiaries much more slowly than it did operations in Japan—even though both employed the same system for collecting and reporting data.

Once collected, the data were also used more effectively by the Japanese plants. In the United States, reports on in-plant and field failures were normally monitored by different groups within the plant, limiting their usefulness. In-plant failures were tracked by the quality department, while field failures were tracked by field service, a branch of the marketing department. These two groups seldom compared figures or met together, for the implicit assumption was that little could be learned by matching the two sets of data.

All of the Japanese plants in the industry assumed otherwise. In every case, a single department—quality—was responsible for tabulating both in-plant and field failures. The two were considered to be closely related, with each offering clues to better understanding the other. Faced with unexpected field problems, a plant's first step was often to check the offending units' serial numbers and then to review the defect sheets from the same production lot. Some insights would be gained if similar problems had been encountered at in-process inspection and subsequently repaired. At least one plant took the process a step further, using recent defect rates and the historical relationship between in-plant and field failures to predict the field performance of its newest models. These practices, and others like them, help to explain the extremely strong positive correlation between in-plant and field failures displayed by Japanese plants in the industry, and the weaker correlation, noted in Chapter 7, displayed by American plants.[10]

A related aspect of Japanese quality management was the use of "early warning systems" to provide an initial screening of field problems. At several plants in the industry, incoming field data were reviewed immediately by the quality department, and problems were assigned to one of two categories: "Routine" problems were considered to be of little urgency, while "emergencies" demanded immediate attention. The former normally involved a small number of units from isolated production lots; because of their random character, these problems were viewed as unrelated and were resolved by following normal corrective action procedures.

Emergencies were handled differently, for in most cases they involved fundamental operating problems traceable to a single production lot. Managers feared that these problems might soon appear in other units already in the field or that similar mistakes might be repeated in subsequent production runs. As a result, special efforts were made to resolve the problems as quickly as possible. Diagnosis began immediately, and teams were often sent into the field to perform further analysis. All units from the same production lot that were still in the warehouse were reinspected. Whenever necessary, parts were replaced, even if that required repairing a unit that had not yet broken down.

The early separation of routine and emergency problems led to relatively efficient remedial action. Potential epidemics—high failure rates attributable to a single persistent problem—were caught much earlier by the Japanese plants in this industry than by many of their American counterparts. Here again, the thoughtful processing of information by the quality department played a central role in ensuring low failure rates.

Such data were also essential to the proper functioning of quality control circles. All the Japanese plants in this industry relied heavily on QCCs to generate suggestions for process improvement and defect reduction; in the United States, only two plants were experimenting with QCCs, and on a limited basis. At the Japanese plants, at least 80 percent of the work force was involved in circle activities. To support them, plants routinely collected extensive quality data. Information on defects was compiled daily and analyzed for trends. Perhaps most important, the data were made easily accessible to line workers, often in the form of publicly posted charts. More detailed data were available to QCCs on request. Such practices illustrate a crucial difference between U.S. and Japanese approaches to quality management: The Japanese plants consistently pushed quality data down to the lowest possible levels of the organization in order to educate the work force, while the American plants normally aggregated upward in order to provide middle and upper management with useful summaries. The Japanese approach stimulated learning by providing QCCs with the information necessary to analyze problems and propose solutions. The U.S. approach implicitly assumed that quality problems were the responsibility of management and offered line workers little useful information.

Together, these programs, policies, and systems formed the core of company-wide quality control. They gave substance to more ethereal attitudes and philosophies, providing direction and support. Because failure data were detailed and readily accessible, improvement projects were guided by fact rather than supposition; because quality departments were supportive and collaborative, responsibility for quality was shared by multiple functions; and because participation in QCCs was widespread, quality enjoyed a broad base of support among factory workers. In combination, these efforts provided the Japanese companies with a solid foundation for launching more focused quality initiatives in product design, vendor selection and management, and production and work force management.

## PRODUCT DESIGN

For the most part, design practices at Japanese plants in this industry mirrored those of superior U.S. manufacturers. Differences were largely matters of degree. For example, all the Japanese plants paid enormous attention to reliability engineering, noting that high reliability was a "given" in the Japanese market. Designers were under tremendous pressure to reduce the number of parts per unit, following the basic principle of reliability engineering that, everything else being equal, the fewer the parts, the lower the failure rate. Most remaining parts were tested rigorously to see if their reliability could be improved. "Nasty tests" under varying conditions of temperature, humidity, and voltage were used, as were life tests, guided by actual field data showing the number of hours before a component typically failed. Changes in parts were often proposed as a result. These efforts were aided by the Industrial Engineering Bureau of the Ministry of International Trade and Industry (MITI), which required that all electric and electronic components sold in Japan be tested for reliability and have their ratings on file with the bureau. Because the information on file was publicly available, designers no longer needed to test components themselves in order to establish reliability ratings.

The Japanese emphasis on reliability engineering was supplemented by a more thorough review of new designs before units reached production. In both countries, the stages of the design process were similar: concept development, engineering prototypes, pilot runs, and then production units. But in Japan, pretesting and experimentation were far more extensive. American plants in the industry usually built a single prototype before moving to pilot production; the Japanese often repeated the process three or four times. Moreover, all affected departments—quality, purchasing, manufacturing, service, and design engineering—played active roles at each stage of the review process. In the United States, the early stages of review were controlled almost exclusively by engineering. By the time other groups had their say, the process had gained momentum, schedules had been established, and changes had become difficult to make.[11]

Because they feared such results, all the Japanese plants had taken additional steps to ensure that engineering considerations did not rule the design process. They were especially careful to incorporate consumers' views into their products and to conduct extensive market research on quality. One company regularly assessed customers' perceptions of reliability by asking, for various product categories, how frequently a high-quality product was expected to fail. These findings were used to set reliability targets for designers. Other firms questioned consumers about durability and product life; both were matters of guesswork in the United States. Several Japanese companies had even created internal consumer review boards. These were groups of employees, without technical training or QC skills, whose primary function was to act as typical consumers and test and evaluate new products. They were expected to turn on air conditioners and decide if the room was cooled comfortably; play with controls and see if they were well positioned and easy to use; listen to units and determine if they were too noisy; and comment on overall attractiveness and aesthetics. More important, all such groups had final authority over new product release. If they were dissatisfied, redesign was inevitable. The message here was unmistakable: Customers—not the design staff, the marketing team, or the production group—had the final say in determining acceptable product quality.

In combination, these practices led to designs that were easy to manufacture and assemble, with few field problems. Japanese plants reported few difficulties with new models, while U.S. plants reported sharp increases in defect and service call rates. Narrower product lines were not the explanation, for in this industry, unlike many others in Japan, product variety was the rule.[12] Japanese and U.S. room air conditioning manufacturers had remarkably similar profiles: The Japanese plants averaged 5.8 chassis sizes and 84 models, while the U.S. plants averaged 5.7 chassis sizes and 81 models.[13] New designs, however, accounted for a far higher proportion (nearly a third) of the Japanese models offered each year. Their smooth introduction was proof that careful reliability engineering, multifunctional design teams, and exhaustive shakedowns of new products were effective in limiting quality problems even in an environment of rapid change.

## VENDOR SELECTION AND MANAGEMENT

Careful selection and management of vendors were equally important to the Japanese approach. Considerable time and resources were devoted to both—far more than in the United States. Vendor selection, for example, was often a drawn-out affair. One Japanese plant reported that it spent several years monitoring performance before signing up a new supplier; others in the industry reported reviews lasting several months. At most plants the reviews focused initially on vendors' management philosophies: their attentiveness to quality or, as one manager put it, "their eagerness to understand what QC means." Other items of interest were a vendor's QC organization; its process for handling quality complaints; its manufacturing methods; its use of statistical quality control; and its trend and dispersion of quality over time. None of these categories received comparable attention at U.S. plants in the industry.

Once vendors were selected, large resources were devoted to maintaining and improving their quality. Receiving inspection was a primary tool. The Japanese plants in this industry devoted six times as many people to receiving inspection as U.S. manufacturers: on average, nineteen people versus three.[14] But in their hands, inspection was less an end in itself than a means to an end. Receiving inspectors acted less as policemen than as consultants to vendors, mimicking the behavior of their counterparts on the assembly line. That was especially true when subcontractors were involved, for they were considered part of the company "family." They were brought into the design process early and were active in prototype and pilot production.[15] Their personnel were often trained by the buying plant in statistical quality control. If receiving inspection turned up problems, buying plants thought nothing of stationing quality experts at the supplier plants for weeks at a time.

At several Japanese plants, incoming materials arrived directly at the assembly line without inspection. New vendors, however, first had to pass rigorous tests: Their products initially received 100 percent inspection. Once all problems were corrected, sampling inspection became the norm. Only after an extended period without a rejection were vendors allowed to send their products directly to the assembly line. At the first sign of deterioration in vendor performance, more intensive inspection resumed. Thus, if sampling inspection was being practiced when problems arose, 100 percent inspection began again; and if no inspection was being practiced, sampling methods resumed. By applying such rolling standards, plants maintained tight control over incoming quality with minimal inspection. One representative plant was able to bring 70 percent of its purchased parts and materials directly to the assembly line without problems.

Despite these advances, Japanese and American approaches to vendors were similar in important respects. Supply relationships were of roughly the same duration. Japanese plants estimated an average of ten years per supplier, while U.S. plants estimated an average of 12.5 years.[16] Single sourcing was more widely practiced in Japan, but not uniformly. Three Japanese plants single sourced less than 20 percent of their purchased parts and materials, placing them below the U.S. average. And cooperative relationships with vendors, while typical, were not universal in Japan. At least one Japanese plant disciplined suppliers by taking away business; several others refused to bring parts and materials to the assembly line without some form of receiving inspection.

These practices suggest that the usual picture of Japanese supply relationships—a long-term collaboration between buyers and trusted, sole-source vendors—may be overstated.[17] They cannot be necessary conditions for superior performance, because several Japanese plants in the industry achieved outstanding quality records without them. Rather, they appear to be secondary and supportive conditions, adjuncts to the more critical activities of careful vendor selection, early involvement in new designs, exhaustive screening of vendors' first shipments, and long-term oversight and support.

## PRODUCTION AND WORK FORCE MANAGEMENT

Conventional wisdom holds that much of Japan's quality and productivity advantage comes from robots and advanced technology. Success and superior equipment are thought to be intertwined. Yet surprisingly, in the room air conditioning industry U.S. and Japanese facilities were much alike. Plants were of comparable ages; automation was limited; and manufacturing followed a similar sequence of operations. Especially in final assembly, where such manual operations as hand brazing and the insertion of color-coded wires were the norm, processes were little different.[18] Japanese plants did use some automated transfer lines and packaging equipment, but only in compressor manufacturing and case welding was the difference in automation at all significant.

In most cases, Japanese managers explained their low levels of automation by pointing to their "high" defect rates. Implicitly, they were voicing a basic principle of Japanese factory management: Automation should follow, rather than lead, quality improvement. First, production processes were to be brought under control; only then were robots or automated devices to be introduced. Otherwise, quality problems were inevitable, for even advanced equipment was limited in its ability to handle variation. According to one firm's quality control manual:

> When automation is introduced to the manually operated factory without locating and grasping the vital points which [affect] quality . . . such automated machines will only manufacture defective products, automatically.[19]

Tight process control was therefore a necessary first step. At most plants, that meant a manufacturing operation that was predictable, with limited variation. Care was taken to keep the process running smoothly, and plants relied heavily on control charts to monitor day-to-day production. Monitoring was often remarkably focused. In one representative case, leak rates were plotted separately for five different tubing joints. Charts were also prominently displayed, so that all employees could track performance.[20]

To improve process control, the Japanese plants often focused on aspects of production management that received little attention in the United States. Housekeeping and preventive maintenance were two obvious examples; another, less commonly noted, was product handling.[21] All of the Japanese plants in the industry were far more careful in their handling of incoming parts and materials, work-in-process, and finished products than were their counterparts in the United States. At one Japanese plant, assembly line workers wore thin gloves to ensure that products remained clean; at another, special cushioning material had been designed to protect products in storage. To ensure the proper alignment of parts during final assembly, the Japanese plants employed fixtures to a much greater extent than did U.S. manufacturers. Two of the Japanese companies had created corporate packaging laboratories to develop more impact-resistant containers; most had also conducted careful studies to determine the best way to stack units in order to minimize damage.

Product handling, then, was viewed by Japanese managers as simply one more variable requiring tight control if consistent quality was to be maintained. The same was true of assembly activities, which the Japanese attempted to control through "foolproofing."[22] In that approach, an operation or process was designed to make human error impossible. At one plant, fans were attached to subassemblies using a torque wrench hanging from the ceiling; it was located so that bolts could not be overtightened. At another plant, each unit on the assembly line was accompanied by its own box of parts. Incorrect attachments were thus eliminated, even during changeovers. Occasionally, foolproofing was impossible because of technical limitations. Then an even stronger principle was invoked: Eliminate the problem by eliminating the offending operation. Substantial product redesign was often required, but improvements could be equally significant. At one plant, such efforts had reduced the number of brazers on the assembly line—a prominent cause of leaks—to the lowest in the industry.

Defects, however, were seldom eliminated completely. Production processes still—occasionally—fell out of control. To monitor and correct these problems, Japanese plants relied on quality audits and tests. Tests were usually more rigorous than in the United States. Processes were automated; results were plotted on control charts; and in-house equipment was used. Leak booths appeared to be more tightly sealed. But otherwise, tests were roughly similar in the two countries and included checks of cooling capacity, voltage, mechanical functioning, and the like. Quality audits, however, were far more extensive in Japan; they required three to four hours per unit, as against an hour or less at U.S. plants. A wide range of performance tests were normally involved. Moreover, audits were clearly viewed by the Japanese as methods of process control, not as predictors of field performance, as they were in the United States. Without prompting, several Japanese managers commented on the tenuous connection between audit results and first-year service call rates.

All these efforts—housekeeping, preventive maintenance, product handling, control charting, foolproofing, quality auditing, and testing—were regarded by the Japanese plants as means to an end: a stable and error-free production process. Variability was tightly controlled and, whenever possible, eliminated. In that respect, workers posed the greatest challenge, for they were far less predictable than machines. Problems were especially likely on first job assignments, where inexperience could lead easily to inadvertent mistakes. Training was therefore extensive. In addition, all the Japanese plants in the industry assigned new employees to existing teams of experienced workers or else paired them with supervisors. These teams, and not the new employees themselves, were held responsible for the quality of output. Only after new workers had demonstrated their competence were they permitted to work independently.

Such efforts added further control and stability to Japanese production processes. The Japanese system of permanent employement was similar in impact. As Chapter 8 has indicated, several American managers cited manpower moves—and the resulting inexperience and lack of product familiarity among workers—as a leading source of their quality problems. The Japanese, with low absenteeism and turnover, faced fewer problems of this sort. Japanese plants had a median turnover of 3.1 percent; the comparable figure for U.S. plants was two times higher. Even more startling were the figures on absenteeism: a median of 3.1 percent for American plants and *zero* for the Japanese.[23]

Stability was encouraged in other ways as well. Bumping, for example, was slight or nonexistent. Key jobs like brazing were certified, ensuring that inexperienced workers were never involved. Demand surges were met by adding overtime hours rather than new employees. If necessary, work days were lengthened by one or two hours, spreading the load evenly to reduce fatigue. Schedules were often frozen in advance—at one plant three months ahead, and at another one month ahead—to encourage forward planning and avoid pressures for short-term adjustment. One result was much longer production runs: an average of 2,500 units per model in Japan, compared with 1,319 units per model in the United States.[24] As Chapter 8 has indicated, longer runs allow experience to accumulate and thus lead to lower failure rates. Differences in run length were of great importance in explaining quality variations in the United States; they were of equal significance in comparisons of the United States and Japan, for assembly lines were otherwise managed quite similarly in the two countries. Their length, speed, and capacity utilization rates were much alike.[25] The main difference in U.S. and Japanese approaches to assembly-line management was the number of units per production run.

Overall, the Japanese plants had distinctly superior production and work force management. Their manufacturing processes were more stable and predictable, and tight control was the norm. Strict process limits had been established using statistical techniques; handling damage, worker inexperience, and other sources of variability had been regulated to the extent possible; rigorous audits and tests ensured that deviations were quickly discovered and reported; and long production runs built up learning and accumulated experience. The resulting manufacturing operations had few defects that could be traced to process-related problems.

## A SYSTEM OF QUALITY MANAGEMENT

The Japanese have developed a remarkably integrated system of quality management. This chapter has focused on attitudes and practices at the factory level; Chapter 10 has described the overarching principles and institutions. Together, they show that micro- and macro-policies have been well coordinated. Process control has been emphasized on the factory floor and in Japanese Industrial Standards; attention to quality has been fostered by management interest and national prizes; quality improvement programs have combined the efforts of line workers, quality control departments, and the Union of Japanese Scientists and Engineers; and product redesign and corrective action programs have been supported by public and private data. In the room air conditioning industry, the result has been failure rates significantly lower than those achieved by U.S. plants.

There is no single secret to the Japanese success in quality management. Rather, a web of mutually reinforcing practices has been responsible. All share an attention to detail—a willingness to delve into the fundamentals of design, marketing, and manufacturing practice. Any one of these efforts might have been of some help in improving Japan's quality performance; as a seamless whole, their impact has been greatly magnified.

There is an important lesson here for U.S. industry. Any single solution to America's quality problems—the proliferation of quality control circles, the creation of national awards for quality, the collection of more accurate quality statistics—is unlikely to be very effective in closing the large quality gap separating American and Japanese firms. A one-dimensional approach will not produce the same results as a more integrated strategy. To match the Japanese, U.S. industry will have to create a quality system of its own, backed by unswerving commitment at the factory level.

# Conclusion

Quality is both a problem and an opportunity for American companies: a problem because foreign competitors are often far ahead in offering products and services of superior quality, and an opportunity because American consumers are increasingly concerned with the quality of what they buy. Closing the gap is likely to be difficult, for it will require a new approach to quality management. The traditional tools have been tried, with only limited success; they address pieces of the problem but are incomplete. Simple solutions and packaged programs will have to be replaced by a deeper understanding of quality and an appreciation of its history, meaning, measurement, and sources. Only then will managers by able to move decisively on the quality front.

## SUMMARY AND REVIEW

The task is formidable, because quality is such a complex and multi-faceted concept. For this reason, Part I began with a broad overview: a combined history, taxonomy, and summary of the literature on quality. Chapter 1 reviewed the history of the quality movement in the United States, tracing its evolution from inspection to statistical quality control and quality assurance. Over time, quality evolved from a narrow technical discipline whose mandate was to detect manufacturing problems to a broader field encompassing all stages from design to market. Responsibility for quality shifted from the inspection department to manufacturing and engineering groups, and quality professionals became more active in measurement, planning, and program design. A number of new tools emerged: process control charts, sampling methods, cost of quality calculations, and

216

reliability engineering. Yet, despite these changes, the field remained largely defensive throughout the 1950s and 1960s. Quality was still seen as a problem to be solved rather than a potential competitive weapon.

That view changed sharply in the 1970s and 1980s. The rise of Japanese imports, demanding new federal and state programs, and increased customer sensitivity awakened U.S. managers to quality's competitive significance. At a small number of leading companies, a new approach emerged: strategic quality management. As described in Chapter 2, it differed from the preceding eras in several critical respects. Quality was defined from the customer's point of view; was linked with profitability on both the market and cost sides; was viewed as a competitive weapon (suggesting the need for continuous improvement and quality levels that exceeded rather than matched competitors'); was built into the strategic planning process; and was obtained through an organizationwide commitment, spearheaded by top management.

To implement this new approach, companies first needed to understand what quality meant to their customers. Because they have often lacked the necessary vocabulary, two chapters were devoted to definitional matters. Chapter 3 reviewed various definitions of quality that have appeared in the literature: the transcendent (quality is innate excellence); product-based (quality is a measure of the quantity of some ingredient or attribute possessed by a product); user-based (quality is a reflection of consumers' preferences); manufacturing-based (quality is conformance to specifications); and value-based (quality is performance or conformance at an acceptable price or cost). These definitions were important for understanding the different perspectives on quality often held by members of engineering, manufacturing, and marketing departments, who frequently accepted one definition but not others. Chapter 4 expanded on this approach, breaking quality into eight separate dimensions: performance, features, reliability, conformance, durability, serviceability, aesthetics, and perceived quality. An important strategic point emerged from the analysis: Companies choosing to compete on quality could do so in several ways. They did not—and often could not—pursue all eight dimensions at once. Rather, they were likely to benefit from focusing on a narrow quality niche, paying less attention to those aspects of quality already provided by other companies or of slight interest to consumers.

The same framework was used in Chapter 5 to examine the corre-

lates of quality. The evidence connecting quality and price, advertising, market share, cost, productivity, and profitability was reviewed,
but few unambiguous results were found. Only when quality was
defined as either conformance/reliability or the PIMS measure of
relative quality were consistent relationships observed. Confor-
mance/reliability was negatively related to total quality costs and
positively related to productivity; the PIMS measure of quality was
positively related to both market share and profitability. Most other
relationships were weak or highly variable, primarily because quality
had not been defined carefully or the dimensions of quality had not
been treated separately.

With this background, Part II turned to the narrower topic of
quality performance in a single U.S. industry. Room air conditioners
were selected for study because of their simple designs, straightforward production methods, and large number of manufacturers. In
Chapter 6, the eight dimensions of quality were applied to this industry; performance was found to be the attribute most desired by consumers, followed by reliability and durability. Consumers' brand
quality rankings, however, were less revealing. They differed sharply
from the rankings of three expert panels: *Consumer Reports,* appliance servicemen and -women, and first-line supervisors. Most differences were traced to the varying definitions of quality used by each
group and their varying levels of experience with multiple brands.

Chapter 7 presented objective measures of quality for the same
industry. Field quality was measured by the service call rate under
first-year warranty coverage, and in-plant quality was measured by
defect rates at incoming inspection, subassembly, final assembly, and
quality audit. On all measures, there were wide and persistent gaps
between the best and poorest plants in the industry. The poorest
plants averaged service call rates that were five times higher and defect rates that were an astonishing twenty times higher. Moreover,
poor performance on in-plant measures was generally associated
with poor performance on field measures, despite extensive inspection and end-of-the-line quality audits. Audit results, in fact, were
commonly misused by managers, who saw them as predictors of field
performance rather than signals that production processes had fallen
out of control.

The sources of superior quality were examined in Chapters 8 and 9
using additional data from the U.S. room air conditioning industry.
Plants were first grouped into four categories of quality performance—best, better, fair, and poor. Practices at superior plants were

then contrasted with practices at less successful performers in order to isolate the most important contributors to quality. Often, reality diverged from conventional wisdom. Managers at several plants cited conservative engineering, vice presidents of quality, and lengthy performance and run tests as keys to their superior quality; none of these practices, however, varied systematically by categories of quality performance. Rather, the best and better plants used reliability engineering when designing new products; offered narrower product lines; monitored incoming shipments using statistical sampling plans; tracked problem suppliers using "hit lists" and "Ten Most Wanted Lists"; set goals for incoming quality and involved purchasing departments in quality improvement; scheduled longer production runs per model; conducted more rigorous quality audits; collected more detailed data on defects and field failures and reported them to higher levels in the organization; and used more advanced inspection and test equipment. Their managements were also more deeply committed to quality improvement and had more effectively communicated their concern through such measures as annual quality goals. The best U.S. plants were distinctive in another important respect: They had organized their quality efforts around a single, dominant theme—in one case, reliability engineering, and in the other, superior process design and equipment—which they pursued with great intensity. In these areas, the best plants were far ahead of their U.S. competitors.

Part III expanded the analysis to include Japanese companies. Chapter 10 began by reviewing the history of the Japanese quality movement and then contrasted it with the U.S. movement described in Chapter 1. There were striking similarities. Both movements were guided initially by the same concepts and philosophies; started with inspection and evolved toward strategic quality management; obtained direction from nonprofit national organizations; and focused heavily on education and training. But the Japanese movement was far more successful and was diffused more rapidly among firms. A host of factors were responsible: top management leadership; education and training aimed at generalists rather than specialists; coordination and credibility provided by the Union of Japanese Scientists and Engineers and the Industrial Standardization Law; and innovations in quality management such as quality control circles and company-wide quality control. Together they produced a revolution in quality attitudes and unprecedented change.

Chapter 11 examined Japanese quality management at the factory level. Using data from the room air conditioning industry, it compared seven Japanese plants with the eleven U.S. plants discussed in Chapters 6 through 9. The Japanese plants had vastly superior quality, with failure rates that were seventeen to sixty-seven times lower. They achieved these results through innovative methods, such as foolproofing to prevent assembly errors, early warning systems to distinguish routine problems from emergencies, and internal consumer review boards, as well as traditional techniques. Reliability engineering, statistical quality control, training and education, preventive maintenance, and supplier oversight were all widely practiced at Japanese plants in the industry. None of these methods is especially new, yet each contributed in some way to the superior quality performance of the Japanese. In combination, they led to designs that were simple to manufacture, with few field problems; production processes that were stable and predictable; workers who were skilled at their jobs and attuned to quality; and organizations that viewed defect-free production as a necessary and desirable end.

## IMPLICATIONS FOR PRACTICE

Perhaps the strongest conclusion that emerges from this analysis is the need for top managers to become involved in quality activities. That is a widely accepted truth, but here it takes on added force. Strategic quality management poses special challenges. It requires a clear sense of direction, a recognition that quality control and quality assurance are at best partial solutions, a sensitivity to quality's multiple dimensions, and the support of functions throughout the organization. Responsibilities of this order cannot be delegated; as Japan's quality movement has shown, top managers must be the architects of change.

Nevertheless, middle- and lower-level managers have important roles to play. They are responsible for identifying and leading quality projects in such departments as design, purchasing, and manufacturing. In each of these areas, *Managing Quality* has identified practices associated with superior U.S. performance. These practices fall into several distinct categories. Some, such as reliability engineering and statistical sampling, have long been recommended by quality experts on theoretical grounds. Others, such as careful monitoring of vendors, precise information systems, and internally developed equipment, have often been associated with excellence in manufacturing. But a few, such as long production runs, limited bumping, the order of assembly operations, and narrow product lines, have rarely appeared in the literature. They are therefore findings of special significance.

Companies in industries other than room air conditioning would undoubtedly benefit from many of these practices. Because they represent basic "blocking and tackling"—simple ideas, carefully executed, day after day—they should transfer readily to other industry environments. And should companies already be matching best U.S. practice, they can still learn from the Japanese, who remain leaders in quality management. Progress is possible on many fronts, including the pretesting of designs prior to release, the use of rolling inspection standards, and the tightening of process control in manufacturing. Such improvements require that firms develop a shared responsibility for quality, with each function contributing in its own way.

In fact, a primary goal of *Managing Quality* has been to isolate the contributions of individual functions. But an equally important goal has been to test the conventional wisdom about quality, for a vast mythology now surrounds the subject. It takes many forms: the belief that quality is undefinable and impossible to discuss objectively; that high quality is always associated with high costs; that automation is the key to Japan's superior quality; and that vice presidents of quality are required for superior results. None of these assumptions was supported by the evidence. Managers' assessments of the sources of quality were equally inaccurate. They vastly overestimated the impact of conservative engineering and inspection and test procedures, while underestimating the impact of long production runs.

These findings suggest an important caveat: If quality is to be managed, it must first be understood. Conventional wisdom is seldom sufficient. It frequently points in the wrong direction or is otherwise incomplete. If managers hope to succeed, they must first move aggressively to improve their understanding of quality practices and performance. They need to acquire more detailed information about consumers' views, competitors' quality levels, and especially the sources of their own quality performance. Conscious experimentation may well be required to distinguish effective from ineffective practice. Such efforts are likely to be costly and time-consuming, but they are essential if real progress is to be achieved.


## IMPLICATIONS FOR RESEARCH

Given its long history, surprisingly little is known about quality management. Academic research on the subject is in its infancy. The analysis of this book suggests a number of directions for further research, each likely to be of some benefit to managers.

There is a clear need for more precise measures of quality. Few studies have recognized the multiple dimensions of quality, and still fewer, the possibility that quality may have different meanings in different industries. Much of the empirical research reviewed in Chapter 5 needs to be replicated with these distinctions in mind. Similarly, analysts need to determine if the various dimensions of quality move together or separately, for otherwise managers will be unable to position their companies to exploit particular quality niches.

These questions suggest two possible avenues of research. The first would focus on the determinants of consumer satisfaction, consumer perceptions of quality, and the relative importance of the various dimensions of quality in shaping buyer behavior. For example, marketing scholars have observed that alternative measures of consumer satisfaction are not well correlated.[1] Is the same true of measures of quality? Does each of the dimensions play a different role in shaping overall quality perceptions? Do the relationships vary with segments of the population? Chapter 6 has addressed these questions in a preliminary fashion, but much additional work remains to be done.

A second line of research would focus on manufacturing tradeoffs. Traditionally, analysts have argued that manufacturing operations could be effective only if they pursued a limited set of objectives.[2] Low cost, high quality, rapid delivery, flexibility to volume changes, and flexibility to new product introductions were thought to be mutually incompatible. Tradeoffs were unavoidable, and any one goal could be achieved only at the expense of others.

Japanese manufacturers, however, have succeeded in producing products that meet the twin objectives of high quality (conformance and reliability) and low cost. Their ability to do so has forced analysts to reconsider the concept of manufacturing tradeoffs, for many traditional assumptions no longer apply.[3] This area clearly warrants further research. Tradeoffs among the various dimensions of quality and between each dimension and the objectives of cost, flexibility, and delivery must be better understood. Which of the dimensions of quality require unique forms of expertise, and which respond to common influences? Which of the dimensions are primarily a reflection of manufacturing skills, and which reflect design, engineering, or purchasing expertise?

A final line of research would focus on the sources of quality in the United States and Japan. The room air conditioning study has provided much insight, but it remains grounded in a single industry. The same analysis has to be replicated in other settings, such as high technology, complex products, process industries, and services. Industry-specific factors would then become more visible, as would findings of wider applicability. At the same time, narrower quantitative analysis must be pursued to isolate the precise contribution to quality of individual policies and practices. The room air conditioning study has identified patterns of behavior, but it has neither assigned weights nor ranked practices by their relative importance. Weights and rankings are necessary if managers are to develop a clear sense of priorities; they are likely to emerge from more focused studies, drawing on fewer variables.

Overall, quality remains a fertile area for research. Its technical tools may be well developed, but its theory and practice lag far behind. The concept of quality is only dimly understood. Links to market share, cost, and profitability are unclear. Measurement is complex, and anecdotes remain the source of most recommendations. The challenge facing researchers is immense, as is the challenge facing managers.

# Appendix
# A

## The Room Air Conditioning Study

Much of the evidence in this book comes from a study of the room air conditioning industry conducted in 1981 and 1982. Appendix A describes the project and research methods and includes copies of the four questionnaires used.

Nine U.S. companies and seven Japanese companies participated in the study. In 1981, they ranged in size from small air conditioning specialists with total sales under $50 million to large home appliance and consumer electronics manufacturers with annual sales of more than $200 million in this product line alone. In most cases, plants were the primary unit of analysis, rather than companies, because practices differed within firms. Two of the American companies operated two plants apiece; otherwise, each company employed a single plant. In total, eighteen plants were involved in the study, eleven of them American and seven Japanese. Together, they accounted for approximately 90 percent of the shipments of room air conditioners in each country.

Cooperation was obtained by first writing a letter to each company's president or vice president of manufacturing, explaining the purpose of the research and promising that a complete set of industry statistics would be provided after the study was completed. Once U.S. companies had agreed to participate, a questionnaire was sent to them requesting background information on their product line, production practices, vendor management practices, quality policies, and quality performance. (See Table A.1 for a copy of the questionnaire.) Site visits were then arranged to review the questionnaire results, collect additional data, tour the factories, and conduct interviews with key personnel. The interviews were open-ended and

TABLE A.1    *The Plant Questionnaire*

For 1981, please provide the following information about your plant and its products:

*General Background*
1. What was your plant's total sales volume?
   In dollars?
   In units?
   By product line (dollars and units) and Btu capacity?
2. How many different products were produced by your plant? (Please do not count minor variations in styling or finish.)
   How many different models?
3. How many employees (on average) did your plant have?
   Total?
   Direct labor?
   Indirect labor?
   First-line supervisors?
   Quality control (assurance)?
4. Where is your plant located?
   City?
   State?
   Rural, urban, or suburban area?
5. How large is your plant (square footage)?

*Labor Force*
6. Are your employees represented by a union?
   If "yes," please state the union involved and the date it was voted in.
7. What was the average turnover rate of your plant's direct labor force?
   Average absenteeism?
8. How long did it take, on average, for a newly hired direct laborer to reach full efficiency (100% of standard)?
9. How many new employees were hired in 1981?
   How many of these were direct laborers?
   Indirect laborers?
   First-line supervisors?
10. How many hours of overtime did your direct labor force work?
11. How many shifts did your plant normally run?
12. What percent of your direct labor force was paid by piece rates?
    What percent was paid by hourly wages?
13. Were there any layoffs?
    If "yes," how many workers were involved?

TABLE A.1  *(Continued)*

*Quality Policies*
14. Did your plant have a formal, written statement of quality policy?
15. Were line managers and first-line supervisors formally evaluated on the quality of their output?
16. Did your firm/plant have a designated V.P. for quality?
17. To whom did the director of the quality control (assurance) department report?
18. Was the quality control (assurance) department empowered to stop production if output did not meet quality standards?
    If "yes," did it ever exercise that authority? (Please describe the circumstances.)
19. Did your plant employ quality circles?
    Observe a Zero Defects Day?

While we are interested in your plant's performance generally, we are especially interested in its production of the following products: _____ . Because our study is focusing on the quality records of different manufacturers of room air conditioners, it is especially important that we collect accurate data on these products. If you have plantwide data available for each of the categories indicated below, however, we would also be interested in securing that information as a basis for comparison.

*Product Characteristics*
20. How many separate parts does the product contain?
21. When was the product first manufactured at your plant?
22. Were any changes made in the product's design in the last year?
    If "yes," please indicate how many, and whether these were major or minor changes.
23. Approximately how many units of the product have been sold since it was first introduced?
24. What was the product's average factory price? Its retail price?

*Product Performance*
25. What was the assembly line reject rate (total defects per unit produced)?
    What percentage of these defects required off-line repair?
    What percentage of these defects involved leaks? Electrical problems?
26. What was the field failure (service call) rate for the product?
    What percentage of these failures involved compressors? Thermostats? Fan motors?

*(continued)*

TABLE A.1    *(Continued)*

27. What were the total warranty costs incurred by the company for this particular product?

28. Based on historical experience, what is the product's estimated (operating) life span?

*Manufacturing Practices*

29. What kind of production process is used to assemble the product—job shop, batch, or assembly line? (If some combination of these different processes is involved, please explain.)

30. What was last year's production capacity for the product?

31. Was production reasonably stable over the course of the year, or were there seasonal peaks and valleys?
    If there were peaks and valleys, by what amount did peak production exceed production in the low period?
    If there were peaks and valleys, was peak production achieved by using overtime, by hiring new workers and laying them off in low periods, or by subcontracting?

32. What was the average batch size or run length for the product?

33. Were standard (MTM) or actual task times used for scheduling and planning?
    If standard times were used, when were they last updated?

34. Was the product produced in a separate work area/dedicated assembly line, or were multiple products assembled in the same work area or the same assembly line?

*Vendor Relations*

35. What percentage of the product's materials was purchased from outside vendors?
    What percentage was purchased from other subsidiaries of the same parent firm?

36. What percentage of purchased parts and materials was single sourced?

37. What percentage of purchased materials was subject to 100% inspection?
    To statistical sampling?

38. What percentage of incoming parts and materials was rejected as being below standards?

39. What was the average amount of time that the plant had been served by its major vendors?

TABLE A.1    *(Continued)*

*Costs of Quality*

40. What were the total costs of quality (prevention, appraisal, internal failure, and external failure costs) attributable to room air conditioning manufacturing?
As a percentage of sales?
As a percentage of applied direct labor costs?
What percentage of these costs fell in each of the following categories:
Prevention?    Appraisal?    Internal failure?    Scrap?
Rework?    External failure?    Warranty?    Product liability?

41. What was the average (warranty) cost per service call?
What percentage of these costs was due to labor costs?
To the cost of replacement parts?

*Assembly Line Characteristics*

42. How many workers were assigned to each room air conditioner assembly line?
How many of these were direct laborers?    Indirect laborers?
Inspectors/testers?    Repairmen?    Group leaders?
First-line supervisors?

43. What was the average cycle time (line speed) of the assembly line?

44. What is the length of each of your room air conditioner assembly lines?

*Component Parts*

45. What was the average wall thickness of the tubing used in your condenser and evaporator coils?
Were aluminum or copper coils employed?

46. What type of fan motors (shaded pole or split capacitor; open or sealed) was employed in your products?

47. What type of thermostats (bimetallic or vapor-filled bulb) was employed in your products?

48. What type of compressors (piston or rotary) was employed in your products?

---

unstructured, although similar questions were posed at each plant. A typical visit lasted two days and included interviews with managers in the quality, manufacturing, purchasing, engineering, and service departments, as well as several hours spent walking the factory floor.

Preliminary analysis of the interviews and questionnaires showed that plants neither employed the same conventions in reporting data nor answered questions in the same degree of detail. Each plant

TABLE A.2.   *The Supervisor's Questionnaire*

All questionnaires included the ten items listed below. Supervisors were asked to respond to items 1, 2, 3, 5, 7, and 10 using a 7-point scale, with 1 indicating the lowest performance, pressure, or understanding and 7 the highest. Item 4 required respondents to assign percentages, while item 6 required them to assign ranks. Items 8 and 9 required yes or no responses. The complete list of questions was as follows:

1. I would rate the quality of my firm's products in relation to its competitors: much worse (1) to much better (7).

2. I am feeling pressure to increase the quality of my firm's products: very little pressure (1) to a lot of pressure (7).

3. I feel that we are at the following stage in understanding our quality problems: we have very little idea why they occur (1) to we pretty much know why they occur (7).

4. If I were to break the "causes" of our quality problems down into areas and then try to assign a percentage to them, I would rate them as follows (please be sure the total adds to 100%): (a) workmanship/work force problems; (b) materials/parts we purchase; (c) maintenance/adjustment of process or equipment; (d) poor design of process or equipment; (e) poor product design; (f) inadequate systems or controls; (g) management errors (including providing insufficient instructions to the work force); (h) other (please specify).

5. The management of my company *acts* as though it considers the manufacturing objectives listed below to have the following weight—relatively unimportant (1) to extremely important (7): (a) low-cost production; (b) meeting the production schedule; (c) producing high-quality (defect-free) products; (d) improving worker productivity.

6. If the management of my company were asked to rank its manufacturing objectives in order, I feel that they would respond as follows: (a) low-cost production; (b) meeting the production schedule; (c) producing high-quality (defect-free) products; (d) improving worker productivity.

7. I feel that the production workers in my company: care very little about product quality (1) to care a great deal about product quality (7).

8. When my on-the-job performance is evaluated, I am held responsible for my people's performance in the areas of: (a) the amount of rework required; (b) scrap costs; (c) rejection (defect) rates; (d) other quality measures (please specify).

9. I have/have not seen the formal quality statement of my firm.

10. I think my company pays: too little attention to product quality (1) to too much attention to product quality (7).

therefore received its own set of follow-up questions to fill in gaps and make the data more comparable. In addition, to develop further information on quality perceptions and attitudes, each plant was asked to administer a brief questionnaire to all of its first-line production supervisors.[1] (See Table A.2.) The number of supervisors surveyed at each U.S. plant ranged from six to forty-two, with a median of sixteen; in total, 199 U.S. supervisors were surveyed.[2]

A similar approach was followed with the Japanese manufacturers, although time constraints limited the amount of information that could be collected. This phase of the project was coordinated by the Nomura School of Advanced Management in Tokyo. Experts at Nomura translated the plant and supervisor's questionnaires into Japanese; contacted the Japanese room air conditioner manufacturers; and arranged for visits by the author, accompanied by a translator. Six of the seven Japanese plants completed the same basic questionnaire as their American counterparts; the other plant provided partial data. Six plants also administered the supervisor's questionnaire to a small sample of their first-line supervisors. The number of supervisors surveyed at each Japanese plant ranged from one to seven, with a median of six; in total, twenty-nine Japanese supervisors were surveyed. To guide the interviews at Japanese plants, a third questionnaire was developed; it too was translated into Japanese and sent ahead to managers. That questionnaire appears in Table A.3.

TABLE A.3 *Questions for Interviews with Japanese Room Air Conditioner Manufacturers*

*Quality Management*
1. How is the quality department organized at your plant? Which departments have responsibility for improving product designs, controlling rejects, reducing scrap, and resolving field problems? What are the roles of the engineering, manufacturing, marketing, and purchasing departments in these areas?
2. How is the customer (field) service department organized? What role does it play in managing product quality?
3. Are goals set for incoming (supplier) quality? For rejection rates in the plant? For field failures (service call rates)? If so, who is involved in the goal-setting process, and precisely how are the goals established?

*(continued)*

TABLE A.3　*(Continued)*

4. What kind of information is normally collected on rejects, field failures, and other quality problems? How detailed are those data? Are the data computerized in any form? To whom are they regularly reported?

5. Are statistical quality control techniques used in managing the quality area? In what areas? Are Acceptable Quality Levels (AQLs) and process capability studies normally employed? What type of statistical training is provided to the work force?

*Work Force Policies and Attitudes*

6. How is a commitment to quality instilled in your work force?

7. What role do Quality Control Circles (QCCs) play in your plant? How many workers are involved, and what type of training are they offered? To what extent have QCCs led to improvements in the quality of your firm's products?

*Quality Systems*

8. Does your firm employ a Total Quality Control system? If so, how is it organized, and when was it first introduced?

9. Does your firm employ a quality cost reporting system? If so, how is it organized, and when was it first introduced?

10. Do you perform a quality audit on a small sample of finished goods? What evaluation system is used to rate those products? How do these ratings correlate with the incidence of field failure problems? If defective units are found in quality audits, what remedial action is taken?

*Vendor (Supplier) Quality Management*

11. What steps are taken to insure that suppliers provide only high-quality components? What action is taken if a supplier fails to provide satisfactory products? How are nonconforming parts handled (i.e., are they generally shipped back to the supplier, "used as is" or scrapped)?

12. Are visits commonly made to suppliers' production facilities to assess their manufacturing and quality control methods? If so, who is involved in these trips, and what are the visitors generally looking for?

13. What role does the purchasing department play in insuring the quality of purchased parts? Are buyers trained in the area of quality, or is that responsibility left to engineering and quality control departments? Are buyers evaluated at all on quality (for example, on the number of incoming lots rejected because of defective parts)? Is there a special position in the purchasing department responsible for vendor quality management?

14. What types of quality data (on rejects, scrap rates, field failure rates, etc.) are routinely reported to the purchasing department?

TABLE A.3    *(Continued)*

*Product Design*

15. What is the sequence that a new product typically goes through from conception to first production run? At what stage are prototypes built, field tests conducted, pilot units built from tooling, and customer satisfaction evaluated? Which departments are involved at each stage of the process (and, in particular, at what point do the quality, customer service, and purchasing departments become involved)? How long does the process normally take?

16. What process is followed for introducing engineering changes to a product? How much pretesting is involved, and what departments (quality, manufacturing, etc.) are involved in the approval process?

17. Is "Failure Mode and Effects Analysis" (FMEA) or a similar technique employed in an effort to predict failure rates prior to the introduction of a new product? Are warranty costs ever estimated during the design phase?

Finally, to obtain quality perceptions and rankings from a group of independent experts, a fourth questionnaire was developed and sent to appliance servicemen and -women in September 1982. A geographically balanced sample of five hundred was first generated from the circulation list of *Appliance Service News,* the industry trade journal; each individual was then sent a covering letter and the questionnaire in Table A.4. One hundred and two questionnaires

TABLE A.4    *The Servicemen and -Women's Questionnaire*

All questionnaires included the fourteen items listed below. Items 1, 2, 3, 4, 10, and 11 were accompanied by lists of the major brands of room air conditioners to ensure complete coverage. Items 2, 3, 10, and 11 were scored using a 7-point scale, similar to the supervisor's questionnaire. Items 4 and 9 required respondents to assign ranks, while items 7 and 8 required them to assign percentages. All other items involved simple filling in the blanks. The complete list of questions was as follows:

1. Please indicate (with a ✓) all brands of room air conditioners that you service and also indicate (with an X) any brands that you sell.

The following questions are designed to get your views on the differences between the various *brands* of room air conditioners. Although there are likely to be variations in the performance of different models sold under

TABLE A.4    *(Continued)*

the same brand name, please try to answer each question for the product line *as a whole.*

2. For each brand of room air conditioner that you service, please give your estimate of how frequently the brand requires repair: relatively few repairs (1) to very frequent repairs (7).

3. For each brand of room air conditioner that you service, please indicate whether you feel that the brand's repair frequency is greater than, less than, or the same as it was five years ago: requires less frequent repair (1) to requires more frequent repair (7).

4. Please rank each of the brands you service on the following dimensions: longest product life; easiest to repair; least costly to repair; quietest; best engineering design; best overall quality.

5. Please complete the following sentence: I define a quality room air conditioner as one that _____.

6. Please complete the following sentence: A room air conditioner takes me an average of ____ hours to repair and costs the customer (or the company, if the unit is covered by warranty) ____ dollars to fix.

7. Based on repairs that you have performed, please break the "causes" of room air conditioner quality problems into categories and assign a percentage to each. (Please make sure that the total adds up to 100%): (a) poor product design; (b) poor workmanship or construction; (c) poor components or materials; (d) poor packaging or shipping damage; (e) faulty installation by the customer; (f) other (please specify).

8. Based on repairs that you have performed, please estimate what percentage of the units you service have required only a single service call, and what percentage of units have required multiple repairs or more than one service call (again, please make sure that the total adds up to 100%): (a) units requiring a single repair/service call; (b) units requiring two repairs/service calls; (c) units requiring three repairs/service calls; (d) units requiring four repairs/service calls; (e) units requiring five or more repairs/service calls.

9. Please indicate the most frequent service problems you have encountered during the (i) first year; (ii) second–fifth year; and (iii) sixth year to end of use of room air conditioner life (please rank the most frequent problems during each period with a "1", the next most frequent with a "2", etc.): (a) compressor problems; (b) fan motor problems; (c) thermostat problems; (d) wiring or electrical problems; (e) fan or blower wheel rubs; (f) leaks; (g) other (please specify).

10. For each brand of room air conditioner that you service, please give your estimate of the responsiveness of that company's service organization to newly discovered field problems: takes a long time to diagnose

TABLE A.4  *(Continued)*

and correct problems (1) to diagnoses and corrects problems quickly (7).

11. For each brand of room air conditioner that you service, please give your estimate of the amount of contact you have with that company's field service staff or customer service representatives: very little contact or communication (1) to extensive contact and communication (7).

12. Please complete the following sentence: If I were to go out today and buy a room air conditioner for my own use, it would be one made by ————— .

13. I do/do not own a room air conditioner. If you do own a unit, please indicate the brand.

14. Please feel free to add any additional comments you'd like concerning the quality of room air conditioners, the quality of other major home appliances that you service, product improvements that you'd like to see, repair problems, warranty provisions, and any other issues related to product quality.

were returned, a response rate of 20 percent. Of these, thirteen were not complete, either because respondents had retired or because they were no longer servicing room air conditioners. The total number of usable questionnaires was eighty-nine, or 18 percent of the original sample.

# Appendix
## B

# Classifying Plants
# by Quality Performance

To identify patterns of behavior, plants were first grouped into categories according to their performance on two dimensions: in-plant and field quality. The classification scheme is described at length in this appendix.

Table B.1 presents the basic U.S. data on field quality. (Note that plants appear here in a different order from the tables of Chapter 7.) Field quality has been measured in two ways: by the service call rate for units under first-year warranty coverage (the total number of service calls recorded in 1981 divided by the number of units in the field with active warranties) and by the service call rate for units under first-year warranty coverage less "customer instruction calls" (only those service calls that resulted from a faulty unit, not from a customer who was using the unit improperly or had failed to install it correctly). Both measures have already been described in Chapter 7. Plants were classified on the basis of the second of these measures and then grouped into categories according to their actual levels of field failures. In most cases, the dividing lines were clear, although there were some borderline cases. For example, plant 8 had a total service call rate well above the industry median, yet after subtracting customer instruction calls, its failure rate differed little from the other fair performers. Because the second figure more accurately reflected the incidence of true product problems, plant 8 was classified as having fair, rather than poor, field quality. A number of companies with high failure rates did not break out customer instruction calls separately. They have been classified as poor performers because their customer instruction calls would have to have been two

TABLE B.1    *Field Quality of U.S. Plants, 1981*

| Plant Number | Service Call Rate, First-Year Warranty Coverage | | Service Call Rate, Less Customer Instruction Calls | |
|---|---|---|---|---|
| | *Percentage* | *Rank* | *Percentage* | *Rank* |
| 1 | 5.3% | 1 | <5.3% | 1 |
| 2 | 8.7 | 2 | <8.7 | 2, 3 |
| 3 | 9.2 | 3 | 5.6 | 2, 3 |
| 4 | 10.5 | 4 | 9.8 | 5 |
| 5 | 11.1 | 5 | 9.3 | 4 |
| 6 | 11.4 | 6 | 10.5 | 6 |
| 7 | 12.6 | 7 | 10.5 | 6 |
| 8 | 16.2 | 8 | 11.8 | 8 |
| 9 | 17.5 | 9 | 13.8 | 9 |
| 10 | 22.9 | 10 | <22.9 | 10 |
| 11 | 26.5 | 11 | <26.5 | 11 |

| | Ranking of Plants on Field Quality | | |
|---|---|---|---|
| | *Good* | *Fair* | *Poor* |
| Plant number | 1, 2, 3 | 4, 5, 6, 7, 8 | 9, 10, 11 |

SOURCE: Company records and questionnaires distributed by the author.

or three times as frequent as the highest rate recorded in 1981 for them to have warranted a fair ranking.

A similar procedure was used to classify U.S. plants on in-plant quality. The results appear in Table B.2. Several indexes were used to ensure consistency, for plants differed in how they defined and recorded defects. Plants were ranked first on their total assembly line defect rates (every defect recorded at every station along the assembly line, divided by the number of units produced), and then by the number of defects requiring off-line repair. The second index more accurately reflects the incidence of serious problems. Minor adjustments and touch-ups can generally be made without pulling a unit off the line; more serious problems normally require off-line repair. Measured on this basis, the high total defect rates of Plant 1 and 9 appear to be much less of a problem.

Because several plants had to estimate the off-line repair rate, a third index, the number of repairmen per assembly line direct laborer, was also used to measure defect seriousness. The proportion

TABLE B.2   *In-Plant Quality of U.S. Plants, 1981*

| Plant Number | Assembly Line Defects per 100 Units | | Assembly Line Defects per 100 Units Requiring Off-Line Repair | | Repairmen per Assembly Line Direct Laborer | |
|---|---|---|---|---|---|---|
| | *Number* | *Rank* | *Number* | *Rank* | *Number* | *Rank* |
| 1 | 150 | 9 | 34 | 5, 6 | .06 | 3 |
| 2 | 8 | 1 | 8 | 2 | .05 | 2 |
| 3 | 10 | 2 | 10 | 3 | .04 | 1 |
| 4 | N/Aª | N/A | N/A | N/A | .09 | 8 |
| 5 | 57 | 5 | 47 | 7 | .13 | 9 |
| 6 | 70 | 6 | 67 | 8 | .06 | 3 |
| 7 | 26 | 4 | 7 | 1 | .08 | 6 |
| 8 | 18 | 3 | 11 | 4 | .08 | 6 |
| 9 | >100 | 7 | >30 | 5, 6 | .16 | 11 |
| 10 | 165 | 10 | 165 | 10 | .13 | 9 |
| 11 | 135 | 8 | >68 | 9 | .07 | 5 |

| | Ranking of Plants on In-Plant Quality | | |
|---|---|---|---|
| | *Good* | *Fair* | *Poor* |
| Plant number | 2, 3, 7, 8 | 1, 4(?), 5, 6 | 9, 10, 11 |

ªN/A = Not available.

SOURCE: Company records and questionnaires distributed by the author.

of the work force engaged in repair activities, including workers assigned to separate rework lines and to rework activities in the warehouse, is likely to correlate well with the incidence of serious defects, for more serious problems usually require more time to correct and necessitate a larger repair staff. This measure provided important additional information, confirming the conclusions about Plant 1 (its high total defect rate appears to include a large number of minor problems) but contradicting those about Plant 9 (its large number of repairmen suggests that defects were, in fact, a serious problem, despite the small proportion of units requiring off-line repair).

Plants were assigned to groups using much the same procedure as before. A composite ranking was computed for each plant by averaging together the three rankings of Table B.2. Dividing lines between groups were then drawn by following the absolute levels of the indexes for each plant. Once again, some judgment was involved, particularly for plants 4, 5, and 9. Plants 5 and 9 were borderline cases, candidates for ranking as either fair or poor in-plant quality. The former was classified as fair, even though its overall rank was low, because its absolute scores on the first two measures were quite close to the median. Plant 9 was classified as poor because its absolute scores on both the first and third measures were so high. Plant 4 presented a different problem, for it provided no information at all on assembly line defects. Rather than classifying the plant on the basis of the third index alone, supplementary data were used. Based on its defect rate at the end-of-the-line quality audit and its rework and scrap costs as a percentage of sales, both of which were quite close to figures reported by other plants with fair in-plant quality, Plant 4 showed up as a fair performer.

Combining in-plant and field quality ratings produced overall rankings for each plant. They are summarized in Table B.3. In most cases, success on in-plant quality implied success on field measures, although the correlation was not perfect, as plants 1, 7, and 8 demonstrate. All of the Japanese plants were in a category of their own, for on both in-plant and field measures they were at least twice as good as the best U.S. plant. Their service call rate under first-year warranty coverage ranged from .04 to 2.0 percent, while their assembly line defect rate per 100 units ranged from 0.15 to 3.0.

Because several of the U.S. plants were borderline cases, experi-

TABLE B.3   *Classification of Plants on In-Plant and Field Quality*

|  | Field Quality | | | |
|---|---|---|---|---|
|  | *Poor* | *Fair* | *Good* | *Excellent* |
| In-plant quality: |  |  |  |  |
| Poor | Plants 9, 10, 11 |  |  |  |
| Fair |  | Plants 4, 5, 6 | Plant 1 |  |
| Good |  | Plants 7, 8 | Plants 2, 3 |  |
| Excellent |  |  |  | All Japanese plants |

*Note:* Overall quality rankings·
  Poor U.S. plants:   9, 10, 11
  Fair U.S. plants:   4, 5, 6
  Better U.S. plants:   1, 7, 8
  Best U.S. plants:   2, 3

ments were conducted with two alternative classification schemes: combining the better and fair plants into a single category and leaving the other categories unchanged; and combining the best and better plants into one category and the fair and poor plants into another. Neither method was especially helpful. When statistical analyses were performed, they produced few significant changes in results.

# Appendix
# C

---

# Statistical Analyses

This appendix contains statistical analyses supporting Chapters 5, 6, 7, 8, and 9. The results for each chapter are discussed in turn.

## CHAPTER 5: HEDONIC REGRESSIONS

Hedonic regressions relate product prices to product attributes using multivariate statistical techniques. Table C.1 reports hedonic regressions for various models of room air conditioners. All data, with the exception of service call rates, which were collected by the author, have been drawn from *Consumer Reports*.[1] In each case, the dependent variable was list price and the independent variables were as follows:

| | |
|---|---|
| BTUCAP | = Btu capacity |
| EER | = energy efficiency ratio |
| WEIGHT | = weight, in pounds |
| OVQLTY | = overall quality ranking by *Consumer Reports* (i.e., units were ranked only by general categories, with no distinction between models with the same general ranking) |
| SPECQLTY | = specific quality ranking by *Consumer Reports* (i.e., units were ranked from first to last within general categories, as well as between them) |
| RELIAB | = service call rates under first-year warranty coverage, 1981 (overall rate for brands, not specific models) |

Equations 1 and 2 were estimated with pooled data from 1979, 1980, and 1982. Equations 3, 4, and 5 were limited to 1982 data, because

241

TABLE C.1 *Hedonic Regressions for Room Air Conditioners, 1979–82*

| Equation number: | Independent Variables | | | | | | | Summary Statistics | | | |
|---|---|---|---|---|---|---|---|---|---|---|---|
| | Constant | BTUCAP | EER | WEIGHT | OVQLTY | SPECQLTY | RELIAB | $R^2$ | $\overline{R}^2$ | SEE | N |
| 1 | −90.5 | 0.03[a] | 21.0 | 0.7 | — | — | — | .67 | .65 | 41.4 | 47 |
| | (90.5) | (0.008) | (14.2) | (0.5) | | | | | | | |
| 2 | −76.4 | 0.03[a] | 19.2 | 0.7 | −0.9 | — | — | .67 | .64 | 41.8 | 47 |
| | (108.3) | (0.009) | (16.2) | (0.5) | (3.8) | | | | | | |
| 3 | 167.8 | 0.03 | −4.6 | 1.1 | — | −5.3 | — | .55 | .32 | 38.2 | 13 |
| | (479.8) | (0.07) | (46.5) | (0.8) | | (3.4) | | | | | |
| 4 | −763.5 | 0.17[b] | −47.3 | 1.7[b] | — | — | 6.2[b] | .88 | .76 | 25.6 | 9 |
| | (425.9) | (0.06) | (33.3) | (0.6) | | | (1.7) | | | | |
| 5 | −445.5 | 0.14[b] | −47.6 | 1.3[b] | — | −3.4 | 5.8[b] | .93 | .81 | 23.7 | 9 |
| | (462.4) | (0.06) | (30.7) | (0.6) | | (2.6) | (3.7) | | | | |

*Note:* Standard errors are in parentheses.
[a]Significant at the 1 percent level.
[b]Significant at the 5 percent level.

242

specific quality rankings were available for that year only and because complete data on service call rates were available for 1981 only.

In these equations, Btu capacity and weight explained most of the variance in prices.[2] Neither of the *Consumer Reports* quality rankings contributed much to the regressions. Both appeared with the expected signs but were statistically insignificant. The results for reliability, however, were quite different. Higher service call rates (implying lower reliability) were associated with higher prices, and at statistically significant levels. These results were unanticipated and remain difficult to explain.

## CHAPTER 6: INTERCORRELATIONS OF BRAND QUALITY RANKINGS

Chapter 6 contained comparisons of brand quality rankings by consumers, *Consumer Reports,* appliance servicemen and -women, and first-line supervisors. Table C.2 presents the supporting statistical analysis: Spearman rank correlations, which measure the degree of association between ordinal or ranked data. The table shows a very weak relationship between the rankings of the different groups. Although servicemen and -women and first-line supervisors ranked brands similarly, and both consumers and servicemen and -women reported comparable rankings for the best quality brand and the brand they would buy, none of the other correlations in Table C.2 was statistically significant.

## CHAPTER 7: INTERCORRELATIONS OF PLANT DEFECT RATES

Chapter 7 included a discussion of plant defect rates, measured at four points along the production chain: incoming inspection, subassembly, final assembly, and quality audit. Table C.3 shows the degree of association among these measures using Pearson correlations. Most correlations were statistically significant, with two exceptions: Quality audit results were only weakly associated with other defect measures, and incoming and assembly line defect rates were unrelated.

TABLE C.2  *Spearman Rank Correlations of Brand Quality Rankings*

| | Consumers | | | Servicemen/-Women | | First-Line Supervisors |
|---|---|---|---|---|---|---|
| | Best Quality | Brand They Would Buy | Consumer Reports | Best Quality | Brand They Would Buy | |
| Consumers | | | | | | |
| Best quality | — | | | | | |
| Brand they would buy | .87[a] | — | | | | |
| Consumer Reports | −.32 | −.25 | — | | | |
| Servicemen/-women | | | | | | |
| Best quality | .21 | .25 | −.05 | — | | |
| Brand they would buy | .23 | .12 | −.10 | .73[a] | — | |
| First-line supervisors[c] | −.04 | −.06 | .30 | .90[a] | .70[b] | — |

[a]Significant at the 1 percent level.
[b]Significant at the 5 percent level.
[c]First-line supervisor rankings for General Electric were based on a simple (unweighted) average of the scores of its two plants.

244

TABLE C.3  *Pearson Correlations of Plant Defect Rates*

| | Incoming | Subassembly | Assembly Line | | | | |
| | | | Total | Off-Line | Leaks | Electrical | Quality Audit |
|---|---|---|---|---|---|---|---|
| Incoming | — | | | | | | |
| Subassembly | .70[a] | — | | | | | |
| Assembly line: | | | | | | | |
| Total | .10 | .65[b] | — | | | | |
| Off-line | .18 | .65[b] | .74[a] | — | | | |
| Leaks | .73[a] | .52 | .33 | .17 | — | | |
| Electrical | .67[a] | .72[a] | .67[a] | .77[a] | .75[a] | — | |
| Quality Audit | .25 | .17 | .32 | .49 | -.24 | .01 | — |

[a]Significant at the 5 percent level.
[b]Significant at the 10 percent level.

## CHAPTER 8: AN INDEX OF VENDOR QUALITY MANAGEMENT

Chapter 8 described an index developed to measure a plant's overall approach to supplier quality. The index was formed by coding vendor selection and vendor management variables in 1/0 form, depending on whether a practice was or was not observed at a plant. Unfortunately, the analysis suffered from a large number of missing observations. Neither of the best plants was represented, and only a small subset of all vendor management variables was used. The index included the following variables: whether the quality control department was involved in vendor selection, whether site visits were mandatory in selecting new vendors, whether quantitative goals were set for incoming quality, whether the purchasing department had a special position for vendor quality management, whether the purchasing department was involved in design reviews, whether the purchasing department received regular reports of field failure rates, and whether the purchasing department was primarily a buying function or was sensitive to quality issues. The last variable was based on subjective assessments by the author. A composite index formed from these variables was strongly related to overall quality performance. An analysis of variance testing for differences in scores on this index by quality categories yielded an F-value of 19.7, which is significant at the 1 percent level. The more conservative Kruskal-Wallis H-test yielded an H-value of 5.8, which is significant at the 6 percent level.

A number of additional experiments were conducted with these variables to see if they conformed to a Guttman scale. Such a scale orders variables by their degree of difficulty. In this case, ordering would require that plants reporting a more difficult vendor management practice also reported having those of less difficulty; conversely, the absence of a less difficult practice would mean the absence of practices of greater difficulty. Applying this procedure to the data on vendor selection and management led to the following classification of variables:

easy:     whether the quality control department was involved in selecting new vendors

medium:   whether quantitative goals were set for incoming quality, whether the purchasing department was involved in design reviews, and whether the purchasing department was primarily a buying function or was sensitive to quality issues

hard:    whether site visits were mandatory in selecting new vendors, whether the purchasing department had a special position for vendor quality management, and whether the purchasing department received regular reports of field failure rates

In this analysis, the coefficients of reproducibility (which measures how well the scale predicts) and scalability (which shows whether the scale is unidimensional and cumulative) were both equal to one, indicating a perfect Guttman scale.[1]

## CHAPTER 8: REGRESSIONS OF DEFECT RATES ON RUN LENGTHS

Chapter 8 noted a strong relationship between assembly line defect rates and average run lengths. Longer runs were associated with fewer defects. Table C.4 presents the supporting statistical analyses: a series of bivariate regressions. Equations 1 and 2 were estimated with data from all plants in the industry, while equations 3, 4, and 5 were estimated with data from a single plant but multiple models. The following variables were employed:

AL DEFECTS   = assembly line defects per 100 units (plantwide average, all models)

LAL DEFECTS = logarithm of assembly line defects per 100 units

AL LEAKS     = assembly line leaks per 100 units (single plant, one model only, individual production runs)

RUNLTH       = average run length (number of units per production run)

LRUNLTH    = logarithm of average run length

1/RUNLTH   = reciprocal of average run length

All five equations showed a strong negative relationship between assembly line defect rates and run lengths, whether industrywide or plant-specific data were used. The best results were obtained with logarithmic or reciprocal transformations, suggesting a nonlinear relationship between the two variables. But whatever the functional form, differences in average run length explained a significant proportion of the variance in assembly line defect and leak rates, both among plants and within a single facility.

TABLE C.4  *Regressions Linking Defect Rates and Run Lengths*

| Equation number: Dependent Variable | Independent Variables | | | | Summary Statistics | | | |
|---|---|---|---|---|---|---|---|---|
| | Constant | RUNLTH | LRUNLTH | 1/RUNLTH | $R^2$ | $\bar{R}^2$ | SEE | N |
| 1  AL DEFECTS (all plants) | 127.7[a] (32.8) | −.04[c] (.02) | — | — | .29 | .20 | 55.4 | 10 |
| 2  LAL DEFECTS (all plants) | 458.9[a] (165.5) | — | −54.8[b] (23.7) | — | .40 | .33 | 50.9 | 10 |
| 3  AL LEAKS (Model A) | −.72 (1.7) | — | — | 23920[b] (6892) | .71 | .65 | 2.5 | 7 |
| 4  AL LEAKS (Model B) | 2.2[b] (.9) | — | — | 5443[b] (1745) | .55 | .49 | 1.9 | 10 |
| 5  AL LEAKS (Model C) | 1.7 (1.2) | — | — | 4743[a] (1116) | .72 | .68 | 2.7 | 9 |

*Note:* Standard errors are in parentheses.
[a]Significant at the 1 percent level.
[b]Significant at the 5 percent level.
[c]Significant at the 10 percent level.

# CHAPTER 9: AN INDEX OF QUALITY INFORMATION SYSTEMS

Chapter 9 described an index developed to measure a plant's quality information system. Like the vendor management index, it was formed by coding quality information system variables in 1/0 form, depending on whether a practice was or was not observed at a plant. In this case, interval variables were involved as well; they were coded 1 or 0 depending on whether they fell above or below the sample median. The following variables were included: whether or not the plant had an informal system for collecting SCR data; whether or not the plant had a computerized system for collecting SCR data; whether or not the plant projected failure rates from limited data; whether or not meetings were held to discuss SCRs; how frequently meetings were held to discuss SCRs; the number of categories the plant used to classify quality audit problems; whether or not the service department was in the same building as the engineering and manufacturing departments; whether or not meetings were held to discuss defect rates; how frequently meetings were held to discuss defect rates; and the highest level in the organization to which defect rates were reported. A few variables discussed in the text were omitted because of missing observations, but a composite index formed from the included variables was still strongly related to overall quality performance.

An analysis of variance testing for differences in scores on this index by quality categories yielded an F-value of 14.6, which is significant at the 2 percent level. The corresponding Kruskal-Wallis H-value was 8.0, which is significant at the 5 percent level. A valid Guttman scale, however, could not be developed from these variables, because a consistent ordering could not be found.

# Notes

INTRODUCTION

1. S. L. (Red) Binstock, "Americans Express Dissatisfaction with Quality of U.S. Goods," *Quality Progress,* January 1981, p. 13.
2. These findings have been compiled from printouts provided by the Roper Center for Public Opinion Research at the University of Connecticut.
3. *Ibid.* The findings for consumer electronics—stereos, radios, and televisions—were quite similar. In 1973, 24 percent of consumers felt that Japanese stereos, radios, and televisions were of better quality than American-made products; in 1983, the figure was 40 percent.
4. For a splendid takeoff on this theme, see John Guaspari, *I Know It When I See It* (New York: AMACOM, 1985).

CHAPTER 1. HISTORY AND EVOLUTION

1. A number of authors have divided the history of the quality movement into distinct periods, although they have frequently used only two categories, quality control and quality assurance. See Robert A. Abbott and David C. Leaman, "Quality Control and Quality Assurance," in Carl Heyel, ed., *The Encyclopedia of Management,* Third Edition (New York: Van Nostrand Reinhold, 1982), pp. 998-1009; Everett Adam, Jr., "Quality Assurance Broadens the Concept of Quality Control," *The Pulse Report,* American Productivity Center, January 1984, p. 4; "ASQC: 40 Years of Growth and Change," *Quality Progress,* May 1986, pp. 56-67; Lawrence R. Dorsky, "Management Commitment to Japanese Apple Pie," *Quality Progress,* February 1984, pp. 14-18; Debra A. Owens, "QA/QC and ASQC History," unpublished paper, American Society for Quality Control, undated; and Jack Reddy, "Incorporating Quality in Competitive Strategies," *Sloan Management Review,* Spring 1980, pp. 53-60.

251

2. Alfred D. Chandler, Jr., *The Visible Hand* (Cambridge, Mass.: Belknap Press, Harvard University Press, 1977), pp. 50–64.

3. J. M. Juran, "Consumerism and Product Quality," *Quality Progress,* July 1970, p. 20, and Debra A. Owens, Director, Technical Programs, American Society for Quality Control, personal communication, April 18, 1984.

4. William J. Abernathy and John E. Corcoran, "Relearning from the Old Masters: Lessons of the American System of Manufacturing," *Journal of Operations Management,* August 1983, pp. 155–68; David A. Hounshell, *From the American System to Mass Production, 1800–1932* (Baltimore: Johns Hopkins Press, 1984), pp. 15–17; and Merritt Roe Smith, *Harpers Ferry Armory and the New Technology* (Ithaca, N.Y.: Cornell University Press, 1977), esp. chs. 3–5. While the initial breakthroughs involving interchangeable parts have often been associated with Eli Whitney, recent research suggests that his role has been overstated. See Robert S. Woodbury, "The Legend of Eli Whitney and Interchangeable Parts," *Technology and Culture,* Summer 1960, pp. 235–53, as well as the above sources.

5. Hounshell, *From American System,* pp. 6, 34–35.

6. *Ibid.,* p. 34.

7. Frederick Winslow Taylor, *Shop Management* (New York: Harper & Brothers, 1919), p. 101. See also Chandler, *Visible Hand,* pp. 275–77, and Frank Barkley Copley, *Frederick W. Taylor: Father of Scientific Management* (New York: Harper & Brothers, 1923), I:324.

8. G. S. Radford, *The Control of Quality in Manufacturing* (New York: Ronald Press, 1922). The book is predated by an earlier article on the subject by the same author. See G. S. Radford, "The Control of Quality," *Engineering Magazine,* October 1917.

9. Radford, *Control of Quality in Manufacturing,* p. 36.

10. *Ibid.,* p. 5.

11. Charles A. Bicking, "The Technical Aspects of Quality Control," *Industrial Quality Control,* March 1958, p. 7.

12. W. A. Shewhart, *Economic Control of Quality of Manufactured Product* (New York: D. Van Nostrand Company, 1931).

13. Abbott and Leaman, "Quality Control" (note 1), p. 1000, and Harold F. Dodge, "Notes on the Evolution of Acceptance Sampling Plans, Part I," *Journal of Quality Technology,* April 1969, p. 77.

14. Shewhart, *Economic Control of Quality,* p. 6.

15. Shewhart in fact developed two charts: the $\bar{X}$ or average chart, and the $\sigma$ or standard deviation chart. The former measured the average level around which dispersion was to be controlled; the latter, the degree of dispersion itself. Standard deviations, however, proved to be difficult

to compute and were shortly replaced by range charts (R), developed in England by Leonard Tippett. See Abbott and Leaman, "Quality Control," pp. 1000–1001, for further discussion of this development. For more on the application of process control charts, see such standard texts as J. M. Juran and Frank M. Gryna, Jr., *Quality Planning and Analysis* (New York: McGraw-Hill, 1980), esp. chs. 12, 13, and 14, and E. L. Grant and R. S. Leavenworth, *Statistical Quality Control,* Fifth Edition (New York: McGraw-Hill, 1980), chs. 2–11. For a more succinct treatment, see *Constructing and Using Process Control Charts* (Boston: Harvard Business School Case Services 9-684-073, 1984).

16. These plans were based on two technical concepts: operating characteristic (OC) curves and lot tolerance percent defective (LTPD). For further discussion, see Dodge, "Notes, Part I," pp. 78–81; Juran and Gryna, *Quality Planning and Analysis,* ch. 17; and Grant and Leavenworth, *Statistical Quality Control,* chs. 12 and 13.

17. Dodge, "Notes, Part I," pp. 82–84, and Harold F. Dodge and Harry G. Romig, *Sampling Inspection Tables* (New York: John Wiley & Sons, 1944).

18. H. F. Dodge, "Notes on the Evolution of Acceptance Sampling Plans, Part II," *Journal of Quality Technology,* July 1969, pp. 155–56.

19. *Ibid.,* pp. 156–59. After years of refinement and revision, these techniques led to Military Standard 105D (MIL-STD-105D), the most widely used acceptance sampling plan in the world. See H. F. Dodge, "Notes on the Evolution of Acceptance Sampling Plans, Part III," *Journal of Quality Technology,* October 1969, pp. 229–32.

20. Abbott and Leaman, "Quality Control," p. 1001.

21. H. F. Safford, "The U.S. Army Ordnance Department Use of Quality Control," *Industrial Quality Control,* January 1946, p. 4. W. Edwards Deming, who would later play a leading role in introducing statistical quality control in Japan, was involved in this effort as Adviser in Sampling to the Chief of Army Ordnance.

22. Eugene L. Grant, "Industrialists and Professors in Quality Control: A Look Back and a Look Ahead," *Industrial Quality Control,* July 1953, p. 31.

23. Holbrook Working, "Statistical Quality Control in War Production," *Journal of the American Statistical Association,* December 1945, pp. 425, 433, 439.

24. One initiator of the OPRD programs has observed that had it not been for the early successes of the Ontario Works of General Electric in applying the techniques of statistical quality control, he might have recommended that the program be curtailed. See Grant, "Industrialists and Professors," p. 33.

25. Abbott and Leaman, "Quality Control," pp. 1001–2; Dodge, "Notes, Part III," p. 228; *Industrial Quality Control,* July 1944; Owens, "QA/QC" (note 1).

26. J. M. Juran, ed., *Quality Control Handbook* (New York: McGraw-Hill, 1951).

27. *Ibid.,* p. 37.

28. Armand V. Feigenbaum, "Total Quality Control," *Harvard Business Review,* November–December 1956, pp. 94, 98 (italics in original). See also Armand V. Feigenbaum, *Total Quality Control* (New York: Mc-Graw-Hill, 1961).

29. Feigenbaum, *Total Quality Control,* pp. 54–57, and Juran, *Quality Control Handbook,* pp. 170–72, 174–77, 281–82.

30. Thomas A. Budne, "Reliability Engineering," in Carl Heyel, ed., *The Encyclopedia of Management,* Third Edition (New York: Van Nostrand Reinhold Company, 1982), p. 1023, and George A. W. Boehm, "'Reliability' Engineering," *Fortune,* April 1963, pp. 124–27, 181–82, 184, 186.

31. *Reliability of Military Electronic Equipment,* Report by the Advisory Group on Reliability of Electronic Equipment, Office of the Assistant Secretary of Defense (Research and Engineering) (Washington, D.C.: U.S. Government Printing Office, 1951). This was the so-called AGREE report.

32. Boehm, "'Reliability' Engineering," p. 127.

33. Budne, "Reliability Engineering," p. 1024. For reasons of clarity, Budne's definition, which parallels that of the AGREE report, has been slightly reworded. See Grant and Leavenworth, *Statistical Quality Control* (note 15), pp. 536–37, for a number of similar definitions.

34. Boehm, "'Reliability' Engineering," pp. 181–82; Budne, "Reliability Engineering," pp. 1024–25; Juran and Gryna, *Quality Planning and Analysis* (note 15), ch. 8; and J. M. Juran, *Quality Control Handbook,* Third Edition (New York: McGraw-Hill, 1974), pp. 22-26–22-27. For an introduction to probability distributions, see any basic statistics text, e.g. Richard I. Levin, *Statistics for Management* (Englewood Cliffs, N.J.: Prentice-Hall, 1978), pp. 136–38.

35. Boehm, "'Reliability' Engineering," pp. 182, 184; Budne, "Reliability Engineering," p. 1026; and Juran and Gryna, *Quality Planning and Analysis,* pp. 182–184.

36. Budne, "Reliability Engineering," p. 1028.

37. The discussion of zero defects is based on James F. Halpin, *Zero Defects* (New York: McGraw-Hill, 1966). At the time the book was written, Halpin was Director of Quality at the Martin Company. He had been one of the founders of its zero defects program.

38. *Ibid.,* p. 15.
39. *Ibid.,* p. 5. See also Captain E. R. Pettebone, "'Zero Defects' Type Programs: Basic Concepts," in Office of the Assistant Secretary of Defense (Installations and Logistics), *Zero Defects: The Quest for Quality* (Washington, D.C.: U.S. Government Printing Office, 1968), pp. 45–60.
40. Philip B. Crosby, *Quality Is Free* (New York: Mentor/New American Library, 1979). For an interesting comparison of Crosby's approach with those of other quality experts, see Charles H. Fine and David H. Bridge, "Managing Quality Improvement," Working Paper 1607-84, Sloan School of Management, Massachusetts Institute of Technology, November 1984, mimeographed.
41. See, for example, Douglas McGregor, *The Human Side of Enterprise* (New York: McGraw-Hill, 1960), and Frederick G. Lesieur, ed., *The Scanlon Plan* (Cambridge, Mass., and New York: Technology Press, John Wiley & Sons, 1958).

## CHAPTER 2. STRATEGIC QUALITY MANAGEMENT

1. For examples of companies that have in recent years taken such approaches to quality improvement, see "American Manufacturers Strive for Quality—Japanese Style," *Business Week,* March 12, 1979, pp. 32C-32V; Thomas A. Barocci, Thomas A. Klein, David A. Sanford, and Kirsten R. Wever, "Quality Assurance Systems and U.S. Management in the 1980s: The Experiences of Eleven High Technology Companies," Working Paper No. 1357-82, Sloan School of Management, Massachusetts Institute of Technology, October 1982, mimeographed; Jeremy Main, "The Battle for Quality Begins," *Fortune,* December 29, 1980, pp. 28–33; and Thomas M. Rohan, "Quality or Junk? Facing Up to the Problem," *Industry Week,* December 12, 1983, pp. 72-79. For the views of three leading quality consultants whose widely used programs first took shape in the 1950s and 1960s, see "Question and Answer: A. V. Feigenbaum, J. M. Juran, Philip Crosby," *Quality Progress,* October 1984, pp. 32-37.
2. Hard evidence of the superiority of Japanese products is surprisingly scarce. Most of the evidence is anecdotal or available only on an unconfirmed basis from companies. Aside from the room air conditioning industry, which is examined in this book, only three industries have been studied in depth: automobiles, color televisions, and semiconductors. The semiconductor data are discussed later in this chapter. The most comprehensive study of quality in the U.S. and Japanese automobile industries is summarized in William J. Abernathy, Kim B. Clark, and Alan M. Kantrow, "The New Industrial Competition," *Harvard Business Review,* September–October 1981, pp. 68-81; more

comprehensive background information can be found in National Academy of Engineering, *The Competitive Status of the U.S. Automobile Industry* (Washington, D.C.: National Academy Press, 1982), pp. 90–108, and William J. Abernathy, Kim B. Clark, and Alan M. Kantrow, *Industrial Renaissance* (New York: Basic Books, 1983). These studies report large gaps in quality performance. In 1979, for example, Toyota averaged .71 defects per vehicle shipped and Honda 1.23 defects per vehicle shipped (measured after one month of service). Comparable figures for the Ford Pinto and the Chevrolet Chevette, two U.S. compacts, were 3.70 and 3.00 defects per vehicle shipped.

Similar data are available for color televisions. In 1979, service call (repair) rates under the first year of warranty coverage for Japanese sets ranged from 3.8 percent for Panasonic to 5.1 percent for Sony; U.S. figures ranged from 6.6 percent for Quasar to 9.7 percent for Magnavox. See Ira C. Magaziner and Robert B. Reich, *Minding America's Business* (New York: Harcourt Brace Jovanovich, 1982), p. 176. Other sources of comparative quality data on the color television industry are J. M. Juran, "Japanese and Western Quality: A Contrast," *Quality Progress,* December 1978, pp. 10–18, and Michael E. Porter, "The U.S. Television Set Market," in *Cases in Competitive Strategy* (New York: Free Press, 1983), p. 511. For a comparison of the quality levels of Japanese *subsidiaries* producing color television sets in the United Kingdom and American and British factories in that country, see Makoto Takamiya, "Japanese Multinationals in Europe: Internal Operations and Their Policy Implications," *Columbia Journal of World Business,* Summer 1981, p. 6.

3. *The Rosen Electronics Letter,* March 31, 1980, pp. 3–5, and Arthur L. Robinson, "Perilous Times for U.S. Microcircuit Makers," *Science,* May 9, 1980, pp. 582–86. For more up-to-date failure data, see William F. Finan and Annette M. LaMond, "Sustaining U.S. Competitiveness in Microelectronics: The Challenge to U.S. Policy," in Bruce R. Scott and George C. Lodge, eds., *U.S. Competitiveness in the World Economy* (Boston: Harvard Business School Press, 1985), p. 168.

4. There are a variety of explanations for the success of Japanese semiconductor manufacturers in this country. Quality is only one of several critical variables. For further discussion, see Daniel I. Okimoto, Takuo Sugano, and Franklin B. Weinstein, eds., *Competitive Edge: The Semiconductor Industry in the U.S. and Japan* (Stanford, Calif.: Stanford University Press, 1984), esp. ch. 3, and T. R. Reid, *The Chip* (New York: Simon & Schuster, 1984), ch. 10.

5. "A Record Year for Recalls," *Dun's Review,* January 1979, p. 31. Many of the recalls were undertaken "voluntarily" by manufacturers, although they were usually influenced in some way by the overseeing agency. Figures for the number of units recalled by the Food and Drug

Administration, the other federal agency heavily involved in overseeing potentially dangerous products, were not available for 1973–78. The number of recall campaigns initiated by the agency, however, dropped slightly during the period, from 1,153 in 1973 to 1,112 in 1978.

6. *Firestone Tire & Rubber Company* (Boston: Harvard Business School Case Services 9-684-044, 1984), p. 3.

7. John E. Calfee and Gary T. Ford, "The FTC's Product Defects Program and Consumer Perceptions of Product Quality," in Jacob Jacoby and Jerry C. Olson, eds., *Perceived Quality* (Lexington, Mass.: Lexington Books, D.C. Heath, 1985), pp. 175–91.

8. The first "lemon laws" were enacted by Connecticut and California in 1982. By September 1983, at least seventeen states had adopted them. For some representative examples, see "Help for Buyers of 'Lemon' Cars Voted in Albany," *New York Times,* June 14, 1983, pp. A1, B6; "Kean Approves a 'Lemon Law' for Auto Buyers," *New York Times,* June 21, 1983, pp. B1, B4; "'Lemon Laws' Gaining Popularity Despite Auto Makers' Opposition," *Wall Street Journal,* July 12, 1983, p. 41; and "Dukakis to Sign 'Lemon' Auto Law," *Boston Globe,* September 15, 1983, pp. 1, 16.

9. Robert H. Malott, "Let's Restore Balance to Product Liability Law," *Harvard Business Review,* May–June 1983, p. 67. In some cases, a fear of liability suits has led companies to discontinue production of a product. See Michael Brody, "When Products Turn into Liabilities," *Fortune,* March 3, 1986, pp. 20–24, for several examples.

10. See, for example, Frank S. Leonard and W. Earl Sasser, "The Incline of Quality," *Harvard Business Review,* September–October 1982, pp. 163–71, and Jack Reddy, "Incorporating Quality in Competitive Strategies," *Sloan Management Review,* Spring 1980, pp. 53–55.

11. John T. Hagan, "The Management of Quality: Preparing for a Competitive Future," *Quality Progress,* December 1984, p. 21.

12. For discussions of the importance of conducting market research to understand the customers' perspective on quality, see Kaoru Ishikawa, "Quality and Standardization: Program for Economic Success," *Quality Progress,* January 1984, p. 18; J. M. Juran, "Mobilizing for the 1970s," *Quality Progress,* August 1969, pp. 9–10; and Technical Assistance Research Programs, Inc. (TARP), "The Bottom-Line Implications of Unmet Customer Expectations and How to Measure Them," Washington, D.C., June 1983, mimeographed.

13. For recommendations on how to conduct market research in this area, see Milind M. Lele and Uday S. Karmarkar, "Good Product Support Is Smart Marketing," *Harvard Business Review,* November–December 1983, pp. 124–32; TARP, "Bottom-Line Implications," and *idem,* "Economic Aspects of Quality Control Decisions (Development of a

Market-Driven Quality Assurance System)," paper presented at educational conference "Statistical Control in Good Manufacturing Practice," sponsored by the American Society for Quality Control, New Brunswick, N.J., October 5, 1982, mimeographed. Relatively few empirical studies have been published on the topic. Four important exceptions are P. Greg Bonner and Richard Nelson, "Product Attributes and Perceived Quality: Foods," in Jacoby and Olson, *Perceived Quality,* pp. 65–79; Consumer Network, Inc., *Brand Quality Perceptions* (Philadelphia: Consumer Network, August 1983); Lele and Karmarkar, "Good Product Support"; and Sunil Mehrotra and John Palmer, "Relating Product Features to Perceptions of Quality: Appliances," in Jacoby and Olson, *Perceived Quality,* pp. 81–96. These studies are discussed at greater length in Chapters 4 and 5.

14. Center for Policy Alternatives, Massachusetts Institute of Technology, *Consumer Durables: Warranties, Service Contracts and Alternatives* (Cambridge: MIT Press, 1978), vol. IV, ch 2; Frank M. Gryna, Jr., "Quality Costs: User vs. Manufacturer," *Quality Progress,* June 1977, pp. 10–13; and Juran, "Mobilizing for 1970s," p. 11.

15. "Making Service a Potent Marketing Tool," *Business Week,* June 11, 1984, pp. 164–70, and TARP, *Consumer Complaint Handling in America: Final Report* (Springfield, Va.: National Technical Information Service, U.S. Department of Commerce, 1979), esp. chs. 3–5. A condensed version of TARP's complaint-handling study is also available. See TARP, "Consumer Complaint Seminar Presented for Nippon Cultural Broadcasting Company," Tokyo, September 4, 1981, mimeographed.

16. The following table, which shows sharp differences in the percentage of customers in several automobile size classes who said they would buy the same make/model again, illustrates the connection between quality and customer loyalty. Imports, which were dominated by the Japanese, fared far better than domestically made cars, which were generally of lower quality.

| | Percentage of Owners Who Would Buy Same Make/Model Again, 1979 | | |
| --- | --- | --- | --- |
| | *Domestic* | *Imported* | *Total* |
| Subcompact | 77.2% | 91.6% | 81.2% |
| Compact | 74.2 | 91.4 | 72.4 |
| Midsize | 75.3 | 94.5 | 76.9 |
| Standard | 81.8 | — | — |
| Luxury | 86.6 | 94.6 | 87.2 |
| Total | 78.7 | 91.8 | — |

SOURCE: National Academy of Engineering, *Competitive Status* (note 2), p. 99.

17. TARP, "Consumer Complaint Seminar," pp. 7–8.

18. Two representative articles based on the PIMS data are Sidney Schoeffler, Robert D. Buzzell, and Donald F. Heany, "Impact of Strategic Planning on Profit Performance," *Harvard Business Review,* March–April 1974, pp. 137–45, and Robert D. Buzzell and Frederick D. Wiersema, "Successful Share-Building Strategies," *Harvard Business Review,* January–February 1981, pp. 135–44.

19. The relationship between quality and productivity is discussed in W. Edwards Deming, *Quality, Productivity, and Competitive Position* (Cambridge: Center for Advanced Engineering Study, Massachusetts Institute of Technology, 1982), ch. 1, and A. V. Feigenbaum, "Quality and Productivity," *Quality Progress,* November 1977, pp. 18–21. As the discussion in Chapter 5 will show, the connection between the two variables is more complex than these (and other) analysts have suggested.

20. Robert E. Cole, "Improving Product Quality Through Continuous Feedback," *Management Review,* October 1983, pp. 8–12, and "Final Report of the American Productivity Center Computer Conference on Quality and Productivity," Washington, D.C., September 22–23, 1983, mimeographed, p. 10.

21. Ralph Barra, "Management Attitude Is the Key Ingredient," in American Productivity Center, *The Pulse Report,* January 1984, p. 7; Lawrence R. Dorsky, "Management Commitment to Japanese Apple Pie," *Quality Progress,* February 1984, p. 18; Hagan, "Management of Quality" (note 11), pp. 23–24; Leonard and Sasser, "Incline of Quality" (note 10), pp. 164–66, 168; and "Quality: The U.S. Drives to Catch Up," *Business Week,* November 1, 1982, pp. 46–47.

22. J. M. Juran, "Product Quality: A Prescription for the West, Part I: Training and Improvement Programs," *Management Review,* June 1981, pp. 9–14.

23. Dorsky, "Management Commitment," pp. 16, 18; Hagan, "Management of Quality," pp. 21–25; and Leonard and Sasser, "Incline of Quality," pp. 164–67.

24. Constantine Pavsidis, "Total Quality Control: An Overview of Current Efforts," *Quality Progress,* September 1984, pp. 28–29.

25. These methods were originally developed by a Japanese statistician, Genichi Taguchi. Much of the subsequent work has been carried out by researchers at Bell Laboratories. See Genichi Taguchi and Yu-In Wu, *Introduction to Off-Line Quality Control* (Nagaya, Japan: Central Japan Quality Association, 1979); G. Taguchi and M. S. Phadke, "Quality Engineering Through Design Optimization," paper prepared for Globecom 84 Meeting of the IEEE Communications Society, Atlanta, November 1984; and M. S. Phadke, R. N. Kackar, D. V. Speeney, and M. J. Grieco, "Off-Line Quality Control in Integrated Circuit Fabrica-

tion Using Experimental Design,'' *The Bell System Technical Journal,* May–June 1983, pp. 1273–1309. For a brief, nontechnical introduction to these issues, see John Mayo, ''Process Design as Important as Product Design,'' *Wall Street Journal,* October 29, 1984, p. 32.

26. The discussion of Hewlett-Packard is based on the following sources: Lee Branst, ''The 3 C's of Quality: Commitment, Communication, Cooperation,'' *Quality,* December 1982, pp. 28–30; Pavsidis, ''Total Quality Control''; Thomas J. Peters and Robert H. Waterman, Jr., *In Search of Excellence* (New York: Harper & Row, 1982), pp. 175–78; Sarah Prestman, ''SQC and JIT: Partnership in Quality,'' *Quality Progress,* May 1985, pp. 31–34; Rick Walleigh, ''Synergy in TQC and JIT: Four Common Action Principles for Manufacturing Success,'' Computer Systems Division, Hewlett-Packard Corporation, mimeographed, undated; John A. Young, ''One Company's Quest for Improved Quality,'' *Wall Street Journal,* July 25, 1983, p. 10; and *idem,* ''Teamwork Is More Easily Praised than Practiced,'' *Quality Progress,* August 1985, pp. 30–34.

27. John A. Young, ''One Company's Quest,'' p. 10.

28. For more on Hewlett-Packard's culture, see William G. Ouchi, *Theory Z* (Reading, Mass.: Addison-Wesley, 1981), pp. 133–39, 143–47, and Rosabeth Moss Kanter, *The Change Masters* (New York: Simon & Schuster, 1983), p. 134.

29. The discussion of the Xerox Corporation is based on the following sources: Don Clausing, ''Product Quality Through Engineering: Dr. Taguchi's Methods,'' Xerox Corporation, mimeographed, April 1983 (revised November 1983); ''The New Lean, Mean Xerox,'' *Business Week,* October 12, 1981, pp. 126–32; Frank J. Pipp, ''A Management Commitment to Quality,'' keynote speech, 37th Annual Quality Congress, American Society for Quality Control, mimeographed, undated; Quality Office, Xerox Corporation, *Competitive Benchmarking: What It Is and What It Can Do for You* (Stamford, Conn.: Xerox Corporation, January 1984); ''Xerox Halts Japanese March,'' *New York Times,* November 6, 1985, pp. D1, D5; and ''Xerox Searches for Life Beyond Boxes,'' *International Management,* June 1986, pp. 24–30. Much of the discussion is drawn from Pipp's speech. At the time it was delivered, Pipp was President of Xerox's Reprographic Business Group.

30. According to David T. Kearns, Xerox's President and Chief Executive Officer: ''If you really want to know how good you have to be to compete, the Japanese are the ones to look at. We want to be remembered as the company that took on the Japanese and were successful.'' *Business Week,* October 12, 1981, p. 126.

31. Pipp, ''Management Commitment,'' p. 12.

32. *Ibid.,* p. 16.

33. The discussion of Corning Glass Works is based on the following sources: *Corning Glass Works: The Z-Glass Project* (Boston: Harvard Business School Case Services 9-681-091, 1981, revised, October 1982); *Corning Glass Works: Tom MacAvoy* (Boston: Harvard Business School Case Services 9-179-074, 1978); Myron Magnet, "Corning Glass Shapes Up," *Fortune,* December 13, 1982, pp. 90–109; personal communication, David B. Luther, Vice President and Corporate Quality Director, Corning Glass Works, May 28, 1986; and Therese Sullivan, "Quality Sharpens Corning's Edge," *Quality,* May 1983, pp. 27–30.

34. "Final Report of the American Productivity Center Computer Conference on Quality and Productivity," p. 11.


CHAPTER 3. CONCEPTS AND DEFINITIONS

1. Robert M. Pirsig, *Zen and the Art of Motorcycle Maintenance* (New York: Bantam Books, 1974), esp. pp. 183–200, 205–15, 223–28, and Barbara W. Tuchman, "The Decline of Quality," *New York Times Magazine,* November 2, 1980, pp. 38–41, 104.

2. Flora Lewis, "The Tiffany Model," *New York Times,* June 7, 1984, p. A31, and Tuchman, "Decline of Quality," pp. 38–40.

3. Scott Buchanen, ed., *The Portable Plato* (New York: Viking Press, 1948), pp. 121–87, and George Dickie, *Aesthetics: An Introduction* (New York: Bobbs-Merrill, 1971), p. 5.

4. "The Cadillac Legacy of Quality," General Motors, undated.

5. Tuchman, "Decline of Quality," p. 39.

6. The essence of this approach can be better understood by examining two recent books: Peter Passell and Leonard Ross, *The Best* (New York: Pocket Books, 1975), and Betty Cornfeld and Owen Edwards, *Quintessence: The Quality of Having It* (New York: Crown Publishers, 1983). Both books rely on "definition by example." The former contains a list of items that the authors deem to be the best in such categories as the best hamburger, the best national park, the best train ride, and the best zoo. While the choices are idiosyncratic and the selection criteria are occasionally obscure, the cumulative weight of evidence suggests an unvarying—if difficult to articulate—concept of excellence.

   Much the same can be said of Cornfeld and Edwards's discussion of "quintessence," a property the authors ascribe to objects as diverse as the Volkswagen Beetle, Crayola Crayons, Swiss Army knives, and Hershey's Chocolate Kisses. All of these objects are

   > . . . things that offer more to us than we specifically ask of them and to which we respond more strongly than is easily explained. What the various things . . . have in common . . . is [that] they

each exhibit a rare and mysterious capacity to be just exactly what they ought to be . . . the way they are now appears self-evident.

While the definition is a bit murky, the examples cited are instantly recognizable and convey a much clearer sense of the concept the authors have in mind.

7. Lawrence Abbott, *Quality and Competition* (New York: Columbia University Press, 1955), pp. 126–27; Zvi Griliches, "Introduction: Hedonic Price Indexes Revisited," in Zvi Griliches, ed., *Price Indexes and Quality Change* (Cambridge, Mass.: Harvard University Press, 1971), pp. 3–15; Kelvin Lancaster, *Consumer Demand: A New Approach* (New York: Columbia University Press, 1971), p. 122; and Keith B. Leffler, "Ambiguous Changes in Product Quality," *American Economic Review,* December 1982, pp. 956–67.

8. Abbott, *Quality and Competition,* p. 129, and Kelvin Lancaster, *Variety, Equity, and Efficiency* (New York: Columbia University Press, 1979), p. 28.

9. David Levhari and T. N. Srinivasan, "Durability of Consumption Goods: Competition Versus Monopoly," *American Economic Review,* March 1969, pp. 102–7; Richard L. Schmalensee, "Regulation and the Durability of Goods," *Bell Journal of Economics and Management Science,* Spring 1970, pp. 54–64; Peter L. Swan, "Durability of Consumption Goods," *American Economic Review,* December 1970, pp. 884–94; Peter L. Swan, "The Durability of Goods and the Regulation of Monopoly," *Bell Journal of Economics and Management Science,* Autumn 1971, pp. 347–57; and Thomas R. Saving, "Market Organization and Product Quality," *Southern Economic Journal,* April 1982, p. 856.

10. Corwin D. Edwards, "The Meaning of Quality," *Quality Progress,* October 1968, pp. 36–39, and Alfred A. Kuehn and Ralph L. Day, "Strategy of Product Quality," *Harvard Business Review,* November–December 1962, pp. 100–110.

11. Kuehn and Day, "Strategy of Product Quality," pp. 101–8; Richard M. Johnson, "Market Segmentation: A Strategic Management Tool," *Journal of Marketing Research,* February 1971, pp. 13–18; Philip Kotler, *Marketing Decision Making: A Model Building Approach* (New York: Holt, Rinehart & Winston, 1971), pp. 491–97; and Brian T. Ratchford, "The New Economic Theory of Consumer Behavior: An Interpretive Essay," *Journal of Consumer Research,* September 1975, pp. 65–75.

12. Edward H. Chamberlin, "The Product as an Economic Variable," *Quarterly Journal of Economics,* February 1953, pp. 1–29; Robert Dorfman and Peter O. Steiner, "Optimal Advertising and Optimal Quality," *American Economic Review,* December 1954, pp. 822–36;

and Lawrence J. White, "Quality Variation When Prices Are Regulated," *Bell Journal of Economics and Management Science,* Autumn 1972, pp. 425–36.

13. J. M. Juran, ed., *Quality Control Handbook,* Third Edition (New York: McGraw-Hill, 1974), p. 2-2, and Harold L. Gilmore, "Product Conformance Cost," *Quality Progress,* June 1974, pp. 16–19.

14. Edwards, "Meaning of Quality," pp. 36–39; Lancaster, *Variety, Equity and Efficiency,* p. 28; and Henri Theil, *Principles of Econometrics* (New York: John Wiley & Sons, 1971), pp. 556–73.

15. E. Sheshinski, "Price, Quality, and Quantity Regulation in a Monopoly Situation," *Economica,* May 1976, pp. 127–37, and White, "Quality Variation," p. 426.

16. Roger B. Yepsen, Jr., ed., *The Durability Factor* (Emmaus, Pa.: Rodale Press, 1982), pp. 12–15.

17. Philip B. Crosby, *Quality Is Free* (New York: New American Library, 1979), pp. 13–20, and Gilmore, "Product Conformance Cost," p. 16.

18. See Roger G. Langevin, *Quality Control in the Service Industries* (New York: AMACOM, 1977), for further discussion of this approach to quality in service businesses.

19. Jack Campanella and Frank J. Corcoran, "Principles of Quality Costs," *Quality Progress,* April 1983, p. 21, and Crosby, *Quality Is Free,* pp. 178–81.

20. Robert A. Broh, *Managing Quality for Higher Profits* (New York: McGraw-Hill, 1982), ch. 1, and Juran, *Quality Control Handbook,* ch. 5.

21. Broh, *Managing Quality,* pp. 3–4, and Armand V. Feigenbaum, *Total Quality Control* (New York: McGraw-Hill, 1961), pp. 1, 13. A more complex discussion of the relationship between quality and value appears in Morris B. Holbrook and Kim P. Corfman, "Quality and Value in the Consumption Experience: Phaedrus Rides Again," in Jacob Jacoby and Jerry C. Olson eds., *Perceived Quality* (Lexington, Mass.: Lexington Books, D.C. Heath, 1985), pp. 31–57. The article also includes a review of the literature on quality, based on a different framework from the one in this chapter.

22. The Consumer Network, Inc., *Brand Quality Perceptions* (Philadelphia, PA: Consumer Network, August 1983).

23. David J. Curry and David J. Faulds, "The Measurement of Quality in Strategic Groups," in Jacoby and Olson, *Perceived Quality,* pp. 280–81, and David J. Curry, "Measuring Price and Quality Competition," *Journal of Marketing,* Spring 1985, pp. 106–17.

24. The idea that there should be links among marketing, engineering, and manufacturing approaches to quality is not new, although it has usually

been formulated differently. Over the years, the idea has appeared in a number of guises. They include a distinction between quality of design, quality of specifications, and quality of conformance; a call for today's quality professionals to work at the interface between functions; a proposal for "structured product analysis" to link customer wants, design logic, and steps in the manufacturing process; recommendations for improved "quality analysis"; and tracings of the new product development process from concept to use. See, respectively, Eugene L. Grant and Lawrence F. Bell, "Some Comments on the Semantics of Quality and Reliability," *Industrial Quality Control,* May 1961, pp. 14–17; John T. Hagan, "The Management of Quality: Preparing for a Competitive Future," *Quality Progress,* December 1984, pp. 21–25; Donald F. Heany and William D. Vinson, "A Fresh Look at New Product Development," *Journal of Business Strategy,* Fall 1984, pp. 22–31; Kaoru Ishikawa, "Quality and Standardization: Program for Economic Success," *Quality Progress:,* January 1984, pp. 16–20; and E. G. D. Paterson, "Quality Control vs. Quality Assurance vs. Reliability," *Industrial Quality Control,* October 1962, pp. 5–9.

25. Ishikawa, "Quality and Standardization," p. 18.

26. One indication of the isolation of departments is the frequent complaint that designers, after completing their work, "throw it over the wall" to manufacturing, which is then held responsible for all problems encountered in production.

27. For more on efforts to shorten development cycles and otherwise improve the new product development process, see W. Earl Sasser and Neil H. Wasserman, "From Design to Market: The New Competitive Pressures," Harvard Business School, 1984, mimeographed.

28. Two important exceptions are Juran and Maynes. See Juran, *Quality Control Handbook,* Third Edition, pp. 2-4–2-9, and E. Scott Maynes, "The Concept and Measurement of Product Quality," in Nelson E. Terleckyj, ed., *Household Production and Consumption* (New York: National Bureau of Economic Research, 1976), pp. 550–54.

## CHAPTER 4. THE MULTIPLE DIMENSIONS OF QUALITY

1. "Survey Shows CEOs Uninformed About Quality," *Quality Progress,* May 1981, pp. 14–17, and S. L. (Red) Binstock, "Americans Express Dissatisfaction with Quality of U.S. Goods," *Quality Progress,* January 1981, pp. 12–14.

2. Jeremy Main, "Toward Service Without a Snarl," *Fortune,* March 23, 1981, pp. 58–66.

3. I am indebted to my colleague Ben Shapiro for this example.

4. There is a clear analogy here to Lancaster's theory of consumer demand. The theory is based on two propositions:

> All goods possess objective characteristics relevant to the choices which people make among different collections of goods. The relationship between . . . a good . . . and the characteristics which it possesses is essentially a technical relationship, depending on the objective characteristics of the good. . . .
>
> Individuals differ in their *reaction* to different characteristics, rather than in their assessments of the characteristics. . . . It is these *characteristics* in which consumers are interested . . . the various characteristics can be viewed . . . as each helping to satisfy some kind of "want." [Kelvin Lancaster, *Consumer Demand: A New Approach* (New York: Columbia University Press, 1971), p. 7. Emphasis in original.]

In these terms, the performance of a product would correspond to its objective characteristics, while the relationship between performance and quality would reflect individual reactions. See Kelvin Lancaster, *Variety, Equity, and Efficiency* (New York: Columbia University Press, 1979), p. 17, and *idem,* "A New Approach to Consumer Theory," *Journal of Political Economy,* April 1966, pp. 132–37, for further discussion.

5. J. M. Juran, *Quality Control Handbook,* Third Edition. (New York: McGraw-Hill, 1974), p. 8–12.

6. "Detroit Woos Younger Car Buyers," *New York Times,* February 11, 1985, pp. D1–D2.

7. "Pushing for Weapons That Work," *New York Times,* July 8, 1984, s. 3, p. 4. The article also cites an Air Force survey showing that maintenance costs accounted for 70 percent of the cost of a typical weapons system in 1980, as opposed to 30 percent in 1960.

8. Philip B. Crosby, *Quality Is Free* (New York; New American Library, 1979), ch. 2, and Harold L. Gilmore, "Product Conformance Cost," *Quality Progress,* June 1974, p. 16. Crosby in fact defines quality as "conformance to *requirements*" rather than as conformance to specifications. That allows him to introduce design issues and to argue that products should be built exactly to requirements "or else the requirements should be changed." In practice, Crosby's definition is virtually identical to approaches based on meeting specifications.

9. L. P. Sullivan, "Reducing Variability: A New Approach to Quality," *Quality Progress,* July 1984, p. 20.

10. Robert W. Hall, *Zero Inventories* (Homewood, Ill.: Dow Jones–Irwin, 1983), pp. 154–55.

11. Genichi Taguchi and Yu-in Wu, *Introduction to Off-Line Quality Control* (Nagaya, Japan: Central Japan Quality Association, 1979). See also the references cited in note 25, Chapter 2. In 1960, Taguchi won Japan's Deming Prize for his statistical work; he has subsequently been awarded three separate Deming literature awards.

12. The evidence on this point is anecdotal. While the Japanese newspaper *Asahi* has published a telling example comparing the quality losses incurred by Sony's U.S. and Japanese color television plants—the U.S. plant incurred a larger number of customer complaints involving color balance, even though its units were all initially within specification; the Japanese plant had a more tightly centered distribution and incurred lower quality losses, but shipped a small number of units whose color balance was initially out of specification—there have been few other direct comparisons of the two approaches. See Sullivan, "Reducing Variability," p. 19, and M. S. Phadke, "Quality Engineering Using Design of Experiments," Proceedings of the American Statistical Association, Section of Statistical Education, 1982, p. 11, for discussions of the Sony example, and Taguchi and Wu, *Off-Line Quality Control,* chs. 2–3, for several other examples.

13. Victor E. Kane, "Process Capability Indices," *Journal of Quality Technology,* January 1986, pp. 41–52; Sullivan, "Reducing Variability," p. 17; and Joe De La Rosa, "Process vs. Specification," *Quality,* April 1985, pp. 57–58. An example used by Sullivan shows the importance of these measures. In the three diagrams below, all items meet specifications. Quality measures based on simple counts of the number of defects therefore treat the three processes as identical, for each is responsible for zero defects. Process capability ratios, however—defined as the ratio of specification width to process width—tell a different story. These ratios vary significantly and quickly demonstrate the superiority (tightness) of the second and third processes.

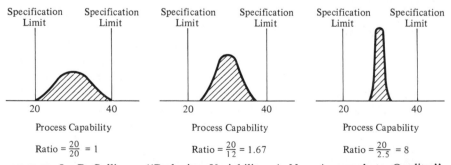

| Specification Limit | Specification Limit | Specification Limit | Specification Limit | Specification Limit | Specification Limit |

| 20    40 | 20    40 | 20    40 |

| Process Capability | Process Capability | Process Capability |
| Ratio = $\frac{20}{20}$ = 1 | Ratio = $\frac{20}{12}$ = 1.67 | Ratio = $\frac{20}{2.5}$ = 8 |

SOURCE: L. P. Sullivan, "Reducing Variability: A New Approach to Quality," *Quality Progress,* July 1984, p. 17. Copyright © 1984 American Society for Quality Control. Reprinted by permission.

14. C. J. Bliss, *Capital Theory and the Distribution of Income* (Amsterdam: North-Holland, 1975), ch. 6.

15. "Why 3M Opted for a 'Lifetime Guarantee'," *Financial Times,* November 9, 1984, p. 12.

16. "Retiring Autos at 14," *New York Times,* April 3, 1983, s. 3, p. 1.

17. Susan W. Burch, "The Aging U.S. Auto Stock: Implications for Demand," *Business Economics,* May 1983, pp. 22–26.

18. Roger B. Yepsen, Jr., ed. *The Durability Factor* (Emmaus, Pa.: Rodale Press, 1982), pp. 190, 197, 200, 203. All estimates were derived from surveys of twenty-five repair people, specializing in the products in question, on the East Coast. Surveys were conducted by telephone in February, March, and April of 1981. Respondents were asked to estimate the average life span for specified brands assuming "reasonable" care by the owner. All refrigerators were 17-cubic-foot, no frills models; the other product categories included a mix of product types (e.g. wringers and automatic washers, compact and full-sized dryers, upright and canister vacuum cleaners). This mixing accounts for some of the variance in durability, although even similar product types showed considerable variation (e.g. the durability of automatic washers ranged from 6.70 years to 11.65 years and the durability of full-sized dryers ranged from 8.38 to 13.52 years).

19. John A. Quelch and Stephen B. Ash, "Consumer Satisfaction with Professional Services," in James H. Donnelly and William R. George, eds., *Marketing of Services* (Chicago: American Marketing Association, 1981).

20. Milind M. Lele and Uday S. Karmarkar, "Good Product Support Is Smart Marketing," *Harvard Business Review,* November–December 1983, p. 127.

21. *Ibid.,* pp. 130–32. For more on the economics of loaning equipment, see Uday S. Karmarkar and Peter Kubat, "The Value of Loaners in Product Support," *IIE Transactions,* March 1983, pp. 5–11.

22. Brian Dumaine, "Chipmaking Machines Come Roaring Back," *Fortune,* October 3, 1983, pp. 87–88. Rapid service is a strategy well suited to the semiconductor manufacturing industry, where the costs of downtime run as high as $5,000 per hour. Yet despite this strategy, GCA has recently suffered severe financial problems, losing ground to its Japanese competitors. See "GCA's Crisis Could Hurt the Industry," *Wall Street Journal,* January 7, 1986, and "GCA Arranges a Refinancing for Its Debts," *Wall Street Journal,* November 4, 1986, p. 18, for further discussion.

23. For data on the incidence of price and nonprice complaints in twenty-six product and eight service categories, see Alan R. Andreasen and Arthur Best, "Consumers Complain—Does Business Respond?" *Har-*

*vard Business Review,* July–August 1977, p. 95. For more detailed data on consumer satisfaction in a single category, television repair, see Center for Policy Alternatives, Massachusetts Institute of Technology, *Consumer Durables: Warranties, Service Contracts and Alternatives* (Cambridge: MIT Press, 1978), vol. III, pp. 3-126–3-144.

24. According to a 1976 consumer survey, consumers' willingness to complain was closely correlated with their expected financial losses from a problem. For potential losses of one to five dollars, 58.7 percent of consumers complained; for potential losses of more than $1,000, 90.5 percent complained. For losses between these two poles, the percentage of consumers complaining generally rose with increasing losses, although there were one or two exceptions. See TARP, *Consumer Complaint Handling in America: Final Report* (Springfield, Va.: National Technical Information Service, U.S. Department of Commerce, 1979), p. 10.

25. Where consumers faced problems with an estimated financial loss of one to five dollars and complaints were satisfactorily resolved, the expected repurchase rate was 70.7 percent; where the estimated financial loss was the same but complaints were unsatisfactorily resolved, the expected repurchase rate was 46.2 percent. Where consumers faced problems with an estimated financial loss of more than $100 and complaints were satisfactorily resolved, the expected repurchase rate was 54.3 percent; where the expected financial loss was the same but complaints were unsatisfactorily resolved, the expected repurchase rate was 19.0 percent. See *ibid.,* pp. 13–14.

26. For a description of ways that businesses deliberately avoid responding to complaints, see Arthur Best, *When Consumers Complain* (New York: Columbia University Press, 1981), ch. 4. For a discussion of complaints as business opportunities, see Tom Peters and Nancy Austin, *A Passion for Excellence* (New York: Random House, 1985), pp. 82–87.

27. "'Humanizing' Corporations," *New York Times,* October 21, 1983, pp. D1, D15; "Making Service a Potent Marketing Tool," *Business Week,* June 11, 1984, pp. 164–70; and "More Firms Use '800' Numbers to Keep Consumers Satisfied," *Wall Street Journal,* April 7, 1983, p. 31.

28. "Why T. Rowe Price Looks Bad but Feels Good," *Business Week,* October 14, 1985, p. 130.

29. Alfred A. Kuehn and Ralph L. Day, "Strategy of Product Quality," *Harvard Business Review,* November–December 1962, pp. 100–110, and Richard M. Johnson, "Market Segmentation: A Strategic Management Tool," *Journal of Marketing Research,* February 1971, pp. 13–18.

30. P. Greg Bonner and Richard Nelson, "Product Attributes and Per-

ceived Quality: Foods,'' in Jacob Jacoby and Jerry C. Olson, eds., *Perceived Quality* (Lexington, Mass.: Lexington Books, D.C. Heath, 1985), pp. 71–74.

31. Donald F. Cox, ed., *Risk Taking and Information Handling in Consumer Behavior* (Boston: Division of Research, Harvard University Graduate School of Business Administration, 1967), ch. 11, and David R. Lambert, ''Price as a Quality Signal: The Tip of the Iceberg,'' *Economic Inquiry,* January 1980, pp. 144–50.

32. ''Imports Alluring to the Consumer,'' *New York Times,* November 14, 1985, pp. C1, C6.

33. Jennifer Pendleton, ''Will Americans Buy an 'Ohio Honda?''' *Advertising Age,* August 29, 1983, pp. M-4, M-5, M-26. Despite its early fears, Honda appears to have met little resistance to its Ohio-built cars. See ''Hondas Built in U.S. Accepted,'' *New York Times,* December 5, 1983, p. D4.

34. Warren O. Hagstrom, ''Inputs, Outputs, and the Prestige of American University Science Departments,'' *Sociology of Education,* Fall 1971, pp. 384–85, and Dean D. Knudsen and Ted R. Vaughan, ''Quality in Graduate Education: A Reevaluation of the Rankings of Sociology Departments in the Cartter Report,'' *American Sociologist,* February 1969, p. 18.

35. Carl Shapiro, ''Premiums for High Quality Products as Returns to Reputations,'' *Quarterly Journal of Economics,* November 1983, pp. 659–79.

36. ''Improved Tires Add to Mileage,'' *New York Times,* August 9, 1984, p. D2. The complexity of rating tire quality is suggested by the industry's strong opposition to the government's tire grading program. See ''Tire Grading Is Criticized,'' *New York Times,* February 17, 1981, pp. D1, D4, for further discussion.

37. ''How to Recognize Quality Furniture: A Buyer's Guide,'' *New York Times,* August 16, 1984, pp. C1, C10.

38. C. L. (Skip) Carpenter, Jr., and Gerald E. Murine, ''Measuring Software Product Quality,'' *Quality Progress,* May 1984, pp. 16–20.

39. Corwin D. Edwards, ''The Meaning of Quality,'' *Quality Progress,* October 1968, p. 38.

40. Tom Alexander, ''Cray's Way of Staying Super-Duper,'' *Fortune,* March 18, 1985, p. 76.

41. Jack Gillis, *The Car Book* (New York: E. P. Dutton, 1984); ''Japanese Autos Get Low Ratings in Insurance Study,'' *Wall Street Journal,* August 20, 1985, p. 10; ''Small, 2-Door Autos Listed as Worst in Study of Safety,'' *New York Times,* October 9, 1983, p. C3; and Yepsen, *Durability Factor* (note 18), p. 69.

42. *Steinway & Sons* (Boston: Harvard Business School Case Services 9-682-625, 1981), p. 5.

43. "Cross' Write Approach," *Boston Globe,* February 24, 1981, pp. 33, 39; "The Rolex: How the Swiss Sell Status," *New York Times,* October 19, 1980, s. 3, p. 6; and "Rolls-Royce: Top of the Class," *New York Times,* April 5, 1981, s. 5, p. 9.

44. Michael E. Porter, "How to Attack the Industry Leader," *Fortune,* April 29, 1985, pp. 153–54. See also Michael E. Porter, *Competitive Advantage* (New York: Free Press, 1985), ch. 15.

45. Brian O'Reilly, "Lessons from the Home Phone Wars," *Fortune,* December 24, 1984, pp. 83–86.

46. TARP, "The Bottom-Line Implications of Unmet Customer Expectations and How to Measure Them," Washington, D.C., June 1983, mimeographed, pp. 2–3.

47. Steven B. Johnson, "Comparing R&D Strategies of Japanese and U.S. Firms," *Sloan Management Review,* Spring 1984, pp. 25–34.

48. Bro Uttal, "Japan's Latest Assault on Chipmaking," *Fortune,* September 3, 1984, p. 81.

49. For a general introduction to this problem, see D. Daryl Wyckoff, "Quality Failures," Harvard Business School, August 1983, mimeographed, pp. 12–14.

50. *Ibid.,* pp. 14–15, and *Singapore Airlines* (C) (Boston: Harvard Business School Case Services 9-682-066, 1982).

51. Leonard A. Morgan, "The Importance of Quality," in Jacoby and Olson, *Perceived Quality* (note 30), p. 62, and Hirotaka Takeuchi and John A. Quelch, "Quality Is More than Making a Good Product," *Harvard Business Review,* July–August 1983, p. 139. Such misperceptions are not confined to quality. A study of companies in the forest products industry found that "executive ratings of their own company's social performance [as measured by public affairs' responsibility and responsiveness] did not correspond to . . . outside stakeholder ratings in even a general way. . . . Thus, there is reason to suspect a significant gap in perceptions of the industry from the inside and the outside." See Jeffrey A. Sonnenfeld, "Structure, Culture and Performance in Public Affairs: A Study of the Forest Products Industry," *Research in Corporate Social Performance and Policy,* 4 (Greenwich, Conn.: JAI Press, 1982): 120.

52. The Consumer Network, Inc., *Brand Quality Perceptions* (Philadelphia: Consumer Network, August 1983), pp. 17, 50, 51. These findings should be treated with caution. Only a very small number of executives were surveyed; in addition, the sample of consumers does not appear to be completely random.

53. For an especially clear method of linking consumer preferences with specific dimensions of quality, see TARP, "Bottom-Line Implications," pp. 4-8.

54. Sunil Mehrotra and John Palmer, "Relating Product Features to Perceptions of Quality: Appliances," in Jacoby and Olson, *Perceived Quality,* pp. 81-96.

55. David Mazursky and Jacob Jacoby, "Forming Impressions of Merchandise and Service Quality," in Jacoby and Olson, *Perceived Quality,* pp. 147, 151.

## CHAPTER 5. CORRELATES OF QUALITY

1. Mallory Factor, "Wall Street Must Choose Between Quality and the Fast Buck," *Wall Street Journal,* April 15, 1985, p. 28.

2. Robert Dorfman and Peter O. Steiner, "Optimal Advertising and Optimal Quality," *American Economic Review,* December 1954, pp. 831-33.

3. The classic statement of this problem is George Akerlof, "The Market for Lemons: Quality Uncertainty and the Market Mechanism," *Quarterly Journal of Economics,* August 1970, pp. 488-500.

4. These investments will be made only if prices can be maintained at levels sufficiently above costs for investments to be compensated and if producing high-quality products remains a profitable strategy. These requirements will be met only in certain conditions, which economists have carefully specified. They involve the ease with which competitors can deteriorate the quality of their products without detection by consumers and the credibility of competitors claiming to offer high-quality products at lower prices. See Thomas Nagle, "Economic Foundations of Pricing," *Journal of Business,* January 1984, Part 2, pp. 56-59, for an introduction to these issues. Other important references include Benjamin Klein and Keith B. Leffler, "The Role of Market Forces in Insuring Contractual Performance," *Journal of Political Economy,* August 1981, pp. 615-42, and Carl Shapiro, "Premiums for High Quality Products as Returns to Reputation," *Quarterly Journal of Economics,* November 1983, pp. 659-79.

5. Harold J. Leavitt, "A Note on Some Experimental Findings About the Meanings of Price," *Journal of Business,* July 1954, pp. 205-6. Leavitt's experimental work on the price-quality relationship is predated by Scitovsky's theorizing. See Tibor Scitovsky, "Some Consequences of the Habit of Judging Quality by Price," *Review of Economic Studies,* 1944-1945, pp. 100-105. For more on the multiple meanings of prices, see Benson P. Shapiro, "Price as a Communicator of Quality:

An Experiment," unpublished D.B.A. thesis, Harvard University, Graduate School of Business Administration, 1970, ch. V.

6. Donald F. Cox, ed., *Risk Taking and Information Handling in Consumer Behavior* (Boston: Division of Research, Harvard Business School, 1967), p. 331.

7. Benson P. Shapiro, "The Psychology of Pricing," *Harvard Business Review,* July-August 1968, pp. 17-18.

8. Peter C. Riesz, "Price-Quality Correlations for Packaged Food Products," *Journal of Consumer Affairs,* Winter 1979, p. 244.

9. Because of its limited theoretical foundation, the entire literature on price and perceived quality has been harshly criticized by some marketing scholars. One has even gone so far as to label it "pseudoresearch." See P. Bowbrick, "Pseudoresearch in Marketing: The Case of the Price-Perceived Quality Relationship," *European Journal of Marketing,* 14: 466-70, and Vithala R. Rao, "Pricing Research in Marketing: The State of the Art," *Journal of Business,* January 1984, Part 2, pp. 550-51.

10. Leavitt, "Some Experimental Findings," pp. 205-10; Andre Gabor and C. W. J. Granger, "Price as an Indicator of Quality: Report on an Enquiry," *Economica,* February 1966, pp. 43-70; and J. Douglas McConnell, "An Experimental Examination of the Price-Quality Relationship," *Journal of Business,* October 1968, pp. 439-44.

11. For summaries of the multicue studies, see David R. Lambert, "Price as a Quality Signal: The Tip of the Iceberg," *Economic Inquiry,* January 1980, pp. 144-50, and Kent B. Monroe and R. Krishnan, "The Effect of Price on Subjective Product Evaluations," in Jacob Jacoby and Jerry C. Olson, *Perceived Quality* (Lexington, Mass.: Lexington Books, D.C. Heath, 1985), pp. 209-32.

12. Robert A. Peterson and William R. Wilson, "Perceived Risk and Price-Reliance Schema as Price-Perceived Quality Mediators," in Jacoby and Olson, *Perceived Quality,* p. 248.

13. The most frequently cited studies include Alfred R. Oxenfelt, "Consumer Knowledge: Its Measurement and Extent," *Review of Economics and Statistics,* 1950, pp. 300-314; Monroe P. Friedman, "Quality and Price Considerations in Rational Decision Making," *Journal of Consumer Affairs,* Summer 1967, pp. 13-23; Ruby Turner Morris and Claire Sekulski Bronson, "The Chaos of Competition Indicated by *Consumer Reports,*" *Journal of Marketing,* July 1969, pp. 26-34; George B. Sproles, "New Evidence on Price and Product Quality," *Journal of Consumer Affairs,* Summer 1977, pp. 63-77; Peter C. Riesz, "Price Versus Quality in the Marketplace, 1961-1975," *Journal of Retailing,* Winter 1978, pp. 15-28; and Riesz, "Price-Quality Correlati-

ons," pp. 236-47. The average correlations in these studies range from .09 to .48, with the majority clustering between .25 and .30.

Three related articles of interest are Loren V. Gerstfeld, "The Price-Quality Relationship Revisited," *Journal of Consumer Affairs,* Winter 1982, pp. 334-46, which computes rank order correlations between quality and price using actual rather than list prices and compares the results for different types of stores; John E. Swan, "Price-Product Performance Competition Between Retailer and Manufacturer Brands," *Journal of Marketing,* July 1974, pp. 52-59, which compares rank correlations of price and quality for retailer and manufacturer brands; and Yoshiko Yamada and Norleen Ackerman, "Price-Quality Correlations in the Japanese Market," *Journal of Consumer Affairs,* Winter 1984, pp. 251-65, which compares rank correlations of price and quality for seventy-nine product categories in the Japanese market.

14. Riesz, "Price-Quality Correlations," p. 236, and *idem,* "Price Versus Quality," pp. 25-27. The findings for durables are broadly consistent with research on the purchase decision for major home appliances, which shows consumers well satisfied with the information they had for judging product quality. One study found that 86 percent of recent purchasers of major home appliances and 75 percent of prospective buyers felt that they had no difficulty judging the quality or reliability of competing brands; another found that 85 percent of all buyers of room air conditioners rated the product information available to them as adequate or more than adequate. Where information of this kind is available, theory predicts a positive correlation between price and quality. See Robert A. Westbrook, Joseph W. Newman, and James R. Taylor, "Satisfaction/Dissatisfaction in the Purchase Decision Process," *Journal of Marketing,* October 1978, pp. 54-60, and "The Buying Consumer: Room Air Conditioners," report by *Appliance Manufacturer* (Chicago: Cahners Publishing, 1979).

15. Morris and Bronson, "Chaos of Competition," p. 33. Also see Yamada and Ackerman, "Price-Quality Correlations," p. 254.

16. For an introduction to hedonic price indexes and the associated statistical techniques, see Zvi Griliches, ed., *Price Indexes and Quality Change* (Cambridge, Mass.: Harvard University Press, 1971).

17. See William J. Abernathy, Kim B. Clark, and Alan M. Kantrow, *Industrial Renaissance* (New York: Basic Books, 1983), pp. 145-49, for the study of automobiles, and John C. Weicher, "Product Quality and Value in the New Home Market: Implications for Consumer Protection Regulation," *Journal of Law and Economics,* December 1981, pp. 365-402, for the study of new homes.

18. Weicher, for example, summarizes his results by saying that "there are

relatively few defects in new homes and . . . owners do not think they affect the home's value, or at least not to any appreciable extent. Nor do they affect home repairs, with a few possible exceptions." Weicher, "New Home Market," p. 366.

19. According to data presented in Chapter 7, service call rates for room air conditioners vary by Btu capacity (size). However, the *ranking* of manufacturers by their products' service call rates varies little by the size of unit involved. For that reason, the average service call rates used in the regressions should be acceptable proxies for the rates for individual models, although they may introduce small errors.

20. Another form of the hedonic approach should also be mentioned. It uses the residual of the hedonic regression (that part of the product's price which has not been explained by the specific attributes measured) to form a "quality-adjusted price." That price reflects the premium or discount one pays for a brand over and above what one gets in terms of measurable characteristics. It thus captures quality differences that might otherwise go unrecorded. See Keith Cowling and A. J. Rayner, "Price, Quality, and Market Share," *Journal of Political Economy,* November–December 1970, pp. 1292–1309, and Keith Cowling and John Cubbin, "Price, Quality, and Advertising Competition: An Econometric Investigation of the United Kingdom's Car Market," *Economica,* November 1971, pp. 378–94, for applications of the concept.

21. *America's Search for Quality* (Benton Harbor, Mich.: Whirlpool Corporation, 1983), pp. 37, 47.

22. This argument was first developed by Phillip Nelson and was later refined by Richard Schmalensee. See Phillip Nelson, "Information and Consumer Behavior," *Journal of Political Economy,* March–April 1970, pp. 311–29; *idem,* "Advertising as Information," *Journal of Political Economy,* July–August 1974, pp. 729–54; and Richard L. Schmalensee, "A Model of Advertising and Product Quality," *Journal of Political Economy,* June 1978, pp. 485–504.

23. Schmalensee, "Advertising and Product Quality," pp. 485–86.

24. Steven N. Wiggins and W. J. Lane, "Quality Uncertainty, Search, and Advertising," *American Economic Review,* December 1983, pp. 881–94.

25. When the sample was limited to nationally advertised brands, the rank correlations between advertising and quality ranged from −1.0 to 1.0, with a mean of .27 in 1972 and .21 in 1973. When unadvertised brands were included, the rank correlations ranged from −.2 to 1.0, with a mean of .54 in 1972 and .61 in 1973. See Herbert J. Rotfeld and Kim B. Rotzoll, "Advertising and Product Quality: Are Heavily Advertised Products Better?" *Journal of Consumer Affairs,* September 1976, pp. 33–47.

26. The superiority of nationally advertised brands also appears in a recent consumer survey. Consumers were first asked to name good- and poor-quality brands in twenty-eight product categories. Average scores were then computed for each brand, based on the ratio of good- to bad-quality citations. In twenty-six of the twenty-eight categories surveyed, the average quality scores of nationally advertised brands were higher than the average quality scores of miscellaneous and less-advertised brands. See The Consumer Network, Inc., *Brand Quality Perceptions* (Philadelphia: Consumer Network, August 1983), p. 7.

27. Rotfeld and Rotzoll, "Advertising and Product Quality," p. 46.

28. C. T. Gilligan and D. E. A. Holmes, "Advertising Expenditure and Product Quality," *Management Decision*, 17, no. 5 (1979): 392. For a summary of other studies on the topic, see Paul W. Farris and Mark S. Albion, "The Impact of Advertising on the Price of Consumer Products," *Journal of Marketing*, Summer 1980, p. 23.

29. Paul W. Farris and David J. Reibstein, "How Prices, Ad Expenditures, and Profits Are Linked," *Harvard Business Review*, November–December 1979, pp. 173–84. The methodology of this study may be questioned. Despite the complexity of the underlying relationships, a bivariate regression model (relative price as a function of relative advertising) was used.

30. *Ibid.*, p. 177. Italics in original.

31. Lynn W. Phillips, Dae R. Chang, and Robert D. Buzzell, "Product Quality, Cost Position, and Business Performance: A Test of Some Key Hypotheses," *Journal of Marketing*, Spring 1983, p. 39. This study used a more sophisticated statistical model than the study by Farris and Reibstein.

32. Hiram C. Barksdale *et al.*, "A Cross-National Survey of Consumer Attitudes Toward Marketing Practices, Consumerism, and Government Regulations," *Columbia Journal of World Business*, Summer 1982, p. 78.

33. *America's Search for Quality* (note 21), p. 37.

34. Of course, the relationship is also likely to depend on how broadly markets are defined.

35. Robert D. Buzzell and Frederik D. Wiersema, "Modeling Changes in Market Share: A Cross-Sectional Analysis," *Strategic Management Journal*, 1981, pp. 27–42; Robert D. Buzzell and Frederik D. Wiersema, "Successful Share-Building Strategies," *Harvard Business Review*, January–February 1981, pp. 135–44; C. Samuel Craig and Susan P. Douglas, "Strategic Factors Associated with Market and Financial Performance," *Quarterly Review of Economics and Business*, Summer 1982, pp. 101–11; Bradley T. Gale and Ben S. Branch, "Concentration Versus Market Share: Which Determines Performance and

Why Does It Matter?" *The Antitrust Bulletin,* Spring 1982, pp. 83–105; Phillips, Chang, and Buzzell, "Quality, Cost, Performance," pp. 26–43; and Sidney Schoeffler, Robert D. Buzzell, and Donald F. Heany, "Impact of Strategic Planning on Profit Performance," *Harvard Business Review,* March–April 1974, pp. 137–45.

36. P. Greg Bonner and Richard Nelson, "Product Attributes and Perceived Quality: Foods," in Jacoby and Olson, *Perceived Quality* (note 11), p. 76, and David J. Curry and David J. Faulds, "The Measurement of Quality Competition in Strategic Groups," in *ibid.,* pp. 280–84.

37. *Firestone Tire & Rubber Company* (Boston: Harvard Business School Case Services 9-684-044, 1984).

38. Jack Campanella and Frank J. Corcoran, "Principles of Quality Costs," *Quality Progress,* April 1983, p. 17.

39. This example was provided by Samuel Jay Kalow, formerly manager of office systems at IBM. Personal communication, March 18, 1985.

40. Robert A. Broh, *Managing Quality for Higher Profits* (New York: McGraw-Hill, 1982), ch. 1; Campanella and Corcoran, "Principles of Quality Costs," pp. 17–18; Philip B. Crosby, *Quality Is Free* (New York: New American Library, 1979), ch. 7; A. V. Feigenbaum, *Total Quality Control* (New York: McGraw-Hill, 1961), ch. 5; and J. M. Juran, ed., *Quality Control Handbook,* Third Edition (New York: McGraw-Hill, 1974), ch. 5.

41. Jeremy Main, "The Battle for Quality Begins," *Fortune,* December 29, 1980, p. 33.

42. "Pushing for Weapons that Work," *New York Times,* July 8, 1984, s. 3, p. 4.

43. Robert S. Kaplan, "Measuring Manufacturing Performance: A New Challenge for Managerial Accounting Research," *The Accounting Review,* October 1983, pp. 686–705, and Steven C. Wheelwright, "Japan—Where Operations Really Are Strategic," *Harvard Business Review,* July–August 1981, pp. 70–71.

44. Charles H. Fine, "Quality Improvement and Learning in Productive Systems," *Management Science,* October 1986, pp. 1301–15, and Charles H. Fine, "Quality Control and Learning in Productive Systems," unpublished Ph.D. dissertation, Graduate School of Business, Stanford University, 1983.

45. Phillips, Chang, and Buzzell, "Quality, Cost, Performance," p. 27.

46. Gale and Branch, "Concentration Versus Market Share" (note 35), pp. 96–97.

47. Phillips, Chang, and Buzzell, "Quality, Cost, Performance," pp. 38–39.

48. *Ibid.,* p. 37.

49. Morton E. Bader, *Practical Quality Management in the Chemical Process Industry* (New York: Marcel Dekker, 1983), ch. 1.

50. Charles C. Harwood, "The View from the Top," *Quality Progress,* October 1984, pp. 26–30.

51. While every effort has been made to ensure the accuracy of the Japanese cost of quality figures, they should still be treated with caution. The concept of quality costs is not widespread in Japan; in several cases, the numbers were compiled solely for the purpose of this research. To ensure consistency, each company filled out a questionnaire in advance of a visit by the author, and then the results were reviewed by the author and company managers working together.

52. "Quality Cost Survey," *Quality,* June 1977, pp. 20–22. The survey also found considerable variation in quality costs across industries. At companies with formal programs for assessing quality costs, these costs ranged from 2.45 percent of sales for furniture and fixtures to 14.7 percent of sales for rubber and miscellaneous products. At companies without formal programs for assessing quality costs, rework, scrap, and warranty expenses ranged from 5.7 percent of sales for rubber and miscellaneous products to 11.6 percent of sales for electric and electronic equipment. But because the survey made little attempt to ensure the consistency of data across companies, and because some industries included only a small number of respondents, interindustry comparisons may not be completely representative.

53. Harold L. Gilmore, "Product Conformance Cost," *Quality Progress,* June 1974, pp. 16–19, and Harold L. Gilmore, "Consumer Product Quality Control Cost Revisited," *Quality Progress,* April 1983, pp. 28–33.

54. W. Edwards Deming, *Quality, Productivity, and Competitive Position* (Cambridge: Center for Advanced Engineering Study, Massachusetts Institute of Technology, 1982), pp. 1–2.

55. A. V. Feigenbaum, "Quality and Productivity," *Quality Progress,* November 1977, p. 21, and *idem,* "Total Quality Leadership," *Quality,* April 1986, pp. 18–22.

56. For a summary of recent research on the sources of productivity growth, see Richard R. Nelson, "Research on Productivity Growth and Productivity Differences: Dead Ends and New Departures," *Journal of Economic Literature,* September 1981, pp. 1029–64. The sources of quality improvement are examined in Chapters 8 and 9 of this book. For an effort to link activities in the two areas, see Michael T. Midas, "The Productivity-Quality Connection," *Productivity Brief 2* (Houston: American Productivity Center, June 1981), pp. 2–3.

57. While the concept of total factor productivity is relatively straightfor-

ward, applying it can be difficult. For practical examples, see Charles E. Craig and R. Clark Harris, "Total Productivity Measurement at the Firm Level," *Sloan Management Review,* Spring 1973, pp. 13–29; Robert H. Hayes and Kim B. Clark, "Exploring the Sources of Productivity Differences at the Factory Level," in Robert H. Hayes, Kim B. Clark, and Chistopher Lorenz, eds., *The Uneasy Alliance: Managing the Productivity-Technology Dilemma* (Boston: Harvard Business School Press, 1985), ch. 4; and *A Note on Productivity Accounting* (Boston: Harvard Business School Case Services 9-682-084, 1982).

58. Nelson, "Productivity Growth and Differences," p. 1038.

59. For a discussion of measures that account simultaneously for changes in output and changes in the percent defective, see Everett E. Adam, Jr., James C. Hershauer, and William A. Ruch, *Productivity and Quality: Measurement as a Basis for Improvement* (Englewood Cliffs, N.J.: Prentice-Hall, 1981), ch. 2.

60. Frank T. Curtin, "Automating Existing Facilities: GE Modernizes Dishwasher, Transportation Equipment Plants," *Industrial Engineering,* September 1983, pp. 32–38, and Robert H. Hayes and Steven C. Wheelwright, *Restoring Our Competitive Edge* (New York: John Wiley & Sons, 1984), pp. 403–5.

61. Charles A. Aubrey II and Debra A. Zimbler, "The Banking Industry: Quality Costs and Improvement," *Quality Progress,* December 1983, pp. 16–20. Other examples relating quality and productivity improvement can be found in Deming, *Quality, Productivity,* ch. 1.

62. Hayes and Clark, "Exploring Productivity Differences," ch. 4.

63. W. Bruce Chew, "Productivity and Change: Understanding Productivity at the Factory Level," Harvard Business School, mimeographed, undated.

64. Roger W. Schmenner and Randall L. Cook, "Explaining Productivity Differences in North Carolina Factories," *Journal of Operations Management,* May 1985, pp. 273–89.

65. These figures are simple (unweighted) averages of the factory prices reported by each company. The higher prices of the Japanese units are not due solely to their superior reliability and conformance. Many of the Japanese models include sophisticated microelectronic controls not available on comparable American units; others are complex but quieter split systems seldom built by U.S. manufacturers. Thus, the price differential between the two countries reflects a bundle of characteristics rather than a premium for reliability alone.

66. A hint of the complexity of these relationships can be gained by correlating the productivity measures with separate, unadjusted measures of assembly line defect rates (conformance) and service call rates under first-year warranty coverage (reliability). While all correlations are in

the expected direction—lower defect and field failure rates implying higher productivity—some are higher when quality is measured as conformance and others are higher when quality is measured as reliability. For example, the Pearson correlation between the assembly line defect rate and assembly line output per actual hours worked is −.49; the correlation between the first-year service call rate and the same productivity measure is −.36. The relative strength of these correlations, however, reverses when the same quality measures but other productivity indexes are used. For example, the correlation between the assembly line defect rate and dollar output per employee is −.63; the correlation between the first-year service call rate and the same productivity measure is −.77. A better understanding of these relationships, including the explanation for differences in tightness of fit between various measures of quality and various measures of productivity, requires further study.

67. For a precise mathematical statement of these conditions, see Dorfman and Steiner, "Optimal Advertising," (note 2), pp. 826–36.

68. Craig and Douglas, "Strategic Factors" (note 35), pp. 101–12; Farris and Reibstein, "Prices, Ad Expenditures" (note 29), pp. 180–81; Phillips, Chang, and Buzzell, "Quality, Cost, Performance" (note 31), pp. 26–43; and Schoeffler, Buzzell, and Heany, "Impact of Strategic Planning" (note 35), pp. 137–45.

69. Phillips, Chang, and Buzzell, "Quality, Cost, Performance," pp. 36–42. However, another study using the PIMS data base reached a different conclusion. In a time series analysis of 460 businesses, Wagner found that even though relative quality helped explain initial differences in ROI, it was of little help in explaining improved performance over time. Why the two studies reached different conclusions is not clear, although different samples and methodologies are the most likely explanations. See Harvey M. Wagner, "Profit Wonders, Investment Blunders," *Harvard Business Review,* September–October 1984, pp. 121–35.


## CHAPTER 6. QUALITY IN THE U.S. ROOM AIR CONDITIONING INDUSTRY I: SUBJECTIVE RATINGS

1. For detailed discussions of how air conditioners work, see Seichi Konzo, J. Raymond Carroll, and Harlan D. Bareither, *Summer Air Conditioning* (New York: Industrial Press, 1958), and Martin Mann, *How Things Work* (New York: Thomas Y. Crowell, 1960), ch. 6.

2. There were many more manufacturers of room air conditioners in the late 1960s and early 1970s than there are today. A 1971 survey, for example, counted twenty-three. See *Note on the Major Home Appli-*

*ance Industry* (Boston: Harvard Business School Case Services 6-372-349, 1972, revised March 1973), pp. 20–21.

3. Each of these is evaluated in the product tests performed by *Consumer Reports*. For further discussion, see "Air Conditioners," *Consumer Reports,* July 1979, pp. 404–9; "High Efficiency Air Conditioners," *Consumer Reports,* July 1980, pp. 428–33; and "Air Conditioners," *Consumer Reports,* July 1982, pp. 356–61.

4. All data in this section have been drawn from consumer surveys sponsored by *Appliance Manufacturer* magazine. Complete survey reports, rather than published summaries, served as the basis for analysis. For readers interested in the published summaries, see "The Buying Consumer: Room Air Conditioners," *Appliance Manufacturer,* April 1979; "Air Conditioners: Owners Tell Who Stands to Gain in an Upgrading Market," *Appliance Manufacturer,* May 1980; "The American Consumer Rates Appliance Reliability and Service," *Appliance Manufacturer,* April 1981; and "The American Consumer Rates Reliability and Service: Air Conditioners," *Appliance Manufacturer,* May 1981.

5. Few consumers, however, were able to cite by name the brand that they would purchase instead. Such a response is quite consistent with other surveys, involving multiple products, that show only a small proportion of all consumers able to cite a specific brand as being the one with the best quality.

6. Note that features and aesthetics do not appear separately on this list. Because these two traits are often associated with product performance—especially quietness, which according to manufacturers is extremely important to purchasers—the percentages ascribed to performance alone may be inflated.

7. The differences between owner and nonowner expectations were significant only for air conditioners and washers. See Center for Policy Alternatives, Massachusetts Institute of Technology, *Consumer Durables: Warranties, Service Contracts and Alternatives* (Cambridge: MIT Press, 1978), pp. 3-27–3-29.

8. Robert T. Lund, "Making Products Live Longer," *Technology Review,* January 1977, pp. 50–51. Estimates by room air conditioner manufacturers are quite similar: an average expected life of ten years, with a range of six to thirteen years. See *Appliance: A Portrait of the U.S. Appliance Industry, 1981* (Oak Brook, Ill.: Dana Chase Publications, September 1981), pp. 2–3.

9. The evidence on this point, while limited, suggests that the quality rankings of brands in different size classes are often positively correlated. An early study using data from the 1960s compared the rank correlations of brands of the same product, but frequently of different model sizes and types, that were tested in different years by *Consumer*

*Reports.* For air conditioners, the rank correlations were .41 for 1960 and 1961, .57 for 1961 and 1963, .09 for 1963 and 1965, and .25 for 1965 and 1967. No measures of statistical significance were reported. See Ruby Turner Morris and Claire Sekulski Bronson, "The Chaos of Competition Indicated by *Consumer Reports,*" *Journal of Marketing,* July 1969, p. 31. Applying the same procedure to the most recent *Consumer Reports* rankings of room air conditioners yields much stronger results. In both 1979 and 1980, two distinct size classes were evaluated. The rank correlation of brands appearing in the two 1979 studies was 1; the rank correlation of brands appearing in both 1980 size classes was .95. The former was obviously significant because the correlation was perfect; the latter was significant at the 2 percent level. (Because of the limited overlap of brands within each year's ratings, these correlations are based on a very small number of observations.) Comparing the quality rankings of brands in the most popular 1979 and 1980 size classes produced a rank correlation of .38; the same calculation for 1980 and 1982 produced a rank correlation of .62. The former was not significant, while the latter was significant at the 10 percent level. Thus, in recent years at least, a high *Consumer Reports* ranking in one size class was generally associated with high rankings in others.

10. Although they are nominally members of management, first-line supervisors are frequently characterized as "men in the middle," with little clear allegiance to either management or labor. Supervisors seldom participate in the core decision-making functions of management, nor do they identify closely with the rank and file. For further discussion, see Lester R. Bittel and Jackson E. Ramsey, "The Limited, Traditional World of Supervisors," *Harvard Business Review,* July–August 1982, pp. 26–31, 36; James W. Driscoll, Daniel J. Carroll, Jr., and Timothy A. Sprecher, "The First-Level Supervisor: Still 'the Man in the Middle,'" *Sloan Management Review,* Winter 1978, pp. 25–37; Fritz J. Roethlisberger, "The Foreman: Master and Victim of Double Talk," *Harvard Business Review,* Spring 1945, pp. 283–98; Leonard A. Schlesinger and Janice A. Klein, "The First-Line Supervisor: Past, Present, and Future," in Jay W. Lorsch, ed., *Handbook of Organizational Behavior* (Englewood Cliffs, N.J.: Prentice-Hall, 1986); and Donald E. Wray, "Marginal Men of Industry: The Foremen," *American Journal of Sociology* 54 (1949), pp. 298–301.

11. Rank correlations are statistical measures of the degree of association or similarity between ordinal (ordered) sets of data. See Hubert M. Blalock, Jr., *Social Statistics,* 2d edition (New York: McGraw-Hill, 1972), pp. 415–26, for further discussion.

12. This conclusion is based on a comparison of brand ownership data and brand quality rankings as reported in the 1979 and 1980 *Appliance Manufacturer* surveys.

13. "Air Conditioners: Owners Tell Who Stands to Gain in an Upgrading Market," *Appliance Manufacturer,* May 1980, p. 48.

14. This conclusion is supported by rank correlations computed from the individual responses of servicemen and -women. With few exceptions, the overall quality ranking a serviceman or -woman assigned to a brand was most closely associated with the ranking assigned to product life or engineering design. Only where brands were especially distinctive on another dimension of quality—for example, Emerson Quiet Kool on quietness, and Friedrich, with its slide-out chassis, on ease of repair— were product life and engineering design less dominant.

15. A more subtle statistical issue must also be addressed. Rankings by servicemen and -women servicing different numbers of brands may not be directly comparable. For example, suppose that one respondent, who services five different brands, ranks General Electric fifth in overall quality; another, who services a dozen brands, ranks it fifth as well. Are the two rankings the same? Should they be weighted equally? The first respondent, after all, has ranked the brand last on his list, while the other has ranked it slightly above average. To compensate for this problem, weighting schemes can be used. For example, respondents' ranks might be adjusted according to the following formula:

$$\text{Weighted rank} = \frac{\text{original rank}}{\text{number of brands serviced}}$$

In this formulation, General Electric would be awarded a score of 1.0 (= 5/5) from the first respondent cited above and a score of .42 (= 5/12) from the second respondent. Since lower scores are better, the second respondent, according to this approach, would have ranked General Electric higher than the first respondent. Use of such a scheme produces greater separation in the rankings of brands in each of the six quality categories but few significant changes in position. More complicated weighting schemes yield similar results. Based on this analysis, it seems safe to conclude that the use of unweighted ranks produces few distortions.

16. Servicemen and -women were asked an open-ended question about their definition of room air conditioner quality. Responses were then assigned to broad categories and tallied by frequency. In declining order of the frequency with which they were mentioned, the resulting categories were product performance, serviceability, reliability, excellence in design or construction, durability, and value. Not surprisingly, serviceability was more important to servicemen and -women than it was to consumers. Both groups, however, ranked performance at the top of their lists.

17. The Pearson correlations are .45 and .32 respectively. Both are significant at the 1 percent level.

18. Leonard A. Morgan, "The Importance of Quality," in Jacob Jacoby and Jerry C. Olson, eds., *Perceived Quality* (Lexington, Mass.: Lexington Books, D.C. Heath, 1985), p. 63.

19. The Spearman rank correlations between first-year service call rates and consumers' rankings of brands by best quality, consumers' rankings of brands they would buy, *Consumer Reports* rankings, servicemen's and -women's rankings of brands by best quality, servicemen's and -women's rankings of brands they would buy, and first-line supervisors' rankings were −.23, −.30, .10, −.13, −.19, and .42, respectively. None of these correlations was significant at the 10 percent level.

## CHAPTER 7. QUALITY IN THE U.S. ROOM AIR CONDITIONING INDUSTRY II: OBJECTIVE MEASURES

1. Warranties are legal documents, governed by the Uniform Commercial Code or other statutory law, that specify a manufacturer's responsibility in the event of product failure. Discussions of their meaning and extent in the appliance industry can be found in Center for Policy Alternatives, Massachusetts Institute of Technology, *Consumer Durables: Warranties, Service Contracts and Alternatives* (Cambridge: MIT Press, 1978), vol. II, chs. 2–5; Jennifer L. Gerner and W. Keith Bryant, "Appliance Warranties as a Market Signal," *Journal of Consumer Affairs,* Summer 1981, pp. 75–86; and U.S. Federal Trade Commission *et al.,* "Report of the Task Force on Appliance Warranties and Service," January 8, 1969, mimeographed.

2. Jaguar, the British manufacturer of automobiles, has reported such an example of inaccurate warranty data. In 1980–81, as part of its renewed focus on quality, the company instituted a customer tracking system. Telephone calls were made to new Jaguar buyers in the United States and Britain and were followed up after thirty days and again after nine months. These calls uncovered a large number of headlight bulb failures that had not shown up in warranty claims. Apparently, dealers had been replacing faulty bulbs without applying for reimbursement; they felt the benefits did not justify the additional paperwork. Only after the company had discovered the problems on its own were remedial steps taken. See Geoffrey Hancock, "Quality Brings Sales Dividends at Jaguar," *Quality Progress,* May 1984, p. 32, for further discussion.

3. Three related problems deserve mention, for they may also affect the accuracy of reported service call rates: missizing of units, customer misuse or abuse of units, and customer discretion in requesting service calls. Missizing occurs when units of a certain cooling capacity are purchased for rooms that are either too large or too small. The result is uneven or ineffective cooling and, frequently, a service call. According

to the survey of servicemen and -women, quality problems are often attributable to missizing, especially when they involve thermostats.

Customer misuse or abuse is closely related to missizing. It involves the use of units in applications for which they were never intended or at settings or stress levels for which they were never designed. Both are likely to increase quality problems. According to the survey of servicemen and -women, more than 21 percent of problems were due to customer misuse or abuse (a category that in this survey is likely to include an unknown percentage of failures actually due to missizing).

Finally, service calls may vary because of customer discretion. A product deficiency does not translate immediately into a service call; customers may wait before requesting a repair if the problem is viewed as minor. The reverse is also true. Faced with warranties that are about to expire, customers may trump up service calls in order to have their units checked while costs are still being paid by the manufacturer. Here again, service call rates are imperfect measures of quality, especially if confined to a narrow time period.

These three problems suggest that service call rates should be used with care, for it is likely that they overstate to some degree the actual incidence of product failings. Even so, in each of the three areas problems might well be minimized if manufacturers took a more proactive approach, introducing more sophisticated designs or better instructions accompanying units. Customer misuse, for example, is a fact of life, hardly confined to air conditioners alone. As the R&D director of a major medical instruments manufacturer has pointed out:

> It is not possible to overestimate the user's capacity for abusing the instrument, nor to anticipate the ways that the user will devise for abuse. . . . Manufacturers should design their systems with this potential for abuse in mind. [Robert J. Meltzer, "Diagnostic Planning for Maximum Effectiveness," *MD & DI,* April 1983, p. 53]

Customer instruction calls can be reduced similarly by better training of salespeople and easier-to-read instruction manuals. From this perspective, problems due to customer misuse or missizing can be properly classified alongside other service calls in that they reflect, to some degree, a company's design, marketing, and operating policies.

4. Other measures of field quality have even more serious problems. For example, the deficiencies of consumer complaint counts were discussed in Chapter 4: They convey only limited information and are easily misinterpreted.

5. This finding, when coupled with comparable research on refrigerators and color televisions, suggests that the 1972–75 period might well be the tailing-off of an earlier downtrend. In both refrigerators and color

televisions, quality improved dramatically in the preceding decade. Between 1958 and 1972 first-year service incidence for refrigerators declined 50 percent; similarly, between 1965 and 1972 service incidence for color television sets declined 50 percent. See Robert T. Lund, "Making Products Live Longer," *Technology Review,* January 1977, p. 51, and Center for Policy Alternatives, Massachusetts Institute of Technology, *The Productivity of Servicing Consumer Durable Products* (Cambridge: MIT Press, 1974), pp. 59–74.

6. Note that service call rates are imperfect measures of the incidence of service calls for any single unit. Rates are computed by tallying up all service calls incurred during the first year of warranty coverage and then dividing by the number of units with active warranties. If problem units or "lemons" are producing most of the service calls, the probability that any single unit will have problems is correspondingly reduced. The proportion of lemons in any population is difficult to estimate, although rough proxies, such as the proportion of units requiring multiple service calls, can sometimes be employed. According to the survey of servicemen and -women, 67 percent of the units they repaired involved a single service call, 19 percent involved two service calls, and 12 percent involved three or more service calls (because of rounding, the numbers do not total 100 percent.)

7. 1976 is excluded from discussion because of the small number of plants that provided data.

8. At the end of the period, eight plants had lower service call rates than when they began; most differences, however, were small. These eight plants were the only ones supplying complete data for 1977–81. Their average service call rates during the period were as follows:

| 1977 | 1978 | 1979 | 1980 | 1981 |
|------|------|------|------|------|
| 16.9 | 13.2 | 11.8 | 11.7 | 12.2 |

An analysis of the four plants providing complete data for 1976–81 yielded similar results.

9. Comparisons of the data in Table 7.1 and Figure 7.1 should be treated with caution, because different samples and different reporting schemes are involved. Problems might also arise because of changes in warranty terms during the period. For example, if warranty coverage became more inclusive and encompassed a broader range of problems, service call rates might remain flat even if the incidence of problems in any given category declined. Some changes in warranty coverage undoubtedly occurred during the period, although their impact was probably small. Since the early 1970s, at least 70 to 80 percent of all room

air conditioner warranties have provided full parts and labor coverage during the first year. See Center for Policy Alternatives, *Consumer Durables: Warranties, Service Contracts and Alternatives,* p. 2–24, and personal communication, Paul Roman, Association of Home Appliance Manufacturers, August 12, 1982.

10. This conclusion is not altered by limiting service call rates for later years to the eight firms participating in the earlier AHAM study. Separate data were available for six of these companies; their average 1981 service call rate was 14.0 per hundred units, of which 1.5 were customer instruction calls. The figures are little different from AHAM's results for 1972: a service call rate of 15.0 per hundred units and customer instruction calls of 2.8 per hundred.

11. Lisa Miller Mesdag, "The Appliance Boom Begins," *Fortune,* July 25, 1983, p. 55.

12. The Spearman rank correlation between servicemen's and -women's brand reliability rankings and first-year service call rates was .39, which was not statistically significant at the 10 percent level. Of course, these rates do not capture all aspects of product reliability. While a large percentage of all repairs involve first-year service calls, servicemen and -women might be using a broader frame of reference: repairs over the entire product lifetime. Service call rates during the first year and later years do not necessarily move together; based on limited data, including second-to-fifth year warranty terms that differed among companies, the Pearson correlation between first-year and second-to-fifth year service call rates was − .49. This figure was statistically insignificant, although quite revealing. It suggests that first-year service call rates and a unit's reliability later in life may be inversely correlated. In that case, servicemen and -women might well be more accurate judges of overall brand reliability than Table 7.3 suggests.

13. The Spearman rank correlation was − .19.

14. For a more precise definition of defects, including comparisons with the terms "imperfection" and "noncomformity," see Richard A. Freund, "Definitions and Basic Quality Concepts," *Journal of Quality Technology,* January 1985, pp. 52–54.

15. For an introduction to seriousness rating systems, see J. M. Juran, ed., *Quality Control Handbook,* Third Edition (New York: McGraw-Hill, 1974), pp. 12-20–12-26.

16. *Ibid.,* pp. 12-5–12-11.

17. Multiple regressions relating assembly line defect rates and various measures of inspection intensity were also attempted, but because of missing observations they had too few degrees of freedom to be meaningful.

18. Figures ranged from a low of forty-five listings to a high of 237, with

a median of ninety-four. Of course, other factors, such as the amount of training inspectors receive, their experience, and the amount of communication about quality among plant employees, are as important as the number of check sheet items in determining the accuracy of inspection. But because of difficulties in securing such data on a comparable basis from all companies, these variables were not pursued further.

19. The Pearson correlations between assembly line defect rates and the total number of inspectors divided by daily output, total inspection time, inspection time per defect check sheet item, the number of inspectors, and the number of checksheet items were .49, .47, .31, .001, and −.24, respectively. None of the correlations was significant at the 10 percent level.

20. The correspondence is especially close in service industries such as banking, where the number of unscreened errors is closely linked to levels of service quality. For example, incorrect bank statements almost always result from processing errors that have been committed before statements are mailed to customers but have not been screened out by inspection. See J. Ronald Furman and G. H. Nearing, "Quality Assurance: An Approach to Measuring Customer Service Levels and Reducing Operating Costs," *The Magazine of BANK ADMINISTRATION,* August 1977, pp. 44–48, for further discussion.

21. The only exception would be plants with exceptionally low levels of defects and service calls (that is, superior quality across the board). In that case, in-plant and field quality would be positively related, whether or not inspection was effective.

22. Special purpose tests can sometimes detect field problems before units leave the factory. Among the most popular are shake and impact tests, which subject units to rough handling and then evaluate their performance, and life tests, which run units for extended periods of time and then check for failures. Several such tests are used by room air conditioner manufacturers; they are reviewed in Chapter 9. For a discussion of similar tests in the electronics industry, see Greg K. Hobbs, "Stimulating the Defect," *Quality,* April 1985, pp. 51–52.

23. The Pearson correlation between first-year service call rates and assembly-line defect rates was .46, which is significant at the 10 percent level. The correlation improves slightly if defects are defined only as problems requiring off-line repair. Then the correlation becomes .58, still significant at the 10 percent level.

24. For further discussions of quality audits, see Juran, *Quality Control Handbook,* pp. 21-4–21-20, and A. V. Feigenbaum, *Total Quality Control* (New York: McGraw-Hill, 1961), pp. 576–78.

25. L. W. Miller, "How Many Should You Check?" *Quality Progress,* March 1975, pp. 14–15, and H. A. VanDine, Jr., "Quality Auditing:

Familiar Land Explored," *Quality Progress,* November 1978, pp. 34–37.

26. One quality manager has summarized the proper use of audits in a slightly more technical fashion: "Audit [results] yield greater confidence in event of rejection and substantially less confidence in results that show no problem." See VanDine, "Quality Auditing," p. 34. Miller, "How Many?" p. 15, reaches smilar conclusions:

> First, a small number of observations can be very effectively used for testing the null hypothesis of no change in the status quo. The second important thing to remember is that in any short period of time, the audit results will not give a precise estimate of the exact level of conformance.

27. The Pearson correlation was − .39.

28. Nevertheless, some analysts recommend the use of audit results to predict field problems and warranty expenses. For a typical example, see V. P. Burns, "Warranty Prediction: Putting a $ on Poor Quality," *Quality Progress,* December 1970, pp. 28–29.

29. Defect rates at quality audit were regressed against assembly line defect rates for the same month. The Cochrane-Orcutt technique was used because of the high degree of serial correlation (rho = .53, significant at the 1 percent level). The resulting equation, with standard errors in parentheses, was as follows:

$$\begin{array}{c} \text{Defect rate at} \\ \text{quality audit} \end{array} = \begin{array}{c} 2.72 \\ (1.04) \end{array} + \begin{array}{c} .0012 \\ (.008) \end{array} \begin{array}{c} \text{Assembly line} \\ \text{defect rate} \end{array}$$

The $R^2$ of this equation was .27, the adjusted $R^2$ was .25, and the standard error of estimate was .98. Measuring audit results by the number of demerit points accumulated by units rather than by the percent defective yielded similar results.

CHAPTER 8. THE SOURCES OF QUALITY: FROM DESIGN TO PRODUCTION

1. For a representative sampling of such articles, see any recent issue of the *Journal of Quality Technology.*

2. This process has clear parallels to the design process for refrigerators. See Center for Policy Alternatives, Massachusetts Institute of Technology, *The Productivity of Servicing Consumer Durable Products* (Cambridge: MIT Press, 1974), pp. 55–57, for a brief description.

3. This was manufacturing's earliest *formal* involvement in the design process. All plants claimed that informal discussions began much earlier, usually before drawings were final.

4. Because of scheduling pressures, plants were not always able to produce the desired number of pilot units from tooling. New models were sometimes launched with only limited production experience. This problem was noted by plants at several levels of quality performance; its impact is unclear. Plants also differed in the number of units that they scheduled for pilot production. Reported differences were small, with most plants scheduling six units or less. But because only a few plants provided such data, no firm conclusions can be drawn.

5. Because this approach to reliability so heavily emphasizes engineering skills, it implicitly devalues manufacturing. Analytical techniques and up-front design receive the lion's share of attention. Thus, the plant whose reliability program is described in the text had a strong technical base, plus a predilection for systems and procedures. But its day-to-day factory management, especially in the areas of labor relations and process control, appeared to be average at best. In several areas it was quite weak. For example, supervisors at the plant attributed 36 percent of its quality problems to workmanship or work force, the highest figure in the industry. And the plant's paint line, an especially sensitive and hard-to-adjust manufacturing process, was experiencing a 19 percent rejection rate, also the highest in the industry (based on a sample of six plants).

6. A. V. Feigenbaum, *Total Quality Control* (New York: McGraw-Hill, 1961), p. 419.

7. The compression ratio in question was 3.7:1.

8. The relationship between component choice and system reliability is discussed at length in J. M. Juran and Frank M. Gryna, Jr., *Quality Planning and Analysis,* Second Edition (New York: McGraw-Hill, 1980), pp. 184–85, 188–89.

9. The average first-year service call rate for bulb thermostats was 1.4 percent, and for bimetallic thermostats .8 percent. The average first-year service call rate for open fan motors was .7 percent, and for sealed fan motors 1.2 percent. T-statistics for testing the differences in these means were 1.5 and .8, respectively. Neither was significant at the 10 percent level. Note that component service call rates are approximations, formed by asking plants whether they used bulb or bimetallic thermostats and open or sealed fan motors, and then averaging the component failure rates for all plants in each category. While plants that reported a mix of component types were excluded from the analysis, there is no guarantee that the components in each category were identical, or that plants reporting one type of component did not use others on a small number of models.

10. Plants reported EERs for their product lines ranging from 6.4 to 7.5. In 1981, the industrywide average was just over 7.

11. Because the data on chassis sizes did not appear to be normally distributed, the Kruskal-Wallis H-test, a nonparametric alternative to the analysis of variance, was used. The Kruskal-Wallis H-value for testing differences across quality categories in the number of chassis sizes was 6.5, significant at the 10 percent level. The corresponding Kruskal-Wallis H-value for differences in the number of models was .7.

12. This idea was first developed by Wickham Skinner in his well-known article "The Focused Factory," *Harvard Business Review,* May–June 1974, pp. 113–21.

13. For evidence on the links between focus and various measures of productivity and profitability, see Robert H. Hayes and Steven C. Wheelwright, *Restoring Our Competitive Edge* (New York: John Wiley & Sons, 1984), pp. 110–17.

14. J. M. Juran, "Vendor Relations: An Overview," *Quality Progress,* July 1968, p. 11.

15. The median number of changes has been used, rather than the mean, because one plant reported an unusually large number of changes, forty.

16. Only two plants reported that visits to a potential vendor's factory were mandatory—one of the best plants and one of the better quality plants. The contribution of these practices to quality performance was unclear, since few new vendors had been selected by the two plants in recent years.

17. Note that this is an adversarial model of vendor relations, rather than the cooperative model that has become so popular in recent years. For a comparison of the two approaches, see Roy D. Shapiro, "Toward Effective Supplier Management: International Comparisons," Harvard Business School, mimeographed, undated. For representative examples of the cooperative approach, see "Industry's Quiet Revolution," *Dun's Business Month,* June 1983, pp. 72–73, 75, and "Ford's Q1 Program Drives Suppliers," *Quality,* September 1985, pp. 36–38.

18. John Deere has developed a simple response to the problem: It takes engineers and makes them purchasing agents. See M. R. Montgomery, "Making It Right," *Boston Globe Magazine,* October 3, 1982, pp. 29–30, for further discussion.

19. The importance of purchasing's involvement in new product development is discussed at length in David N. Burt and William R. Soukup, "Purchasing's Role in New Product Development," *Harvard Business Review,* September–October 1985, pp. 90–97.

20. Note that the implications of diverting parts and materials around receiving inspection are quite different from a conscious decision to accept incoming shipments without checking—even though both approaches mean no inspection. The latter practice is but one element in

a larger program for improving vendor quality; it normally follows a steady reduction in incoming rejection rates. The former practice, on the other hand, is a subversion of established procedures and conveys the implicit message that quality is a secondary concern that may be compromised under pressure.

21. For introductions to process design, see Harold T. Amrine, John A. Ritchey, and Oliver S. Hulley, *Manufacturing Organization and Management,* Fourth Edition (Englewood Cliffs, N.J.: Prentice-Hall, 1982), ch. 5; Evan D. Scheele, William L. Westerman, and Robert J. Wimmert, *Principles and Design of Production Control Systems* (Englewood Cliffs, N.J.: Prentice-Hall, 1960), ch. 10; and Howard L. Timms, *The Production Function in Business* (Homewood, Ill.: Richard D. Irwin, 1966), ch. 9.

22. The sequence of operations described here is only a rough schematic. It omits a number of inspection points and also several secondary operations. Not all plants followed the precise pattern that has been outlined. But it does capture the general flow of activities as partially completed units moved down the assembly line.

23. Surprisingly, at many plants line balancing and sequencing were accomplished by manual methods, even though formal algorithms were widely available. See Richard B. Chase, "Survey of Paced Assembly Lines," *Industrial Engineering,* February 1974, pp. 14–18, for further discussion.

24. The fan motor failure rate for the two plants that mounted their fan motors early was .2 percent, while the average at other plants was 1.1 percent. The compressor failure rate for the plants that mounted their compressors early was .7 percent, while the rate at the two companies that attached their compressors late was 1.3 percent.

25. This conclusion applies only to the age of buildings. No data were collected on the age of equipment, although there was a small amount of anecdotal evidence showing building and equipment age to be positively correlated.

26. For valid comparisons, an additional variable should also be considered: the split between subassembly and final assembly tasks. Plants might differ in the amount of work they choose to do on the assembly line. Some tasks might be performed off-line or otherwise built into subassemblies; that would alter the amount of work slated for the assembly line. No direct data were available to compare the split at plants of differing quality performance, so the impact of this variable was impossible to estimate, although practices appeared to be similar across the industry.

27. *A priori,* it is difficult to predict whether a narrow or broad division of labor will result in better quality. The writings of Frederick Taylor and

the scientific management school would support a narrow definition of workers' jobs, while more recent research on job enlargement and worker satisfaction would support a broader definition. See Richard B. Chase, "Strategic Considerations in Assembly-Line Selection," *California Management Review,* Fall 1975, pp. 17–23, for further discussion.

28. With one exception, neither an analysis of variance nor a Kruskal-Wallis H-test showed significant differences among quality categories in the number of assembly lines, assembly line length, or cycle times. The associated F-values were .4, 1.1, and 2.4 respectively, while the Kruskal-Wallis H-values were 1.8, 6.4, and 2.7 respectively. Only the Kruskal-Wallis H-value for differences among categories in assembly line length was statistically significant, at the 10 percent level.

29. See, for example, Richard J. Schonberger, *World Class Manufacturing* (New York: Free Press, 1986), pp. 50–51.

30. The only statistically significant difference, however, involved utilization rates. The F-statistic from an analysis of variance was 4.6, while the Kruskal-Wallis H-value was 6.2. The former is significant at the 6 percent level, the latter at the 10 percent level.

31. This argument is closely analogous to Hayes and Clark's analysis of the link beween productivity and confusion. See Robert H. Hayes and Kim B. Clark, "Exploring the Sources of Productivity Differences at the Factory Level," in Kim B. Clark, Robert H. Hayes, and Christopher Lorenz, eds., *The Uneasy Alliance: Managing the Productivity-Technology Dilemma* (Boston: Harvard Business School Press, 1985), pp. 178–84.

32. Production stability might also be disrupted by the introduction of new equipment. Hayes and Clark, for example, found that new equipment had a strong negative impact on productivity and that the effect persisted for as long as a year. *Ibid.,* pp. 183–84. In the current study, no data were collected on equipment investment, so its impact on quality levels could not be determined.

33. The F-values from an analysis of variance testing for differences across quality categories in absenteeism, turnover, average overtime, new hires as a percentage of direct labor, and layoffs as a percentage of direct labor were .4, 1.4, 4.0, .3, and .6, respectively. The Kruskal-Wallis H-values were 1.2, 3.1, 4.2, 1.0, and .1, respectively. None of these statistics was significant at the 10 percent level.

34. See "Overtime Is Unproductive," *Psychology Today,* August 1981, p. 83.

35. For an introduction to the literature on learning and experience curves, see John M. Dutton, Annie Thomas, and John E. Butler, "The History

of Progress Functions as a Managerial Technology," *Business History Review,* Summer 1984, pp. 204–33, and Louis E. Yelle, "The Learning Curve: Historical Review and Comprehensive Survey," *Decision Sciences* 10 (1979): 302–28.

36. The classic example of disrupted learning and workers starting afresh is the "first day of the week" syndrome. Defect rates are thought to be unusually high on Mondays because workers have been away from the factory for two days and need several hours to polish and rediscover their skills. Only limited data were collected to test the hypothesis, but they point in the same general direction. Defect rates (for identical models) were not universally higher on Monday than they had been the preceding Thursday or Friday; in fact, they were just as likely to be lower. Similar results were obtained by comparing defect rates for startup quarters (after a plant's annual shutdown period) with defect rates for other quarters. At some plants they were higher than average and at other plants they were roughly the same. Thus, the findings provide little support for either the first day of the week or first quarter syndrome.

37. To check on these estimates, a small sample of plants' monthly defect reports were collected and reviewed. All showed a series of pronounced "spikes" where daily defect rates had risen dramatically from previous levels. In most cases, changeovers to a new model family (chassis size) had occurred on the same day. Moreover, the height of the spikes generally corresponded with individual plant estimates of the increase in defects they experienced from changeovers.

38. The F-statistics from an analysis of variance, by quality categories, of the number of model changeovers and chassis changeovers per month were .5 and .4, respectively. The Kruskal-Wallis H-values were .8 and 2.4, respectively. None of these statistics was significant at the 10 percent level.

39. For a rare example of scheduling that includes quality considerations, see *Inland Steel: Quality Scheduling 1985* (Boston: Harvard Business School Case Services 9-686-107, 1986).

40. Linear, logarithmic, and reciprocal transformations of the data were all used. The latter two best approximate the shape of the curve in Figure 8.2. They also provided the best statistical fits. For further discussion of the choice of functional forms when estimating regression equations, see J. Johnston, *Econometric Methods,* Second Edition (New York: McGraw-Hill, 1972), pp. 47–55.

41. In one case, a 10 percent increase in run length meant an 8 percent decline in leak rates; in the other two cases, a 10 percent increase in run length implied a 3 percent decline in leaks. All three of these numbers

are elasticities—the percentage that the dependent variable will change for a percentage change in the independent variable—calculated at the sample means.

42. Run length and changeovers are obviously linked; they are not separate, unrelated variables. Once the daily production rate has been set, increases in either run length or changeovers lead automatically to decreases in the other variable. But since companies in this industry varied widely in their daily production rates, the number of possible combinations of run length and changeovers was large.

43. The F-statistic from an analysis of variance was .8 and the Kruskal-Wallis H-value was 2.1. Neither was significant at the 10 percent level.

## CHAPTER 9. QUALITY POLICIES AND ATTITUDES

1. Frank S. Leonard and W. Earl Sasser, "The Incline of Quality," *Harvard Business Review,* September–October 1982, pp. 164–67.

2. The F-statistics from an analysis of variance testing for differences across quality categories in the total size of quality departments and their size as a percentage of the plant labor force were 1.4 and .5, respectively. The Kruskal-Wallis H-statistics (from a nonparametric test) were 4.2 and 3.5, respectively. None of these statistics was significant at the 10 percent level. Note that in the few cases when inspectors were classified as members of manufacturing departments, they were added to the totals for quality departments to make the figures comparable across companies.

3. The importance of perceived control—even when it is not exercised—is well illustrated by a psychological experiment popularized by the book *In Search of Excellence*. Subjects in the experiment were divided into groups and were given puzzles to solve and proofreading chores; as they worked, their concentration was disrupted by loud background noises. In one group, subjects were provided with a button to turn off the noise, and in the other they were not. Members of the first group solved five times the number of puzzles and made far fewer proofreading errors than members of the second group. More significantly, they did so without even touching the shutoff switch. Apparently, "the mere knowledge that [they could] exert control made the difference." See Thomas J. Peters and Robert H. Waterman, Jr., *In Search of Excellence* (New York: Harper & Row, 1982), pp. xxiii–xxiv, for further discussion.

4. This was true only of production units. Virtually all plants performed life tests on prototypes and new models. But only three plants—one of the best and two that were fair—performed life tests on a small sample of production units.

5. Because of high variance within categories, even differences in the number of calorimeter tests were not statistically significant across quality categories. The F-statistics from an analysis of variance testing for differences across quality categories in the number of on-line leak tests, the daily number of shake and impact tests, the number of shake and impact tests as a percentage of daily production, the daily number of calorimeter tests, and the number of calorimeter tests as a percentage of daily production were 2.7, 2.5, 2.2, 2.1, and .5, respectively. The Kruskal-Wallis H-values were 3.9, 7.5, 6.9, 5.6, and 4.3, respectively. Only the Kruskal-Wallis H-values for the number and percentage of shake and impact tests were statistically significant, at the 10 percent level.

6. In this industry, adjustments were especially likely on the halogen "sniffers" used by most firms. For more on these devices, and a comparison with other methods for detecting leaks, see Therese Sullivan, "Sensing Leakage," *Quality*, December 1982, pp. 18–24.

7. The F-statistics from an analysis of variance testing for differences across quality categories in the number of receiving, coil, and assembly line inspectors were 16.7, 5.8, and 2.2, respectively. The first of these statistics was significant at the 1 percent level, the second at the 6 percent level. The associated Kruskal-Wallis H-values were 6.1, 5.3, and 4.4, respectively, none of which was significant at the 10 percent level. Moreover, when the number of inspectors was divided by daily production rates to adjust for differences among plants in production volumes, the F-statistics from an analysis of variance were no longer significant.

8. Efforts to increase the sensitivity of line workers to quality have been reported in a number of other industries. Bethlehem Steel, for example, reported a sharp increase in quality after employees were sent to visit customers to hear their complaints about quality firsthand. See "Employee Involvement Gains Support," *Wall Street Journal,* December 12, 1984, p. 33. The same approach was used at General Electric's locomotive works in Erie, Pennsylvania. See Thomas M. Rohan, "Quality or Junk? Facing Up to the Problem," *Industry Week,* December 12, 1983, p. 78. Feedback was also increased at the First National Bank of Chicago after a study found that clerks were frustrated by the lack of information showing how their personal efforts translated into quality improvements. See James C. Hershauer, "A Productivity Audit of Lock Box Service Quality: First National Bank of Chicago," *The Magazine of BANK ADMINISTRATION,* October 1978, pp. 43–48.

9. For an unusually detailed discussion of these elements, see R.P. Smith, "Research and Other Data in the Monitoring of Product Quality," *Journal of the Marketing Research Society,* 21: 189–205, which focuses

on the market data that Ford of Europe collects to monitor its quality performance over time.

10. One of the poor plants did track SCRs on a regular basis, but it used the data primarily to control service costs. Computer printouts of service calls were first scanned by the Director of Service to identify repair shops that charged the company for a large number of "no parts" service calls, which were thought to indicate cheating. Field service managers were then notified and asked to visit the repair shops to inquire further. According to the Director of Service, this was one of the chief uses of the SCR report. He claimed that the computer system on which it was based had not been designed to break out SCRs by types of problems or to trigger remedial action, and that it was seldom, if ever, used for that purpose.

11. This was not universally true. One of the best plants received little SCR feedback because the bulk of its units were sold to a private label buyer (a problem reported by several firms in the industry). It therefore tried to monitor field performance through a "constructed service call rate" developed from internal data collected in quality audits.

12. See, for example, Philip B. Crosby, *Quality Is Free* (New York: McGraw-Hill, 1979), pp. 7–8; Armand V. Feigenbaum, "Total Quality Leadership," *Quality,* April 1986, pp. 18–22; "Is Japan Cornering the Market on Product Quality?" *International Management,* January 1981, pp. 22–25; and the references cited in Chapter 2, note 21.

13. The same approach—promoting a quality control manager to plant manager—was used with great success by Sanyo, the Japanese consumer electronics giant, in turning around the color television plant it purchased from Warwick Electronics in 1977. See *Sanyo Manufacturing Corporation, Forrest City, Arkansas* (Boston: Harvard Business School Case Services, 9-682-045, 1981).

14. The importance of committing management time to quality improvement has been well summarized by the chairman of Signetics Corporation, the American semiconductor manufacturer discussed in Chapter 5:

> We realized that if we were going to prove that we meant it when we said quality, we were going to have to put time into it. We knew about the "managers' apparent interest index," which says, in effect, "people watch your feet, not your lips." If the boss does a lot of preaching, but doesn't invest a lot of hours of effort himself, people see through it.

See Charles C. Harwood, "The View from the Top," *Quality Progress,* October 1984, p. 28.

15. For a summary of the literature on goal-setting and its impact on performance, see Edwin A. Locke *et al.*, "Goal-Setting and Task Performance, 1969–1980," *Psychological Bulletin,* 90, no. 1: 125–52.

16. One of the poor and one of the fair plants had also set goals for defect rates, but they were not at all systematic. Their numbers were literally plucked out of thin air. In one case, the manufacturing manager had arbitrarily set a target of 3 percent leaks, even though the present rate was eight times higher. Such goals played little role in improvement programs.

17. Because paired ordinal data from a single sample were involved, a one-tailed Wilcoxon matched-pairs ranked-signs test was used to test for significance. The Z-score comparing the ranking of meeting the production schedule with the ranking of producing high-quality (defect-free) products, the objective ranked second by supervisors, was 5.1, significant at the .1 percent level.

18. This problem is hardly confined to the room air conditioning industry. The explosion of the space shuttle Challenger, for example, was linked by the Rogers Commission to intense pressures to maintain a preestablished launch schedule. For a fascinating discussion of production pressures in such complex systems as air, marine, and space transport, see Charles Perrow, *Normal Accidents* (New York: Basic Books, 1984), pp. 148, 158, 172, 174, 176, 179–85, 187–88, 190, 207–8, and 275. For a discussion of production pressures in the semiconductor industry, see Everett M. Rogers and Judith K. Larsen, "Lessons from a Government Lawsuit," *New York Times,* March 25, 1984, s. 3, p. 3.

19. As an internal memorandum at one of the better plants put it, summarizing a survey of shop-floor employees that explored barriers to quality improvement: "What actions would signal to people that management is serious about quality? When they sacrifice output for it."

20. Differences in the weight that supervisors thought their managers attached to producing high-quality products were statistically significant across the four quality categories. The Kruskal-Wallis H-test was used, because ordinal data were involved. The resulting H-statistic was 10.4, which is significant at the .1 percent level.

## CHAPTER 10. THE JAPANESE QUALITY MOVEMENT

1. Kaoru Ishikawa, *What Is Total Quality Control? The Japanese Way* (Englewood Cliffs, N.J.: Prentice-Hall, 1985), p. 15.

2. Personal communication, Kaoru Ishikawa, April 9, 1985.

3.  Koji Kobayashi, who would eventually become chairman of NEC, evidently felt the same way in his early years on the job:

> I joined NEC . . . in 1929. At that time, I was asked by my boss to study statistical quality control. . . . Shortly thereafter, I read a paper on statistical quality control that appeared in the Bell System *Technical Journal.* However, since this paper was based on statistics and contained many difficult formulas, I could not muster a vast amount of interest in it. And since I thought that my job was the development of communications equipment, and not statistics, I stopped studying quality control right then and there.

    Koji Kobayashi, "Quality Management at NEC Corporation," *Quality Progress,* April 1986, p. 18.
4.  Ishikawa, *What Is Total Quality Control?* pp. 14–15, and *idem,* personal communication, April 9, 1985.
5.  This discussion of the Civil Communications Section is based on the pioneering research of Kenneth Hopper. See Kenneth Hopper, "Creating Japan's New Industrial Management: The Americans as Teachers," *Human Resource Management,* Summer 1982, pp. 13–34, and *idem,* "Quality, Japan, and the U.S.: The First Chapter," *Quality Progress,* September 1985, pp. 34–41.
6.  Hopper, "Creating Japan's New Industrial Management," p. 15; Kobayashi, "Quality Management at NEC," p. 19; and Hitoshi Kume, "Quality Control in Japan's Industries," *The Wheel Extended,* Spring 1980, p. 21.
7.  Despite their wide prevalence today, statements of company philosophy were rare in Japan immediately after World War II. According to the chairman of Matsushita Electric, of the companies attending the original CCS seminars, his was the only one that at the time had a formal company philosophy. See Hopper, "Creating Japan's New Industrial Management," p. 28.
8.  *Ibid.,* p. 23.
9.  Hopper, "Quality, Japan, and the U.S.," p. 37.
10. *Ibid.,* p. 38.
11. Hopper, "Creating Japan's New Industrial Management," p. 26.
12. Ishikawa, *What Is Total Quality Control?* p. 6; Kume, "Quality Control," pp. 21–22; and T. R. Reid, *The Chip* (New York: Simon & Schuster, 1984), p. 182.
13. Reid, *The Chip,* p. 179, and Jeremy Main, "The Curmudgeon Who Talks Tough on Quality, *Fortune,* June 25, 1984, p. 120.
14. W. Edwards Deming, "What Happened in Japan?" *Industrial Quality Control,* August 1967, pp. 91–92.

15. *Ibid.;* W. Edwards Deming, *Quality, Productivity, and Competitive Position* (Cambridge: Center for Advanced Engineering Study, Massachusetts Institute of Technology, 1982), pp. 101–4; and "An Interview with W. Edwards Deming: The Roots of Quality Control in Japan," *Pacific Basin Quarterly,* Spring/Summer 1985, pp. 3–4.

16. Ishikawa, *What Is Total Quality Control?* pp. 18–19.

17. *Ibid.,* p. 19, and Kume, "Quality Control," pp. 21–22.

18. For representative examples of Juran's early approach to quality, see J. M. Juran, *Quality Control Handbook* (New York: McGraw-Hill, 1951), and *idem, Managerial Breakthrough* (New York: McGraw-Hill, 1964).

19. Telephone interview with Armand Feigenbaum, August 21, 1986, and Christopher W. L. Hart and Gregory D. Casserly, "Quality: A Brand-New, Time-Tested Strategy," *Cornell H.R.A. Quarterly,* November 1985, p. 54.

20. Robert Doktor, T. Kawase, and J. H. Haig, "Culture as a Constraint on Productivity," *International Studies of Management and Organization,* xv, nos. 3–4 (1986): 14.

21. J. M. Juran, "Product Quality: A Prescription for the West, Part II: Upper-Management Leadership and Employee Relations," *Management Review,* July 1981, p. 61. Hopper draws a similar conclusion about the Civil Communications Section:

    > Though we must admire the dedication of the engineers . . . and though without them much of the advice they gave the Japanese probably would not have arrived in time, it has to be remembered that elsewhere in the world the equivalent of CCS advice was widely available, nowhere more so than in the U.S. itself. If good advice were all that were necessary, America would now be looking back proudly on decades of good productivity growth.

    Hopper, "Quality, Japan, and the U.S.," p. 39.

22. Ishikawa, *What Is Total Quality Control?* pp. 15–16; Kume, "Quality Control," p. 21; and Japanese Industrial Standards Committee, "Industrial Standardization in Japan: 1981," mimeographed, undated, p. 1.

23. Kaoru Ishikawa, "Quality and Standardization: Program for Economic Success," *Quality Progress,* January 1984, p. 18. An interesting extension of this argument is provided by Nathan Rosenberg, who has observed that the United States' first corporate R&D laboratories were dedicated primarily to testing, measuring, grading, and specification writing—activities all related to standardization—and that this was how the laboratories had their earliest impact. See Nathan Rosenberg, "The Commercial Exploitation of Science by American Industry," in Kim B.

Clark, Robert H. Hayes, and Christopher Lorenz, eds., *The Uneasy Alliance: Managing the Productivity-Technology Dilemma* (Boston: Harvard Business School Press, 1985), pp. 19–51.

24. For an early review of comparable U.S. quality standards, see Acheson J. Duncan and William R. Pabst, Jr., "Quality Standards," *Journal of Quality Technology,* April 1972, pp. 102–9.

25. Personal communication, Professor Keinosuke Ono, Graduate School of Business Administration, Keio University, March 4, 1983. Professor Ono notes that

> . . . application to the [JIS] scheme has been voluntary. With this certified mark, however, the certified products have . . . considerable power to gain consumers' confidence in their quality. [This] was especially so in [the] old days, when most of the Japanese did not believe in [the] quality of "made in Japan." As a consumer, I remember that I first checked in buying any industrial product [to see] if the item carried "the mark," and I was willing to pay some premium price for the certified ones.

26. Standards Department, Agency of Industrial Science and Technology, Ministry of International Trade and Industry, "Guide for Application of the JIS Mark," mimeographed, undated, p. 3. Also see Kume, "Quality Control," p. 27.

27. Standards Department, "Guide for Application," pp. 20–21.

28. Kaoru Ishikawa, "Quality Control in Japan," in Naoto Sasaki and David Hutchins, eds., *The Japanese Approach to Product Quality* (Oxford: Pergamon Press, 1984), p. 3.

29. Japanese Industrial Standards Committee, "Industrial Standardization 1981," p. 14.

30. Michael A. Cusumano, *The Japanese Automobile Industry* (Cambridge, Mass.: Harvard University Press, 1985), pp. 322–23; Kume, "Quality Control," p. 21; and Union of Japanese Scientists and Engineers, "JUSE: Organization and Activities," mimeographed, undated, p. 1.

31. Cusumano, *Japanese Automobile Industry,* p. 323; Ishikawa, *What Is Total Quality Control?* pp. 16–19; Masumasa Imaizuma, "History of QC Circles," in *Proceedings of the 1981 International QC Circle Convention* (Tokyo: Union of Japanese Scientists and Engineers, 1981), pp. 1–2; and Kume, "Quality Control," p. 21.

32. Robert E. Cole, "The Macropolitics of Organizational Change: A Comparative Analysis of the Spread of Small-Group Activities," *Administrative Science Quarterly,* December 1985, p. 572, and Cusumano, *Japanese Automobile Industry,* p. 323. For a brief introduction to the

role and activities of Keidanren, see Ezra F. Vogel, *Japan as Number One* (New York: Harper & Row, 1979), pp. 113–15.

33. Cusumano, *Japanese Automobile Industry,* pp. 323–25, and Ishikawa, *What Is Total Quality Control?* p. 21. Ishikawa's ability to gain the cooperation of broadcasters was due, in part, to the fact that his father had been a founder of the Japan National Broadcasting Corporation (NHK) in 1948.

34. Cole, "Macropolitics of Organizational Change," p. 573; Ishikawa, *What Is Total Quality Control?* pp. 4–5; and Union of Japanese Scientists and Engineers, "JUSE," pp. 1–3.

35. Cusumano, *Japanese Automobile Industry,* pp. 332–33, and Ishikawa, *What Is Total Quality Control?* pp. 18–19. For a broad overview of the shifting emphasis of Japanese quality control, see Noriaki Kano, "Evolution of Quality Control with Change of Economic Structure in Japan," *Reports of Statistical Application Research, JUSE,* September 1984, pp. 22–41.

36. Leonard Nadler, "What Japan Learned from the U.S.—That We Forgot to Remember," *California Management Review,* Summer 1984, p. 53.

37. Imaizumi, "History of QC Circles," p. 3, and QC Circle Headquarters, JUSE, *QC Circle Koryo (General Principles of the QC Circle)* (Tokyo: QC Circle Headquarters, JUSE, 1980), pp. 6–7.

38. Ishikawa, *What Is Total Quality Control?* p. 22.

39. Imaizumi, "History of QC Circles," pp. 3–4, 8, and QC Circle Headquarters, *QC Circle Koryo,* pp. 8–9. For a description of a typical presentation at a QC Circle conference, see J. M. Juran, "The QC Circle Phenomenon," *Industrial Quality Control,* January 1967, pp. 329–30. Juran's article is generally thought to have introduced quality control circles to the West for the first time.

40. The classic introduction to these techniques is Kaoru Ishikawa, *Guide to Quality Control* (Tokyo: Asian Productivity Organization, 1976).

41. See, for example, Mamoru Saito, "Nippon Steel's Use of JK Activities," *International Studies of Management and Organization,* Spring 1986, pp. 126–43, and Setsuro Sekiya, "Quality Control at Toyota Motor Corporation," *The Wheel Extended,* July–September 1982, pp. 11–13. Note that QC circles are less prevalent in smaller Japanese companies. See Robert Wood, Frank Hull, and Koya Azumi, "Evaluating Quality Circles: The American Application," *California Management Review,* Fall 1983, p. 42.

42. Cusumano, *Japanese Automobile Industry,* pp. 336–37. Since not all QC circles are registered, the actual number of circles is undoubtedly higher.

43. The first quotation is from Juran, "The QC Circle Phenomenon," p. 333, and the second is from Hirotaka Takeuchi, "Productivity: Learning From the Japanese," *California Management Review,* Summer 1981, p. 8.

44. Wood, Hull, and Azumi ("Evaluating Quality Circles," p. 44), for example, have observed that

> . . . the current state of information regarding the effectiveness of QCs can best be described as a long list of claimed benefits, supported by anecdotal data and isolated cases which do not adequately establish the validity or generality of the benefits claimed.

45. Ishikawa, "Quality Control in Japan," pp. 1–5; *idem, What Is Total Quality Control?* p. 5; and "Father of Quality Control Circles Doubts Their Long-Term Viability in the West," *International Management,* August 1982, pp. 23–24.

46. Masao Kogure and Yoji Akao, "Quality Function Deployment and CWQC in Japan," *Quality Progress,* October 1983, p. 25, and L. P. Sullivan, "The Seven Stages in Company-wide Quality Control," *Quality Progress,* May 1986, pp. 77–78.

47. Unfortunately, confusion between TQC and CWQC is still widespread. Some experts use the terms interchangeably; others see CWQC as a more advanced and comprehensive concept. Kaoru Ishikawa claims that "Japanese-style TQC" (which he also calls CWQC) and "Feigenbaum-style TQC" are different. The latter focuses on the involvement of all functions (e.g. marketing, purchasing, manufacturing) in quality control, while the former requires the involvement of all functions *and* all levels of the company (personal communication, Kaoru Ishikawa, April 9, 1985, and Ishikawa, *What Is Total Quality Control?* pp. 90–91). Feigenbaum, on the other hand, claims that CWQC and his version of TQC are identical and that CWQC is a term seldom used by Japanese companies today (interview with Armand Feigenbaum, August 21, 1986). See also Cusumano, *Japanese Automobile Industry,* pp. 326–27, and Hart and Casserly, "Quality" (note 19), p. 54.

48. "Father of Quality Control Circles," p. 25; Ishikawa, "Quality Control in Japan," p. 2; Kume, "Quality Control" (note 6), p. 24; Wayne S. Rieker, "QC Circles and Company-wide Quality Control," *Quality Progress,* October 1983, p. 15; and Sullivan, "Seven Stages," pp. 80–81.

49. Hirotaka Takeuchi and Ikujiro Nonaka, "The New New Product Development Game," *Harvard Business Review,* January–February 1986, p. 140. A longer version of this article appears as Ken-ichi Imai, Ikujiro Nonaka, and Hirotaka Takeuchi, "Managing the New Product Development Process: How Japanese Companies Learn and Unlearn," in Clark, Hayes, and Lorenz, *Uneasy Alliance* (note 23), p. 337–75.

50. Ishikawa, "Quality Control in Japan," pp. 1–2; Ishikawa, *What Is Total Quality Control?* pp. 21, 91; Rieker, "QC Circles," pp. 15–16; and Sullivan, "Seven Stages," p. 81.

51. Quality Control Center, Production Engineering Division, Matsushita Electric Industrial Co., Ltd., "Basic Concepts of Quality Control and Roles and Duties of Managers," mimeographed, 1982, p. 11.

52. Robert E. Cole, "Improving Product Quality Through Continuous Feedback," *Management Review,* October 1983, pp. 11–12; Robert H. Hayes and Steven C. Wheelwright, *Restoring Our Competitive Edge* (New York: John Wiley & Sons, 1984), pp. 369–71; J. M. Juran, "Product Quality: A Prescription for the West, Part I: Training and Improvement Programs," *Management Review,* June 1981, p. 10; and Richard J. Schonberger, *Japanese Manufacturing Techniques* (New York: Free Press, 1982), pp. 52–54.

53. Ishikawa, "Quality and Standardization," pp. 17–18; *idem, What Is Total Quality Control?* pp. 21, 106–7; Rieker, "QC Circles," p. 15; and Sullivan, "Seven Stages," p. 83.

54. Ishikawa, "Quality and Standardization," pp. 17–18; *idem, What Is Total Quality Control?* pp. 46–49; Kogure and Akao, "Quality Function Deployment," pp. 25–29; L. P. Sullivan, "Quality Function Deployment," *Quality Progress,* June 1986, pp. 39–50; and *idem,* "Seven Stages," p. 83.

55. Fumihiko Adachi, Keinosuke Ono, and Konosuke Odaka, "Ancillary Firm Development in the Japanese Automobile Industry," in Konosuke Odaka, ed., *The Motor Vehicle Industry in Asia* (Singapore: Council for Asian Manpower Studies, 1983), pp. 388–89.

56. *Ibid.,* and Cole, "Macropolitics of Organizational Change" (note 32), p. 567.

57. Deming, "What Happened in Japan?" (note 14), p. 90, and Juran, "Product Quality I" (note 52), p. 12.

58. Deming, *Quality, Productivity, Competitive Position* (note 15), pp. 101–2; Deming, "What Happened in Japan?" p. 90; "Interview with Deming" (note 15), pp. 3–4; Hopper, "Creating Japan's New Industrial Management" (note 5), p. 21; and Juran, "Product Quality II" (note 21), pp. 57–58.

59. Cole, "Macropolitics of Organizational Change," pp. 572–73; Cusumano, *Japanese Automobile Industry* (note 30), pp. 322–24; Deming, *Quality, Productivity, Competitive Position,* pp. 101–2; and "Interview with Deming," pp. 3–4.

60. This orientation is visible in the organization's own writings. See, for example, "ASQC: 40 Years of Growth and Change," *Quality Progress,* May 1986, pp. 56–67.

61. There are in fact two Deming Prizes, one for companies and one for individuals. The Deming Applications Prize is awarded annually to a company that has achieved great success in quality control; it receives the lion's share of publicity. A Deming Prize is also awarded annually to an individual who has made outstanding contributions to the theory, applications, and methods of quality control, usually through published writings. See Kume, "Quality Control" (note 6), p. 22.

62. For discussions of U.S. standardization and certification procedures, see David A. Garvin, "Can Industry Self-Regulation Work?" *California Management Review,* Summer 1983, pp. 37–52; David A. Garvin, "Deregulating and Self-Regulating," *The Wharton Magazine,* Spring 1981, pp. 57–63; and David Hemenway, *Industrywide Voluntary Product Standards* (Cambridge, Mass.: Ballinger, 1975).

63. Ishikawa, *What Is Total Quality Control?* p. 37. See also Juran, "Product Quality I," pp. 10, 13–14.

64. See, for example, Chalmers Johnson, "The 'Internationalization' of the Japanese Economy," *California Management Review,* Spring 1983, pp. 7–9, and *idem, MITI and the Japanese Miracle* (Stanford, Calif.: Stanford University Press, 1982), p. 8.

65. Masanori Moritani, *Japanese Technology* (Tokyo: Simul Press, 1982), p. vii, and interview with Professor Paul Varley, Chairman, Department of East Asian Languages and Cultures, Columbia University, November 29, 1985.

66. Moritani, *Japanese Technology,* pp. 52–53, and personal communication, Professor Keinosuke Ono, Graduate School of Business Administration, Keio University, December 23, 1983. For more on Japan's "culture of shame," see Ruth Benedict, *The Chrysanthemum and the Sword* (New York: New American Library, 1946), pp. 222–27.

67. Johnson, "'Internationalization' of Japanese Economy," p. 7.

68. Tamatsu Goto and Nobukatsu Manabe, "How Japanese Manufacturers Achieve High IC Reliability," *Electronics,* March 13, 1980, pp. 144–45, and Franklin B. Weinstein, Michiyuki Uenohara, and John G. Linvill, "Technological Resources," in Daniel I. Okimoto, Takuo Sugano, and Franklin B. Weinstein, eds., *Competitive Edge: The Semiconductor Industry in the U.S. and Japan* (Stanford, Calif.: Stanford University Press, 1984), p. 62.

69. Weinstein, Uenohara, and Linvill, "Technological Resources," p. 62.

70. William J. Abernathy, Kim B. Clark, and Alan M. Kantrow, *Industrial Renaissance* (New York: Basic Books, 1983), p. 57.

71. Most of the evidence on this point is anecdotal, for few studies have collected comparative quality data. For a discussion of Japanese subsidiaries in the United Kingdom, see Makoto Takamiya, "Japanese Multinationals in Europe: Internal Operations and Their Public Policy

Implications," *Columbia Journal of World Business,* Summer 1981, pp. 5–17. For a discussion of Japanese subsidiaries in Asia and Latin America, see Anant R. Negandhi, Golpira S. Eshghi, and Edith C. Yuen, "The Management Practices of Japanese Subsidiaries Overseas," *California Management Review,* Summer 1985, pp. 93–105. For discussions of Japanese subsidiaries in the United States, see Nina Hatvany and Vladimir Pucik," Japanese Management in America: What Does and Doesn't Work," *National Productivity Review,* Winter 1981–82, pp. 61–74; Richard T. Johnson, "Success and Failure of Japanese Subsidiaries in America," *Columbia Journal of World Business,* Spring 1977, pp. 30–37; Sigmund Nosow, "A Lesson for American Managers: Learning from Japanese Experiences in the U.S.," *National Productivity Review,* August 1984, pp. 407–16; and Martin K. Starr and Nancy E. Bloom, "The Performance of Japanese-Owned Firms in America: Survey Report," Center for Operations, Graduate School of Business, Columbia University, mimeographed, February 1985.

72. On Bridgestone Tire, see "The Japanese Manager Meets the American Worker," *Business Week,* August 20, 1984, pp. 128–29. On Nissan, see Bryan H. Berry, "An American Work Force Produces Japanese Quality," *Iron Age,* July 18, 1986, pp. 44–50. On Matsushita, see J. M. Juran, "Japanese and Western Quality: A Contrast," *Quality Progress,* December 1978, pp. 10–18. On Sanyo, see *Sanyo Manufacturing Corporation, Forrest City, Arkansas* (Boston: Harvard Business School Case Services 9-682-045, 1981). More recent information on Sanyo was provided by Professor Hirotaka Takeuchi, Hitotsubashi University, in an unpublished manuscript.

## CHAPTER 11. CONTRIBUTORS TO JAPANESE QUALITY

1. Service call rates have been reported for only the first year of warranty coverage because that was the only period for which U.S. and Japanese companies offered comparable terms.

2. Quality Control Center, Production Engineering Division, Matsushita Electric Industrial Co., Ltd., "Basic Concepts of Quality Control and Roles and Duties of Managers," mimeographed, 1982, pp. 5, 7.

3. A similar approach has been used by firms in the U.S. electronics industry. Called "strife testing"—standing for "stress plus life"—it involves the application of "external stress (thermal, electrical, mechanical) that slightly exceeds that experienced by the product under normal use conditions [to] reveal areas of weakness. Observed failures are analyzed and corrected to decrease probability of recurrences." Ki Punches, "Burn-In and Strife Testing," *Quality Progress,* May 1986, p. 93.

4. Note that this finding differs from the results for U.S. and Japanese automobile plants, where the Japanese were found to have fewer inspectors. See Michael A. Cusumano, *The Japanese Automobile Industry* (Cambridge, Mass.: Harvard University Press, 1985), p. 329.

5. Continued training has been a hallmark of Japanese industry, whether of blue-collar workers, engineers, or managers. For more on the latter two groups, see Daun Bhasavanich, "An American in Tokyo: Jumping to the Japanese Beat," *IEEE Spectrum,* September 1985, pp. 72–81, and Peter F. Drucker, "What We Can Learn from Japanese Management," *Harvard Business Review,* March–April 1971, pp. 110–22.

6. The goal-setting process described here has close parallels to "phased program planning," an approach used by American companies to manage technological innovation and new product development. See James Bryant Quinn, "Managing Innovation: Controlled Chaos," *Harvard Business Review,* May–June 1985, p. 82.

7. Differences also appeared in the average rankings that supervisors assigned to management's manufacturing priorities. A 1 to 7 scale was used, with 7 indicating the highest priority or greatest weight. Japanese supervisors assigned a score of 6.7 to producing high-quality products; U.S. supervisors assigned a score of 5.9. Japanese supervisors assigned a score of 6.1 to meeting the production schedule; U.S. supervisors assigned a score of 6.5. Both differences were significant using a nonparametric Mann-Whitney U-test, the former at the 1 percent level (U-value of 6.5) and the latter at the 5 percent level (U-value of 12.5).

8. For a detailed discussion of staff as supporting actors, see Richard J. Schonberger, *World Class Manufacturing* (New York: Free Press, 1986), pp. 39–55.

9. The ability of Japanese companies to collect failure data after warranties have expired is due, in part, to their captive service networks. In the United States, appliance repair is more frequently provided by independents. See J. M. Juran, "Japanese and Western Quality: A Contrast," *Quality Progress,* December 1978, pp. 11–12, for further discussion.

10. The correlation between assembly line defect rates and first-year service call rates in Japan was .96; the correlation in the United States was .46. The former was significant at the 1 percent level; the latter at the 10 percent level. Note that two Japanese plants were excluded from this analysis—one because it had recently introduced a "just-in-time" production system and was experiencing an abnormally high level of defects, and the other because it was primarily an assembler and thus purchased virtually all of its parts and subassemblies from outside suppliers, unlike other manufacturers, who were heavily involved in fabrication.

11. For similar conclusions about design practices in the U.S. and Japanese automobile industries, see Robert E. Cole, "The Japanese Lesson in Quality," *Technology Review,* July 1981, p. 31.

12. For a discussion of the link between limited product lines and Japan's superior manufacturing performance, see James C. Abegglen and George Stalk, Jr., *Kaisha: The Japanese Corporation* (New York: Basic Books, 1985), pp. 79–89.

13. Neither difference was significant using either a t-test or a Mann-Whitney U-test. The t-value for differences in the number of chassis sizes was .1 and the U-value was 24.0. The t-value for differences in the number of models was .1 and the U-value was 29.0.

14. This difference was significant at the 1 percent level, using either a t-test or a Mann-Whitney U-test. The t-value was 11.8 and the U-value approximately 0.

15. For more on the role of subcontractors, see Ken-ichi Imai, Ikujiro Nonaka, and Hirotaka Takeuchi, "Managing the New Product Development Process: How Japanese Companies Learn and Unlearn," in Kim B. Clark, Robert H. Hayes, and Christopher Lorenz, eds., *The Uneasy Alliance: Managing the Productivity–Technology Dilemma* (Boston: Harvard Business School Press, 1985), pp. 362–71.

16. This difference was not significant using either a t-test or a Mann-Whitney U-test. The t-value was .9 and the U-value was 20.0.

17. See, for example, Richard J. Schonberger, *Japanese Manufacturing Techniques* (New York: Free Press, 1982), pp. 175–77.

18. For example, Japanese assembly lines averaged 7.3 wirers and 6.8 brazers, while U.S. assembly lines averaged 7.1 wirers and 5.8 brazers. Neither difference was significant using either a t-test or a Mann-Whitney U-test. The t-value for differences in the number of wirers was .1 and the U-value was 13.0. The t-value for differences in the number of brazers was .9 and the U-value was 14.0.

19. Quality Control Center, Matsushita, "Basic Concepts" (note 2), p. 11. The same principle has been recognized by American experts. See Ray Hinson, "Robots Provide Improved Quality in Manufacturing," *Industrial Engineering,* January 1984, pp. 45–46, and Daniel E. Whitney, "Real Robots Do Need Jigs," *Harvard Business Review,* May–June 1986, p. 115.

20. Richard Schonberger has called this approach "easy-to-see quality." See Schonberger, *Japanese Manufacturing Techniques,* pp. 56–59.

21. For more on housekeeping and preventive maintenance, see *ibid.,* pp. 66–68, 136–37, and Robert H. Hayes and Steven C. Wheelwright, *Restoring Our Competitive Edge* (New York: John Wiley & Sons, 1984), pp. 355–57.

22. Schonberger, *Japanese Manufacturing Techniques,* p. 70.

23. Medians have been reported here rather than means, because there were a small number of extreme observations. However, for both turnover and absenteeism, the difference in U.S. and Japanese means was significant at the 5 percent level or better using either a t-test or a Mann-Whitney U-test. The t-value for differences in turnover was 2.3 and the U-value was 9.5. The t-value for differences in absenteeism was 8.3 and the U-value was approximately zero. Note also that the remarkable figure of zero absenteeism reported by Japanese plants has a plausible explanation. Japanese workers do occasionally get sick, but since they seldom use all of their vacation days, those days are used in lieu of absences. In part, this is because Japanese unions have not always succeeded in winning sick leave for their members. See "Japan's Firms Have Found a Friend: The Unions," *Wall Street Journal,* April 28, 1986, p. 28, for further discussion.

24. This difference was significant at the 6 percent level using a t-test (t-value of 2.1) and at the 7 percent level using a Mann-Whitney U-test (U-value of 11.5).

25. Assembly lines averaged 790 feet in the United States and 997 feet in Japan. Cycle times averaged .63 minutes in the United States and .55 minutes in Japan. Capacity utilization rates averaged 70 percent in the United States and 73 percent in Japan. None of these differences was statistically significant using either a t-test or a Mann-Whitney U-test. The t-values were .7, −.4, and .7, respectively. The U-values were 23.0, 37.0, and 33.0, respectively.

CONCLUSION

1. See, for example, Alan R. Andreasen, "A Taxonomy of Consumer Satisfaction/Dissatisfaction Measures," *Journal of Consumer Affairs,* Winter 1977, pp. 11–24.

2. Wickham Skinner, "Manufacturing: Missing Link in Corporate Strategy," *Harvard Business Review,* May–June 1969, pp. 136–45; *idem,* "The Focused Factory," *Harvard Business Review,* May–June 1974, pp. 113–21; and Steven C. Wheelwright, "Reflecting Corporate Strategy in Manufacturing Decisions," *Business Horizons,* February 1978, pp. 57–66.

3. Steven C. Wheelwright, "Japan—Where Operations Really Are Strategic," *Harvard Business Review,* July–August 1981, pp. 70–71.

APPENDIX A. THE ROOM AIR CONDITIONING STUDY

1. The supervisor's questionnaire was an expanded version of a questionnaire first used by Leonard and Sasser. See Frank S. Leonard and W.

Earl Sasser, "The Incline of Quality," *Harvard Business Review,* September–October 1982, p. 164.

2. While sample statistics and tests of significance have been reported for supervisors' responses in several parts of the book, it is important to remember that *all* supervisors were surveyed at U.S. plants. This set of data therefore constitutes a population rather than a sample. Significance tests are difficult to interpret in such circumstances. See Hubert M. Blalock, Jr., *Social Statistics* (New York: McGraw-Hill, 1972), pp. 238–39, for a brief discussion.

## APPENDIX C. STATISTICAL ANALYSES

1. "Air Conditioners," *Consumer Reports,* July 1979, pp. 404–9; "High Efficiency Room Air Conditioners," July 1980, pp. 428–33; and "Air Conditioners," *Consumer Reports,* July 1982, pp. 356–60.

2. These results closely parallel those of another hedonic study of room air conditioners. See Center for Policy Alternatives, Massachusetts Institute of Technology, *Consumer Durables: Warranties, Service Contracts and Alternatives,* (Cambridge: Massachusetts Institute of Technology, 1978), pp. 2-214–2-221.

3. For a further discussion of Guttman scales, see Norman H. Nie *et al., Statistical Package for the Social Sciences,* Second Edition (New York: McGraw-Hill, 1975), pp. 528–33.

# Index

# Index